I0799395

IMAGES
of America

MOUNTAIN TOP

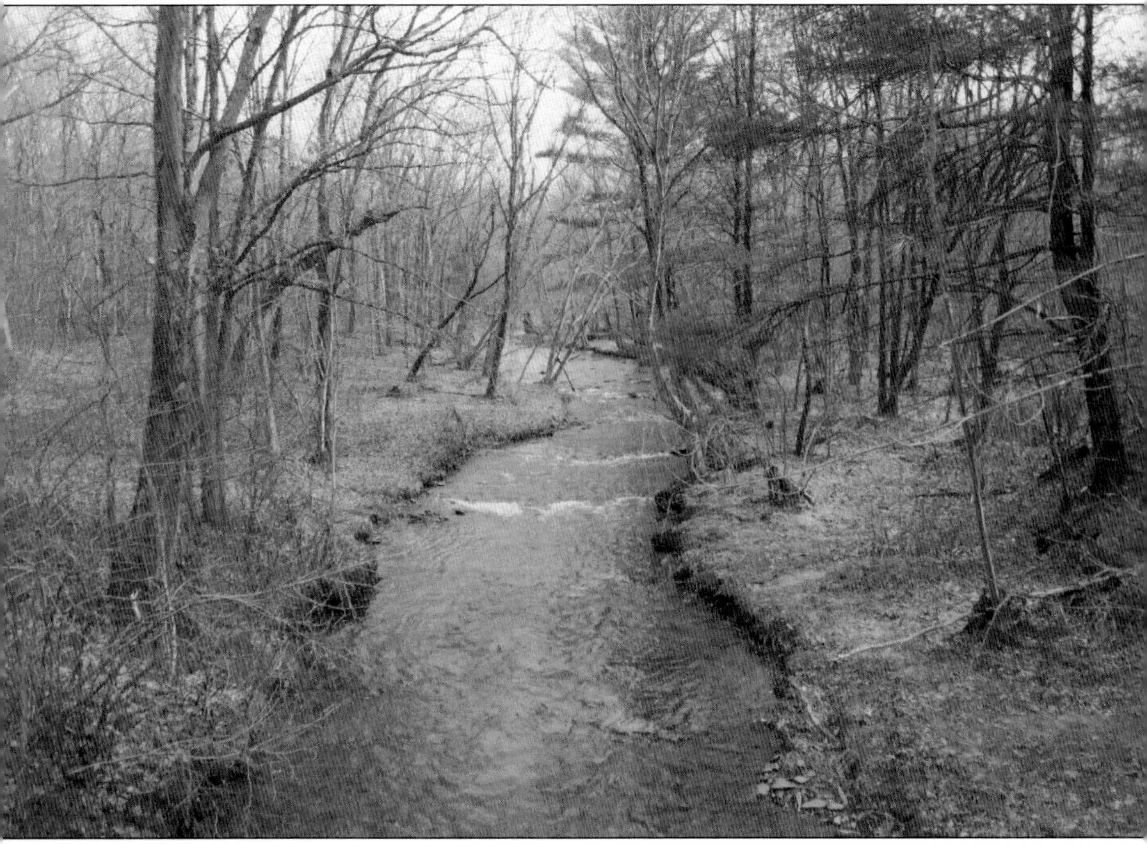

Big Wapwallopen Creek Near American Legion Mountain Post No. 781. Mountain Top is located in the watershed of the Big Wapwallopen Creek, a section of which is designated as a public recreation area provided by the American Legion Mountain Post No. 781 Inc. It is conserved by the North Branch Land Trust and the Bureau of Recreation and Conservation of the Pennsylvania Department of Conservation and Natural Resources. (Courtesy of Darlene Miller-Lanning.)

On the Cover: Mountain View Gas Station. The Mountain View Gas Station was built by Arthur Yocum in 1931 and was operated by James "Fuzzy" Cornelius. Located at the summit of Penobscot Mountain on the newly improved Route 309, the business had many customers and soon became a well-known landmark. Cornelius and his son Jimmy were photographed next to the station's four gas pumps with a 1932 Model A Ford nearby. Today, Jimmy Cornelius is a member of the Mountain Top Historical Society. (Courtesy of George and Mary Hollock.)

IMAGES
of America

MOUNTAIN TOP

Joseph Kubic, Darlene Miller-Lanning,
and the Mountain Top Historical Society

ARCADIA
PUBLISHING

ISBN 978-0-7385-9256-5

Published by Arcadia Publishing
Charleston, South Carolina

Printed in the United States of America

Library of Congress Control Number: 2011945331

For all general information, please contact Arcadia Publishing:
Telephone 843-853-2070
Fax 843-853-0044
E-mail sales@arcadiapublishing.com
For customer service and orders:
Toll-Free 1-888-313-2665

Visit us on the Internet at www.arcadiapublishing.com

To the residents of Mountain Top: past, present, and future

Contents

Acknowledgments

The Mountain Top Historical Society thanks the many community members who have graciously supported this project over the past 10 years. First, we recognize Bob Gaetano and Jim Keiser, teachers at the Crestwood High School in Mountain Top, Pennsylvania, who, in 1997, recruited a team of students, teachers, and residents to compile a history of the area. This initiative resulted in an organization and a publication. The Mountain Top Historical Society, founded during an American Education Week roundtable discussion in 1999, was incorporated in 2001. Shortly thereafter, the book *Pieces of the Past: A History of the Mountain Top Area* was published in 2002. We gratefully acknowledge the efforts of everyone involved in this important initial venture.

Subsequently, the Mountain Top Historical Society produced additional books on community history, authored by Joseph Kubic. These included *Mountain Top Past and Present* (2005), *Mountain Top Historical Business Directory* (2006), *History of Glen Summit Springs* (2008), *Fairview High School Alumni* (2009), and *Railroads Thru Mountain Top* (2010). Kubic's work has also laid the foundation for this publication.

Other references consulted for this book were: Herbert Atkins, *A Picture Tour of Wilkes-Barre and Vicinity* (T-L Printery Inc., 1933); Annie Bohlin, "The History of the Ashley Planes: 1843–1948," *Flags Diamonds and Statues* (Anthracite Railroad Historical Society, Winter 1984); H.C. Bradsby, *History of Luzerne County* (Nelson Publishing Company, 1893); Benjamin H. Carpenter, *History of Glen Summit Springs* (T-L Printery Inc., 1936); Charles H. Eddinger, *Early History of Rice Township* (Rice Township Bicentennial Committee, 1976); "Historical Sketch of Mountain Top," *Fairview High School Annual* (Fairview High School, 1934); "Local Ice Crop is Largest Harvested in Many Years," *Wilkes-Barre Record* (February 20, 1920); Mountain Top Community Association, *Mountain Top: Southern Gateway to the Wyoming Valley* (Square Printing Company, 1935); Stewart Pearce, *Annals of Luzerne County* (J.B. Lippincott and Company, 1860); Cdr. E.J. Quimby, *Wilkes-Barre & Hazleton Railway* (Model Craftsman Publishing, 1972); and Helen Smith Whitebread, *A History of Slocum Township and Its Environs* (Slocum Township Bicentennial Committee, 1976).

We also thank the editors and staff of Arcadia Publishing for helping to make this book a reality.

Introduction

Mountain Top is located between the Penobscot, Wilkes-Barre, and Nescopeck Mountains of northeastern Pennsylvania at the headwaters of the Big Wapwallopen Creek. A census-designated place, the community occupies 70 square miles between the Susquehanna and Lehigh Rivers to the west and east and the cities of Wilkes-Barre and Hazleton to the north and south. It is accessible from Route 309 and Interstate 81; the intersection of Interstates 80 and 81 lies close by. Nearly 17,000 residents live in the community's six municipalities of Wright, Fairview, Dorrance, Slocum, and Rice Townships as well as Nuangola Borough. They are served by the Crestwood School District, which includes Dennison Township and White Haven and Penn Lake Boroughs. Rugged yet promising, Mountain Top's location and landscape have shaped the community's historical growth as a center of lumbering and agriculture, railroading and vacationing, manufacturing and distribution, and residential development, creating connections between neighborhoods and across time.

While the summit of Penobscot Mountain rises over 2,000 feet above sea level, glacial action formed rolling hills between its neighboring mountain ranges. This distinctive topography provided Native Americans and colonial settlers with an access route between the Delaware, Lehigh, and Wyoming Valleys. Native American tribes, including the Iroquois and Lenni Lenape, were active in the area now known as Mountain Top. The Lehigh and Wapwallopen Paths passed through present-day Wright and Slocum Townships, and Native American artifacts have been found near streams, ledges, and fields.

During the 18th century, King Charles II of England, in two overlapping land charters, granted the region to both the Connecticut colony in 1662 and William Penn in 1681. Under the Pennsylvania claim, the territory was designated as Bucks County in 1682, Northampton County in 1752, and Northumberland County in 1772. Under the Connecticut claim, the territory was given to colonists who, chartered as the Susquehanna Company in 1753, attempted to settle the Wyoming Valley in 1762 and 1769. They established Hanover and Newport Townships in 1770 and 1773, parts of which would be included in Mountain Top. Territories held by the Susquehanna Company were attached to Litchfield County, Connecticut, as Westmoreland Township in 1774 and recognized as Westmoreland County in 1775.

By 1769, however, Pennsylvania settlers had moved north along the Susquehanna River. Controversy over land claims resulted in the Yankee-Pennamite War, which was temporarily suspended during the Revolutionary War in 1776 and the Battle of Wyoming in 1778. In 1782, the dispute was addressed at the Continental Congress and the Pennsylvania claim upheld. Unhappy with this decision, Connecticut settlers proposed the creation of a new state, Westmoreland. Instead, a compromise was reached in 1786, and Luzerne County, Pennsylvania, was formed, of which Mountain Top is still a part.

Following the Revolutionary War, settlers moved into remote reaches of the old colonial townships. The region's great forests of pine, oak, and hemlock first attracted hunters and lumbermen. Game and timber were abundant, and mountain streams provided power for sawmills. Cleared land could be farmed, although the rocky terrain made agriculture difficult.

In 1785, settlers from Northampton County traveled north through the Butler Valley to reach the Big Wapwallopen Creek in southern Newport Township. The area in which they settled separated from Newport as Dorrance Township in 1840. Early families included the Woodrings, Eishenbrouts, Rinehimers, Weners, Hellers, Whitebreads, Erohs, Bleims, Englers, Lutzes, and Stuarts.

Also in 1785, William and John Lutsey located in the northern part of Newport Township. By 1800, members of the Alden, Millage, Mullen, Fritz, Winters, Ogin, Weiss, Paine, Fink, Fredericks, and Delamater families resided there. About 1836, John Rosencrans built a sawmill, and William Lutsey erected the first frame house in 1837. In 1838, a school/meetinghouse was constructed on the property of Philip Myers. John Rosencrans was the first teacher and postmaster. Silas Alexander opened a store about 1848. Hiram Rosencrans was the first blacksmith, followed by Benjamin Lear. The settlement broke away from Newport as Slocum Township in 1854.

Venturing from the Wyoming Valley, Conrad Wickeiser cut a road into the mountainous regions of Hanover Township in 1798, settling in what is now Penobscot. In 1820, James Wright followed Wickeiser, opening a tavern and three sawmills. Harvey Holcomb settled nearby, selling his property to Elias Carey in 1833.

Similarly in 1833, Cornelius Garrison constructed a sawmill on the Big Wapwallopen Creek in the area now known as Blytheburn. Garrison made the first farm improvement with crops and an orchard. Soon afterward, Samuel Stivers, William Vandermark, and John Hoffman located south of Triangular Lake, now Nuangola Lake. In 1840, a log schoolhouse was built near the Stivers property. The first teacher was Charles Fine. The pioneer blacksmith, Stephen Lee, operated the first store nearby. The first postmaster, William Albert, kept an office at what is now Albert's Corners.

In 1851, these villages split from Hanover to become Wright Township. Wright Township further divided when the section near Penobscot became Fairview Township in 1889; the Nuangola Lake area, including portions of Slocum Township, became Nuangola Borough in 1908; and lands north of the Big Wapwallopen Creek, including half of Blytheburn, became Rice Township in 1928.

Travel routes developed by early inhabitants of the Mountain Top area were closely followed by 19th-century railroads. In 1837, the Lehigh Coal and Navigation Company moved into the region. Anthracite coal had been discovered in the Wyoming Valley, and the company was anxious to construct a transportation system linking mines in Wilkes-Barre with markets in Philadelphia.

To the southeast, canals were built along the Lehigh and Delaware Rivers. To the northwest, mountainous terrain necessitated construction of the Lehigh & Susquehanna Railroad. This system included a track between Solomon's Gap and White Haven, completed in 1840, and three inclines crossing the Penobscot Mountain, known as the Ashley Planes, completed in 1843. Cars loaded with coal were hauled up the planes by stationary engines, then transported by rail to White Haven, where the contents were shipped via the Lehigh Canal.

After flooding destroyed the canals in 1862, the Lehigh Coal and Navigation Company replaced them with rail lines. The company added a new section of rail around Penobscot Mountain, known as the Back Track, in 1866. Used to carry passenger traffic, westbound freight, and empty cars, this track increased the capacity of the Ashley Planes, which were dedicated to lifting eastbound freight to a weigh station at the top of the mountain.

In 1867, the Lehigh Valley Railroad extended through Penobscot. The beauty of the Wyoming Valley, as seen from the train traveling around the mountainside, inspired the name of Fairview Station at the summit. Further expansion of railroad facilities occurred in 1871 when the Central Railroad of New Jersey leased the Lehigh & Susquehanna Railroad. A station, car shops, and roundhouse constructed at Penobscot Yards provided employment for local residents. Related enterprises included the Crystal Spring Water Company, which built a reservoir on Wilkes-Barre Mountain in 1873 and the DuPont Powder Works at Gracedale.

At the turn of the 20th century, an electric railway also traversed Mountain Top. Beginning in 1903, the Wilkes-Barre & Hazleton Railway, an interurban transit system powered by a "live" third rail, served local stations at Albert, Blytheburn, Pine View, and Nuangola on the route between its namesake cities. Significant features of the 30-mile line, which crossed the Penobscot Mountain to the west near Nuangola rather than to the east at Solomon's Gap, included a power station, two substations, 33 bridges, and a half-mile tunnel. The Wilkes-Barre & Hazleton Railway scheduled both nonstop limited and local runs. Its electric cars carried not only passengers and business travelers from urban centers, but also poultry and dairy products from rural farms. The railway's presence fostered the development of the Crystal Lake and Wilkes-Barre and Hazleton Ice Companies, which, in 1912 and 1916, dammed the Little Wapwallopen Creek to create the Lower and Upper Ice Lakes in what is now Rice Township.

As rail access to its secluded forests and streams improved, Mountain Top became a resort location. Natural resources of timber and water were now also valued for their recreational potential as tourists and vacationers left hot, crowded cities to enjoy Mountain Top's scenic vistas, pristine lakes, and refreshing breezes. The summer colony of Glen Summit grew along the Lehigh Valley Railroad on Nescopeck Mountain. Given its elevation, the mountain crest remained comfortable in humid weather, and its wooded hillsides were watered by springs. Capitalizing on these features, the railroad established the Glen Summit Hotel and Land Company in 1882 and developed properties purchased from the Conety, Derr, and Patterson families. In 1884, the newly constructed three-story Glen Summit Springs Hotel offered luxurious lodging and dining accommodations for 250 people, and provided facilities for hunting, fishing, boating, swimming, horseback riding, tennis, croquet, bowling, billiards, shuffleboard, concerts, and dancing. In that same year, hotel manager Joseph Patterson established the Glen Summit Water Company. Further improvements followed in 1888 when water from the nearby Indian Springs and Twin Springs was directed into a reservoir at Fountain Lake. A rustic chapel and casino were also added. Over the years, cottages at Glen Summit were built by the Farnsworth, Sharpe, Ellis, Hollenback, Welles, and Shoemaker families, among others. Graystone Terrace, constructed in 1914 by five-and-dime store founder Fred Morgan Kirby and his wife, Jessie, was surrounded by Japanese gardens featuring a bamboo teahouse, oriental statuary, and lily ponds.

A resort community also flourished at Nuangola Lake, a natural body of water originally called Three-cornered Pond or Triangular Lake. In 1885, lots were sold on the southwest shore, and cottages were built. The Nuangola Union Chapel, constructed in 1900, was dedicated in 1904. By that time, the Wilkes-Barre & Hazleton Railway provided service to Nuangola, and the lakeside retreat grew in popularity. During this era, John Jennings, a photographer whose family operated a boat rental at Nuangola, published postcard images of the lake and surrounding countryside. In 1910, Amos Storm and his sons Edward and Perry started a general store in Nuangola; in 1934, Perry Storm and his son Foster opened the Grove Theater, home to the Broadway Players summer stock troupe, in a building across the street. Managed by Royal Stout, the husband of Broadway actress Nellie Kennedy Stout, the theater featured well-known performers, including Kirk Douglas, who debuted there in 1941.

Other hamlets served by the Wilkes-Barre & Hazleton Railway included Blytheburn and Pine View. Established in 1911 by developers Thomas and Wells, Blytheburn was located along the Big Wapwallopen Creek. With a lake, dam, and swimming pond, the planned community grew during the 1920s. Pine View began as a collection of summer cottages near the Ice Lakes. Later, residents like Mario Peruzzi, who, with his brother-in-law Amadeo Obici, had cofounded the Planters Peanut Company, and William Schaeffer, president of the Wyoming Valley Trust Company, lived there in elegant permanent homes.

While Mountain Top prospered throughout the 1920s, it could not escape the hardships and changes wrought by the Great Depression. Oil replaced coal as the nation's primary fuel, and railroading declined. Gasoline-powered cars and trucks replaced trains as preferred methods for travel and shipping. Given these circumstances, the Wilkes-Barre & Hazleton Railway ceased operations in 1933. The Central Railroad of New Jersey, which had begun using diesel engines on the Back Track, closed the Ashley Planes in 1948. The Lehigh Valley Railroad conducted the last run of its famous "Black Diamond" passenger train through Fairview in 1959.

Mountain Top's unique location, however, once again shaped the community's fortunes and future. Roads, cut through the mountain passes since colonial times, had been periodically improved. To the east, a log road from Solomon's Gap to Ashley opened in 1866 and later became the Wilkes-Barre and Hazleton Turnpike, along which Horton and Gilchrist operated a stage line. Portions of the road were modified in 1908 to become Ashley Boulevard, which was considered a scenic drive. Between 1926 and 1935, the boulevard was realigned with dramatic ravine fills and rock cuts to become

Route 309. In 1965, it was widened to four lanes. To the west, crossing the Penobscot Mountain near Nuangola, Interstate 81 was constructed through Rice and Dorrance Townships in 1967.

Modern highways provided families and corporations with easy access to Mountain Top, which became a center for suburban development and industrial manufacturing. Soon after the construction of Route 309, Bradley Ayers built single-family homes and multiple-family town houses in Fairview Heights and Fairview Park. Small businesses like the Broadway Tavern, Triangle Restaurant, and Sunset Drive-in, each identified with distinctive roadside signs, opened along Route 309. In 1952, the Crestwood Industrial Park was established in Mountain Top. The Foster Wheeler Corporation located there in 1953, followed by King Fifth Wheel in 1954, Eberhard Faber in 1956, the Radio Corporation of America in 1959, Fibrous Glass Products in 1961, and Dana Perfumes in 1963. These trends continued as the industrial park attracted additional companies and residential developments multiplied. The population of Mountain Top increased significantly after Hurricane Agnes, which, in 1972, caused flooding of the Susquehanna River in the Wyoming Valley and prompted many families to relocate. Because of its proximity to New York City and Philadelphia, the region also attracted commuters who lived in Mountain Top and worked in metropolitan centers.

Mountain Top's educational, religious, civic, and municipal organizations kept pace with community growth. Townships maintained independent one-room schools until 1897, when Fairview School, which included a three-year high school program in addition to an elementary curriculum, was built. Because of a growing population, the school was expanded in the 1930s. Larger, brick-built elementary schools were constructed in Slocum Township, Nuangola Borough, Wright Township, and Dorrance Township in 1925, 1934, 1937, and 1950. St. Jude's Church constructed an elementary school in 1958. In 1955, a jointure of schools from Fairview, Wright, Rice, Dorrance, Slocum, and Dennison Townships as well as Nuangola, White Haven, and Penn Lake Boroughs created the Central Luzerne County Joint School District. A new high school was established on Route 309 in 1962, and in 1969, the district and school adopted the Crestwood name. New elementary schools were built in Rice and Fairview Townships in 1970 and 1973, while the Crestwood Middle School, built as an extension of the Crestwood High School, opened in 2000.

Similarly, early religious organizations expanded and flourished. Congregations met in rural schools and members' homes until they constructed their own buildings or merged to form larger congregations. Their legacies of faith and service continue in the Emmanuel United Church of Christ, St. Mary's Church of Our Lady Help of Christians, and Stairville United Methodist Church of Dorrance Township; Glen Summit Chapel and Mountain Top Presbyterian Church of Fairview Township; Nuangola Chapel of Nuangola Township; Cornerstone Christian Fellowship and St. Martin in the Fields Episcopal Church of Rice Township; Faith United Methodist Church, Grace Bible Baptist Church, Mount Zion Church, Slocum Seventh-day Adventist Church, and Slocum United Methodist Church of Slocum Township; and Christ United Methodist Church, Mountain Top Baptist Church, Mountain Top Family Center Church, New Life Community Church, St. Jude's Church, and St. Paul's Lutheran Church of Wright Township.

For roughly 200 years, people have chosen Mountain Top as a place to find employment and raise families. The distinct yet interdependent neighborhoods they established, guided and enhanced by a variety of civic and municipal organizations, demonstrate the goals and values they shared. Residents of Mountain Top currently support and enjoy the services and benefits of six municipal parks and volunteer fire companies, three township police departments, two ambulance associations, a public library, and a senior citizens' center as well as diverse social groups and numerous school and community sports leagues. "In your search for opportunity in far off places," Lester Zerfoss, principal of Fairview High School, advised the class of 1938, "don't overlook the possibilities of your own homeland gateway. . . . We, ourselves, must build our community, plan its growth, shape its characteristics, set its standards of culture, [and] develop its natural beauty. . . . [We ourselves] must make Mountain Top a beautiful, attractive, and prosperous place to live." As we consistently work to accomplish this goal today, an awareness of our community's past strengthens our vision for its future.

One

Townships and Boroughs

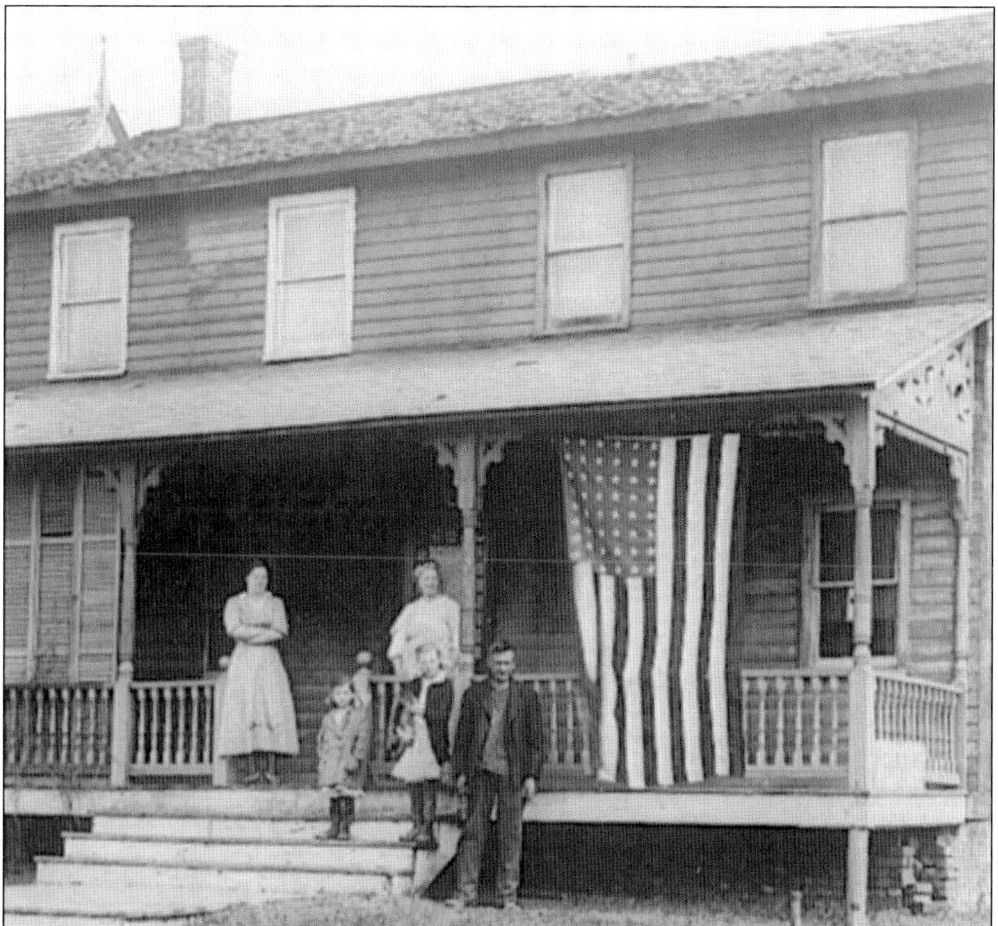

Wetzel House. In the early 20th century, August and Frances Wetzel lived with their daughters Marion, Annie, and Esther in this house on Woodlawn Avenue at Penobscot. The building, which remained in the Wetzel and Lines families for generations, also served as a store. (Courtesy of Redmond Lines.)

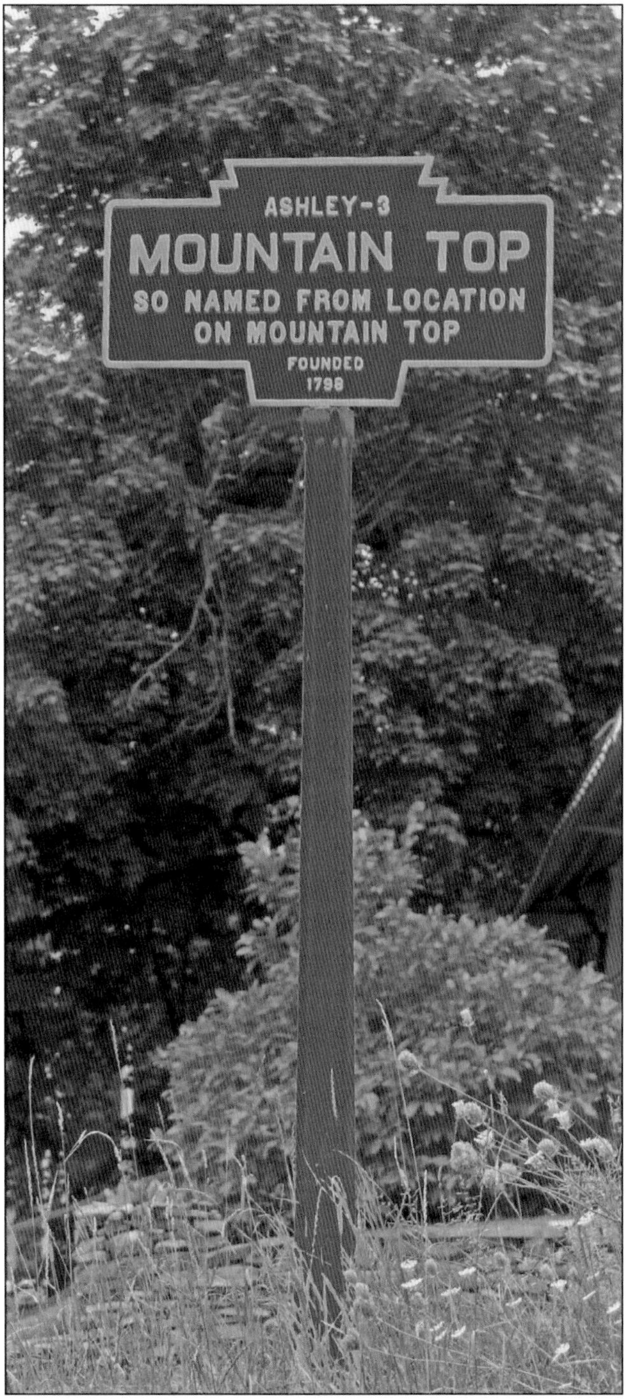

Mountain Top Historical Marker. Mountain Top includes Wright, Fairview, Dorrance, Slocum, and Rice Townships as well as Nuangola Borough. Originally the name Mountain Top referred only to Fairview but was applied to all townships when post offices consolidated there. This state historical marker, originally located on North Main Street in Fairview, now stands at the intersection of Route 309 and Chestnut Street. (Courtesy of Darlene Miller-Lanning.)

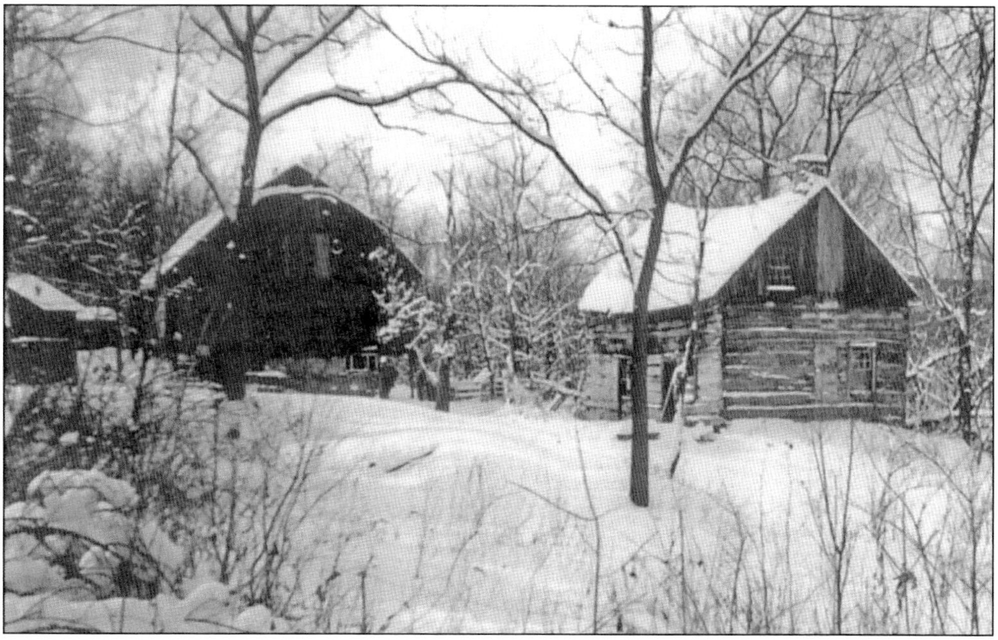

WARNER HOMESTEAD. Areas now included in Mountain Top were taken from two colonial townships. Dorrance and Slocum Townships separated from the older Newport Township in 1840 and 1854, respectively. Lumbering and agriculture were the primary occupations of early settlers, who erected log cabins like the Warner Homestead in Dorrance. (Courtesy of the Mountain Top Historical Society: *Pieces of the Past.*)

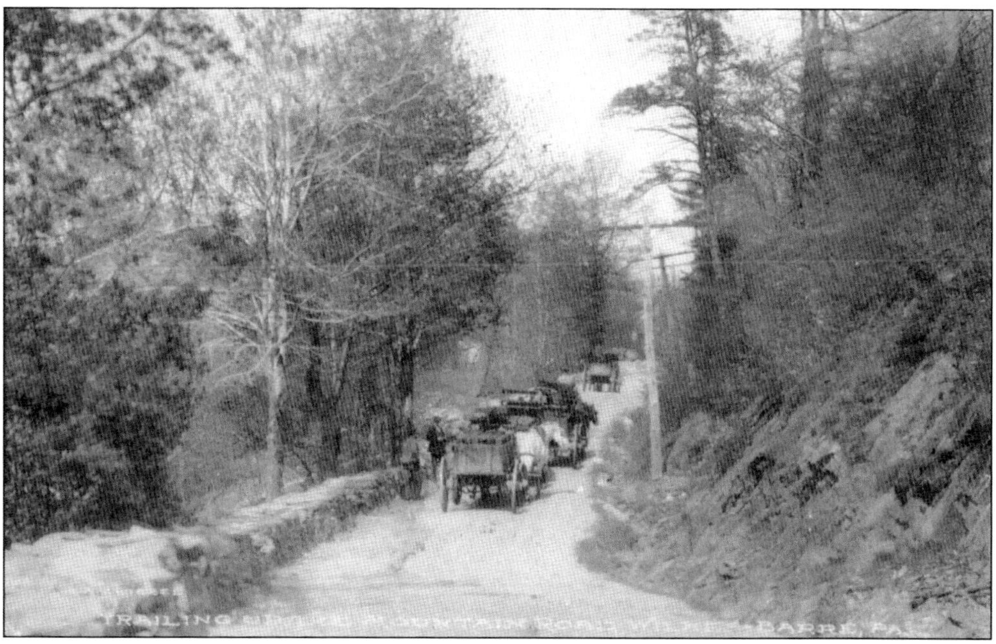

TRAILING UP THE MOUNTAIN ROAD. Land originally included in the colonial township of Hanover was divided into Wright, Fairview, and Rice Townships in 1851, 1889, and 1928. The first settler in the region now known as Fairview was Conrad Wickeiser, who used a team of oxen to cut a log road up the Penobscot Mountain in 1798. (Courtesy of Robert Hatcher.)

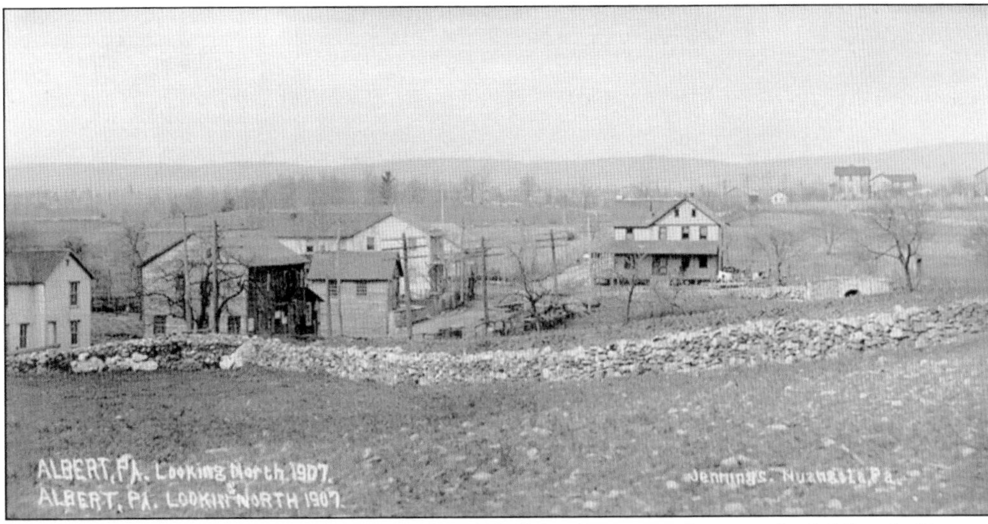

ALBERT'S CORNERS, WRIGHT TOWNSHIP. In 1907, John Jennings photographed Albert's Corners at the intersection of what is now South Main and Church Roads. Based on the federal census of 1910, structures included the Jackel House; Smith's Blacksmith Shop; Smith's Hotel, now called the Crossroads Inn; Cooksey's Inn, later known as the Harry Bower Tavern and Fisher's Café; the Varney Farm; and the Kreuzer Farm. (Courtesy of Sam and Rachel Goyne.)

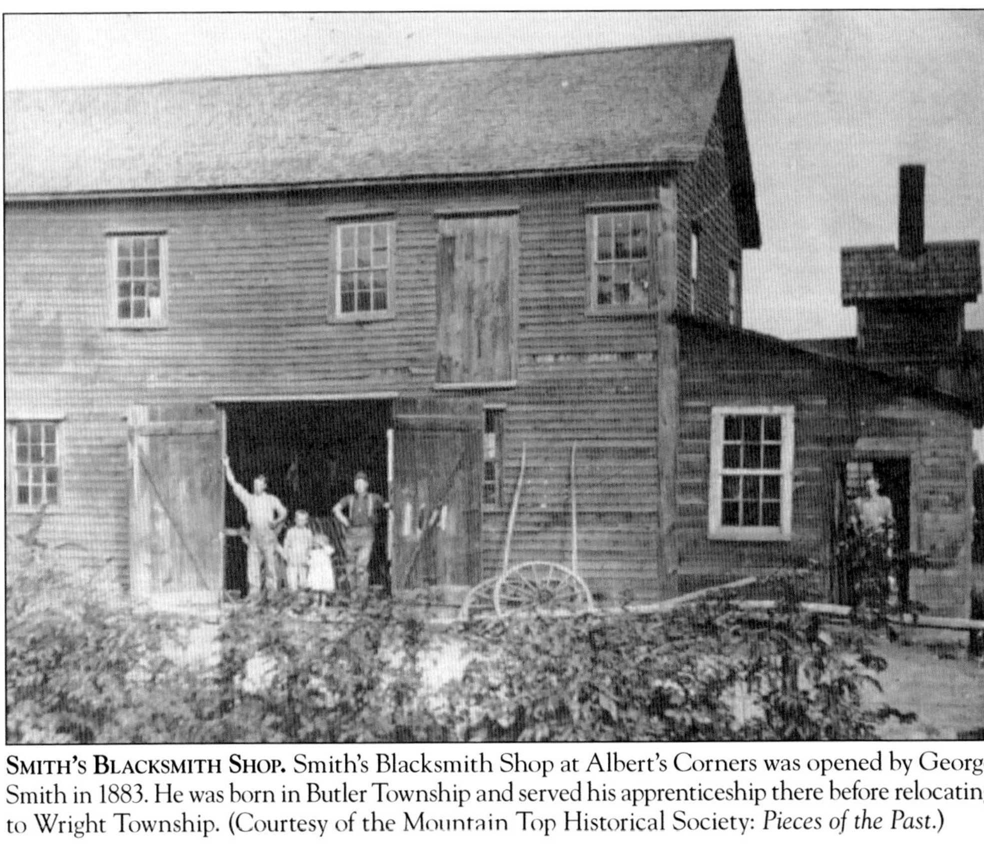

SMITH'S BLACKSMITH SHOP. Smith's Blacksmith Shop at Albert's Corners was opened by George Smith in 1883. He was born in Butler Township and served his apprenticeship there before relocating to Wright Township. (Courtesy of the Mountain Top Historical Society: *Pieces of the Past.*)

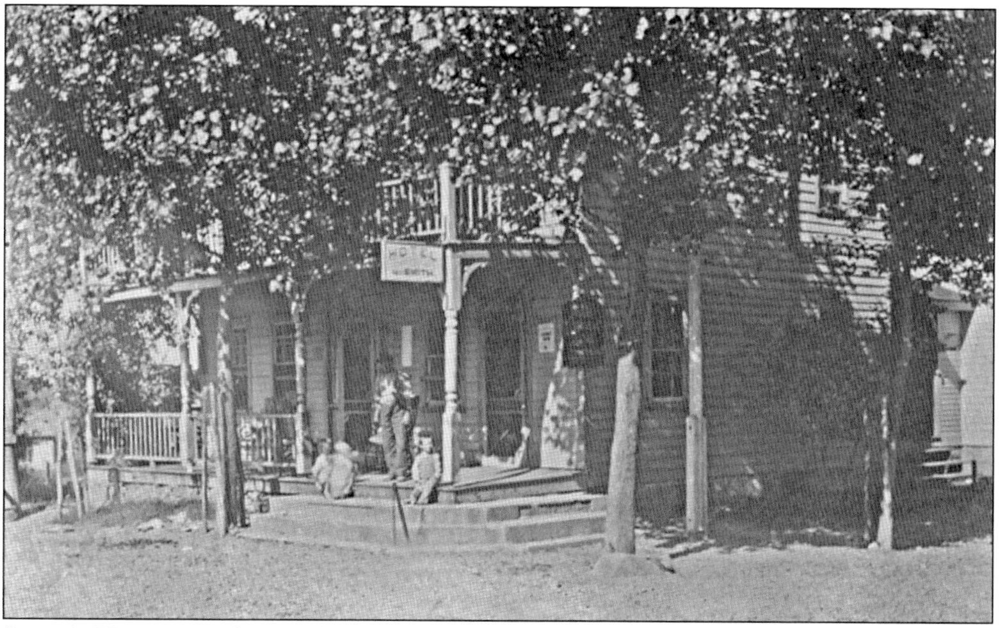

SMITH'S HOTEL. Smith's Hotel served as post office and stagecoach stop on the Wilkes-Barre and Hazleton Turnpike, now Main Road. The establishment, which had many owners before and after the Smiths, was also known as Albert's Hotel and Hildebrand's Hotel. (Courtesy of Sam and Rachel Goyne.)

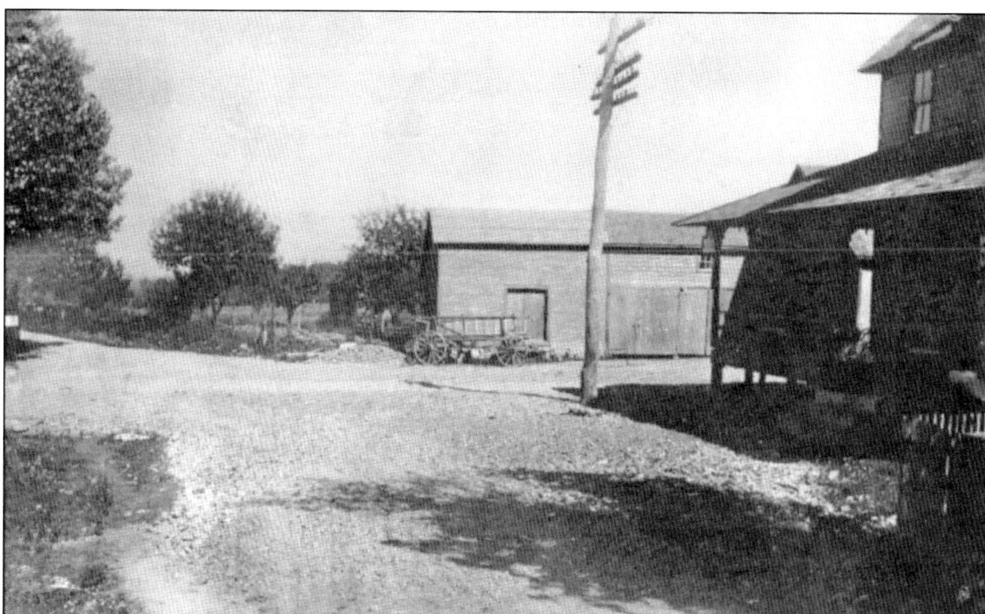

ALBERT'S CORNERS, LOOKING WEST. In this view of Albert's Corners, the Wilkes-Barre and Hazleton Turnpike is shown from left to right. The Harry Bower Tavern is visible on the right, with the Jerry Lutz Garage at center right. In the 1920s, Carl Sachs's gas station would be built on the site of the garage. (Courtesy of Sam and Rachel Goyne.)

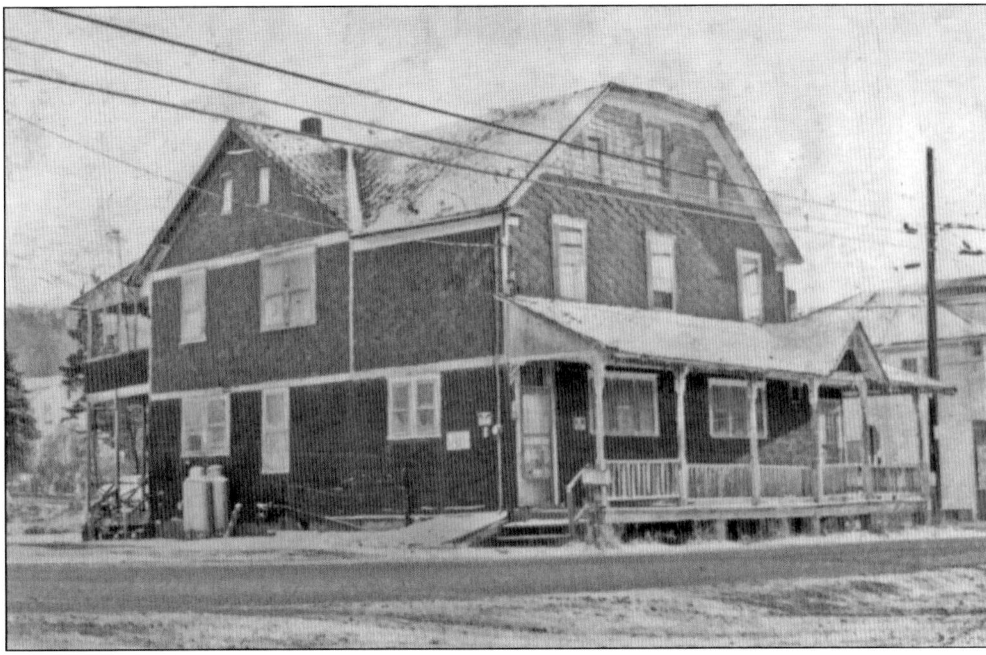

Fisher's Café. Fisher's Café was previously known as Cooksey's Inn, the Zerfoss Tavern, and the Harry Bower Tavern. Frank and Catherine Fisher purchased the business in the 1940s. It remained a well-known gathering place until it closed in the 1980s. The building was torn down, and the lot is now vacant. (Courtesy James and Edith Miller.)

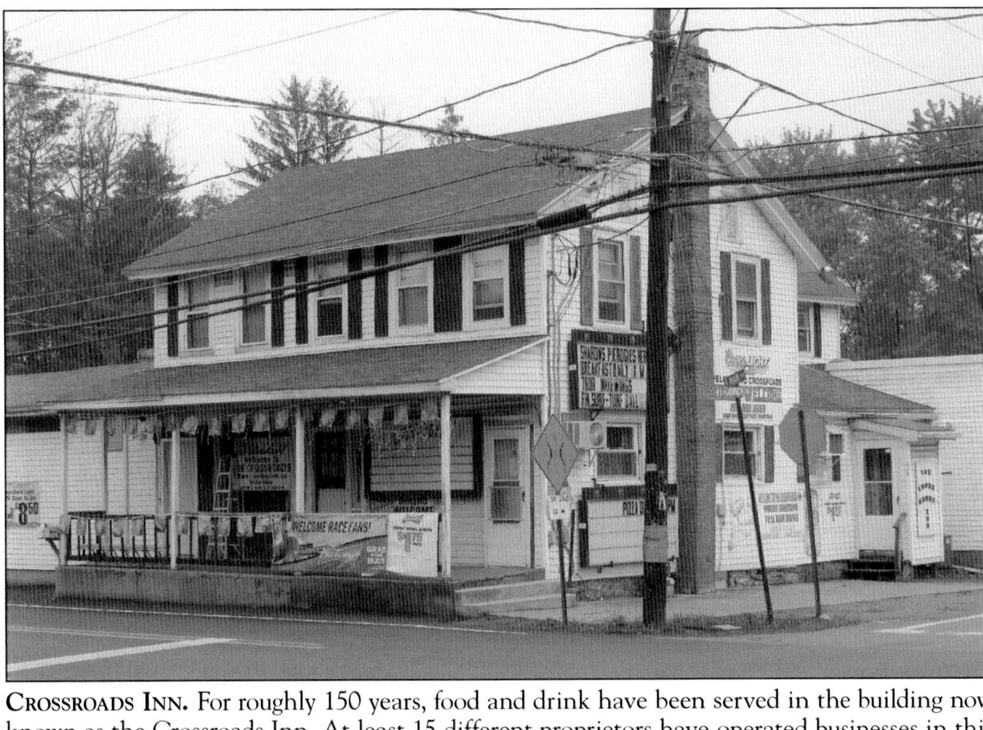

Crossroads Inn. For roughly 150 years, food and drink have been served in the building now known as the Crossroads Inn. At least 15 different proprietors have operated businesses in this structure, one of the oldest in Mountain Top. (Courtesy of Darlene Miller-Lanning.)

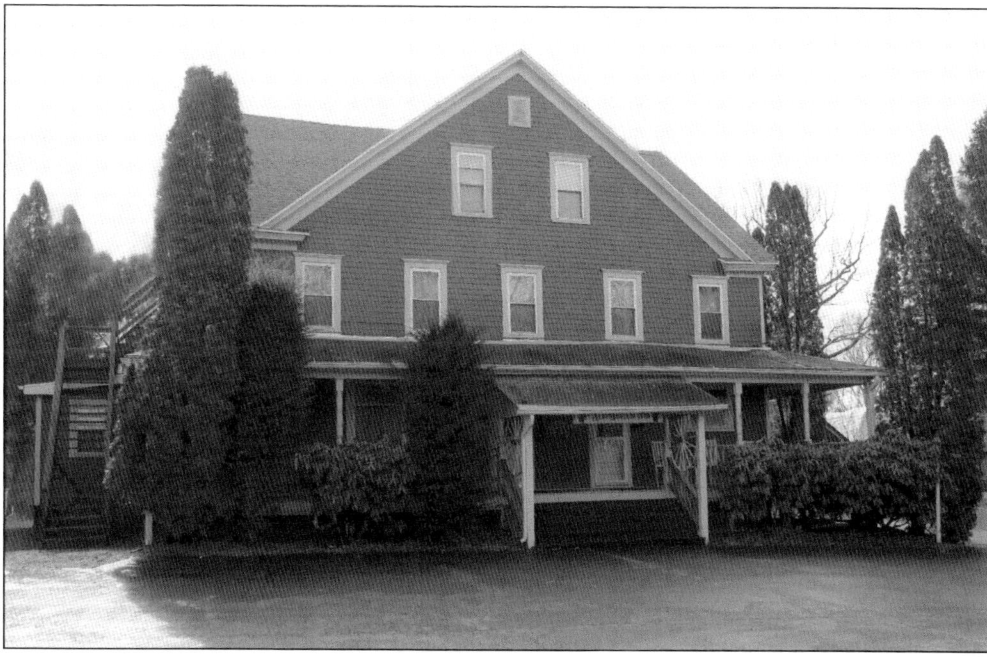

ALBERDEEN INN. The Alberdeen Hotel, built near the Wilkes-Barre & Hazleton Railway station at Albert, was operated by Fred Hendler in the early 1900s. Subsequent owners included Pete and Maggie Jacobs, Ed and Lenore McCabe, and Bill and Annie Macos. (Courtesy of Darlene Miller-Lanning.)

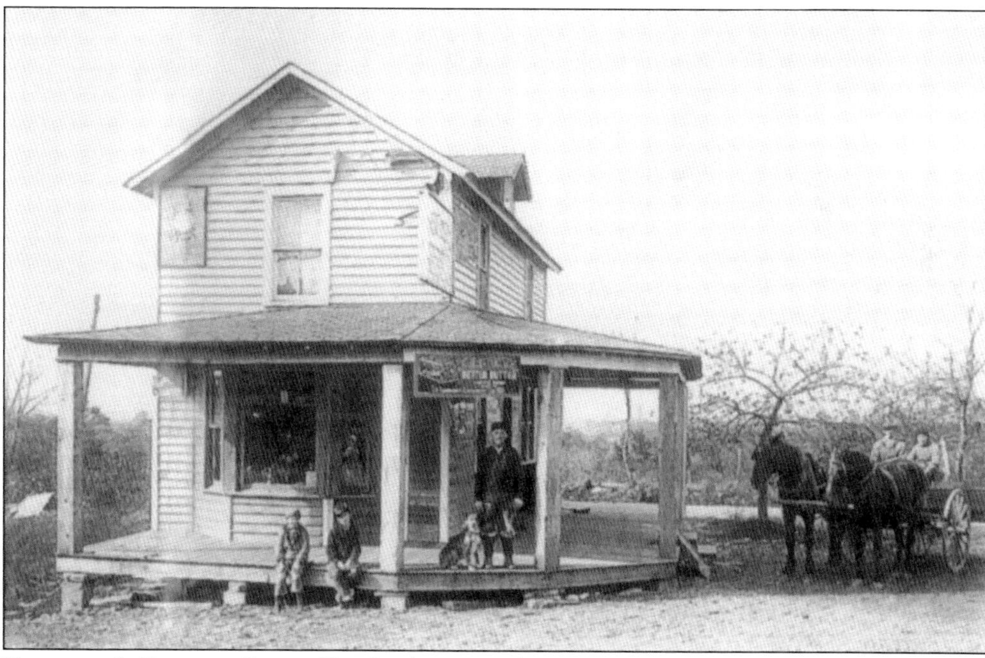

KENTHACK'S GENERAL STORE. Kenthack's General Store was built by Minnie Kenthack in 1919. It was located at the triangular intersection between Main and Alberdeen Roads known as The Point. Today, the site is occupied by the Knights of Columbus Building. (Courtesy of the Mountain Top Historical Society: *Pieces of the Past.*)

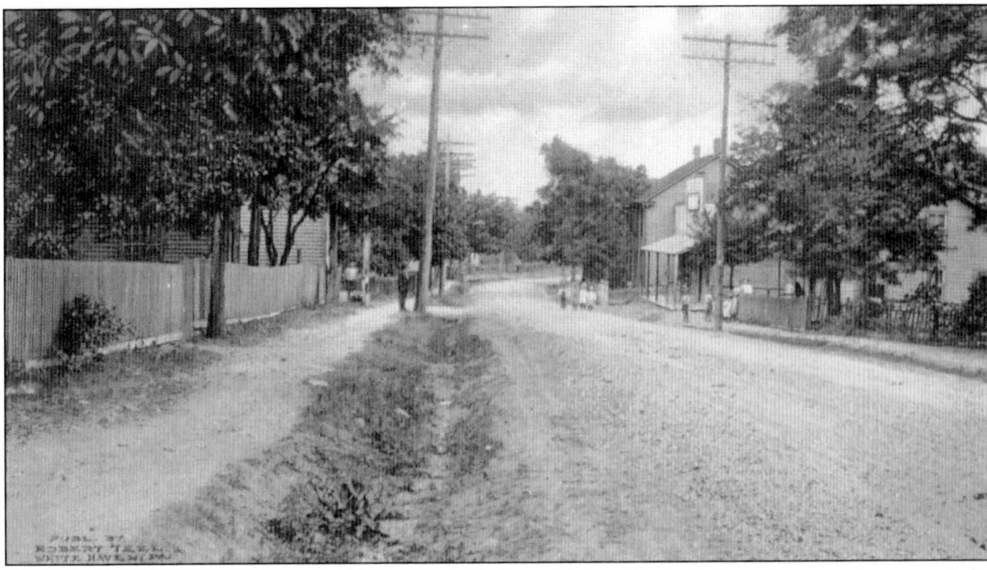

North Main Street, Fairview Township. Robert Teel published this view at the turn of the 20th century. John Snyder's General Store, visible on the right, was located on the site of Jerry Moyer's Barbershop, now owned by John "Zip" Frankenfield. The store was split into two sections, one of which was reconstructed as the Mountain Top Post Office. (Courtesy of the Mountain Top Historical Society: *Past and Present.*)

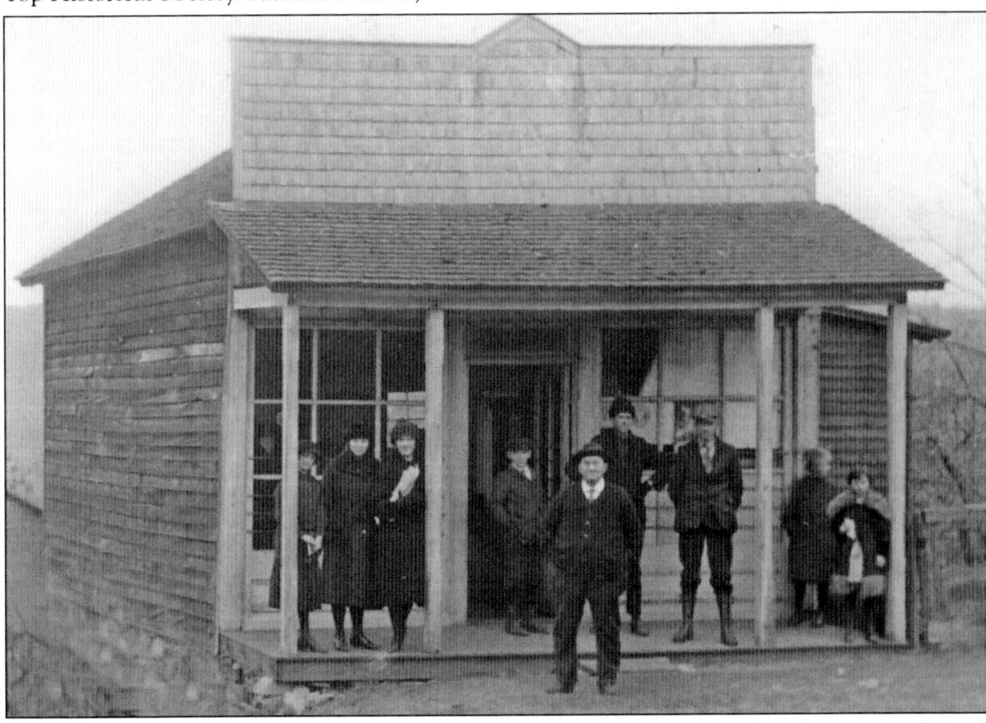

Mountain Top Post Office. The Mountain Top Post Office was located at the corner of North Main and Chestnut Streets. In 1957, the US Postal Service opened a new facility near Abod's Lounge on Kirby Avenue. Later, services were twice moved to the Wideman and Simoncavage Buildings on Kirby Avenue and Route 309, respectively. (Courtesy of James and Edith Miller.)

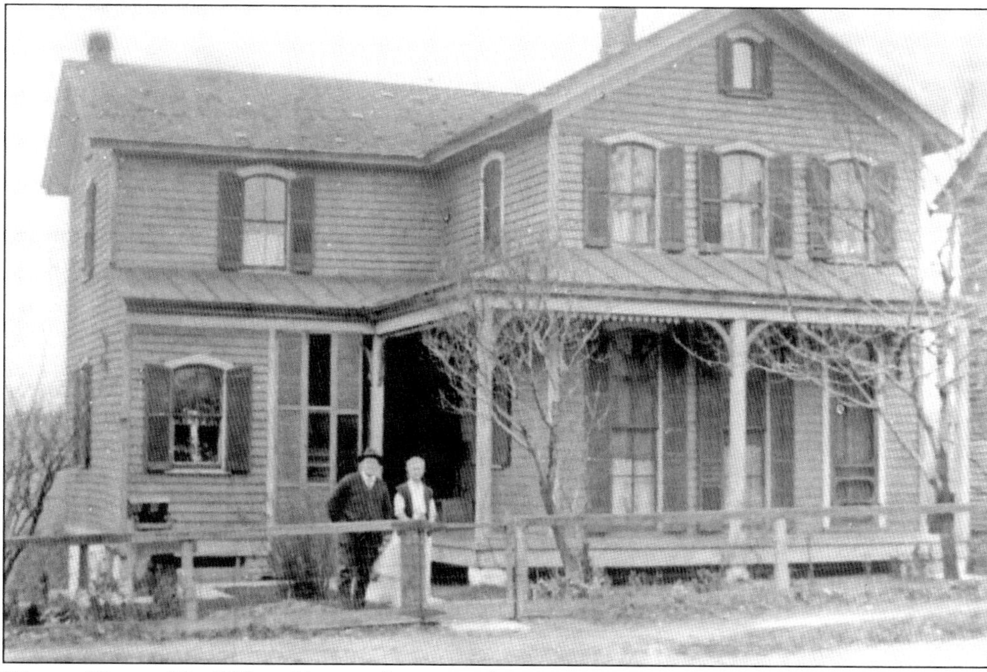

Wilcox House. The Wilcox House, adjacent to the Mountain Top Post Office, served as a residence, store, and butcher shop. Elmer and Adele Wilcox, who also maintained the post office, resided there from the late 19th through the early 20th centuries. (Courtesy of James and Edith Miller.)

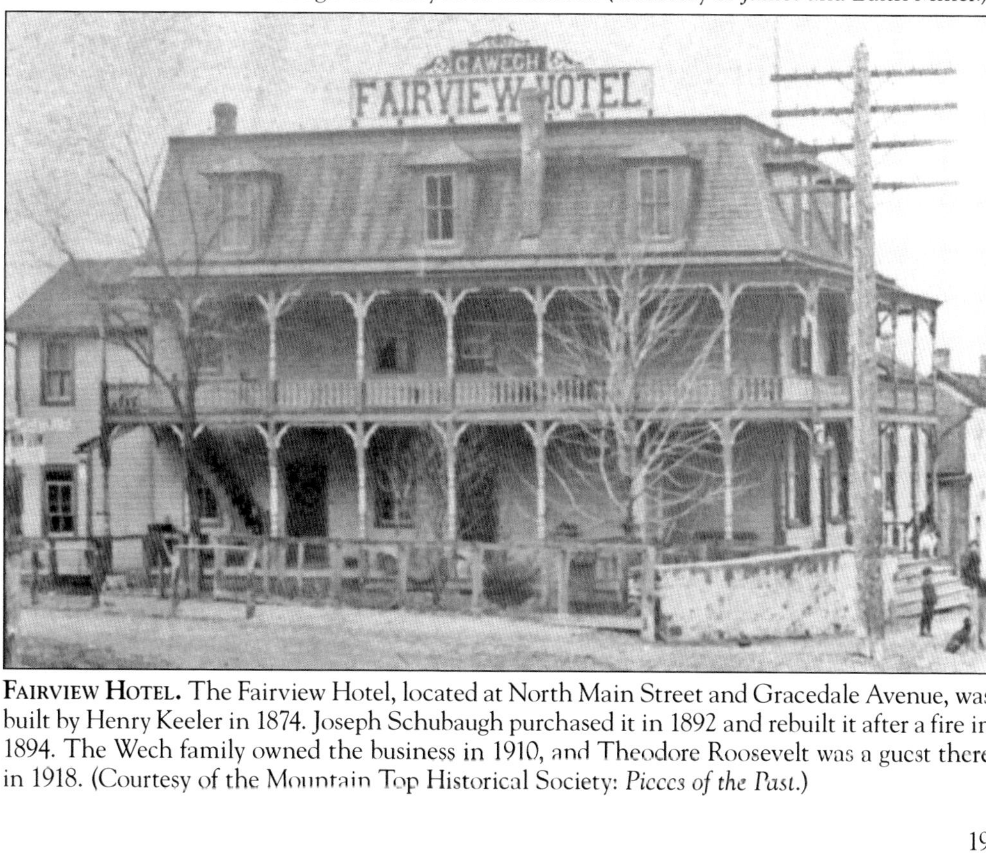

Fairview Hotel. The Fairview Hotel, located at North Main Street and Gracedale Avenue, was built by Henry Keeler in 1874. Joseph Schubaugh purchased it in 1892 and rebuilt it after a fire in 1894. The Wech family owned the business in 1910, and Theodore Roosevelt was a guest there in 1918. (Courtesy of the Mountain Top Historical Society: *Pieces of the Past.*)

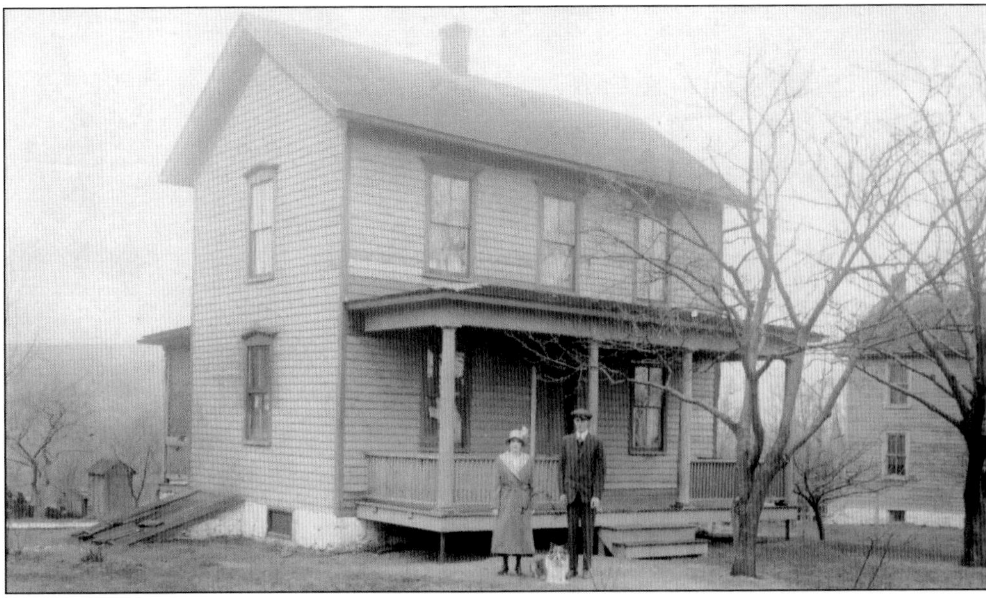

Richards House. The federal census of 1900 reported that Norman and Christiana Richards lived with their 10 children in this house at the corner of North Main and Chestnut Streets. Later, the home was owned by Claude and Margaret Kahley, who also raised a large family there. (Courtesy of Minnie Koons Peters.)

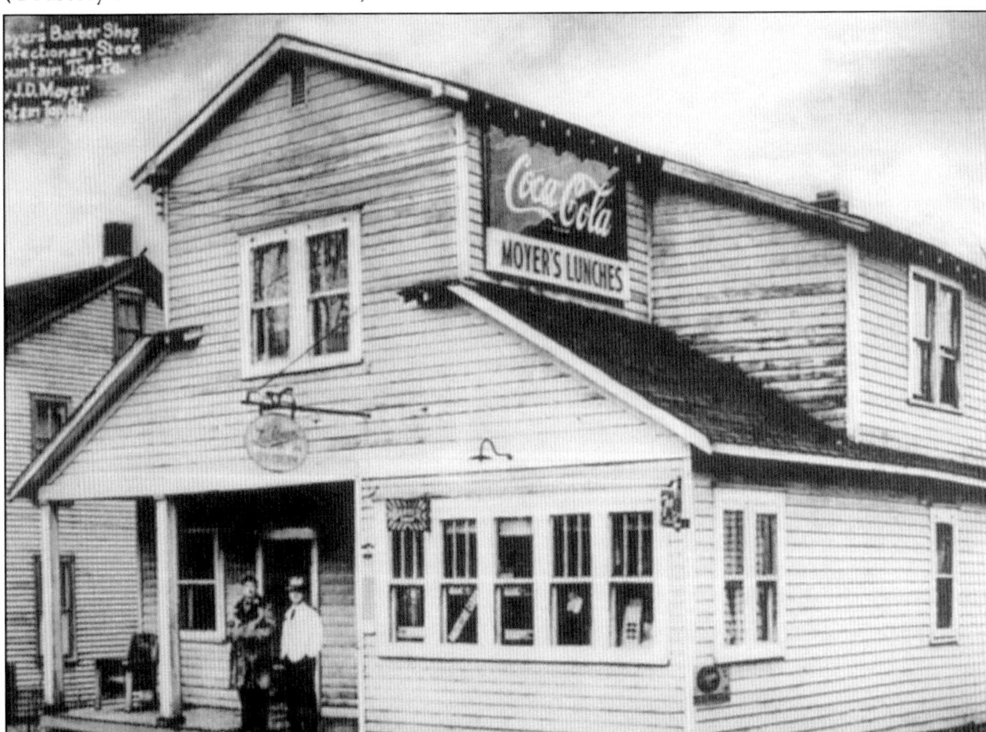

Moyer's Barbershop. During the 1940s and 1950s, customers could get haircuts, ice cream, candy, and soda at Jerry Moyer's Barbershop on North Main Street. Moyer's grandson John "Zip" Frankenfield has continued the family business for more than 45 years. (Courtesy of Leo Brookus.)

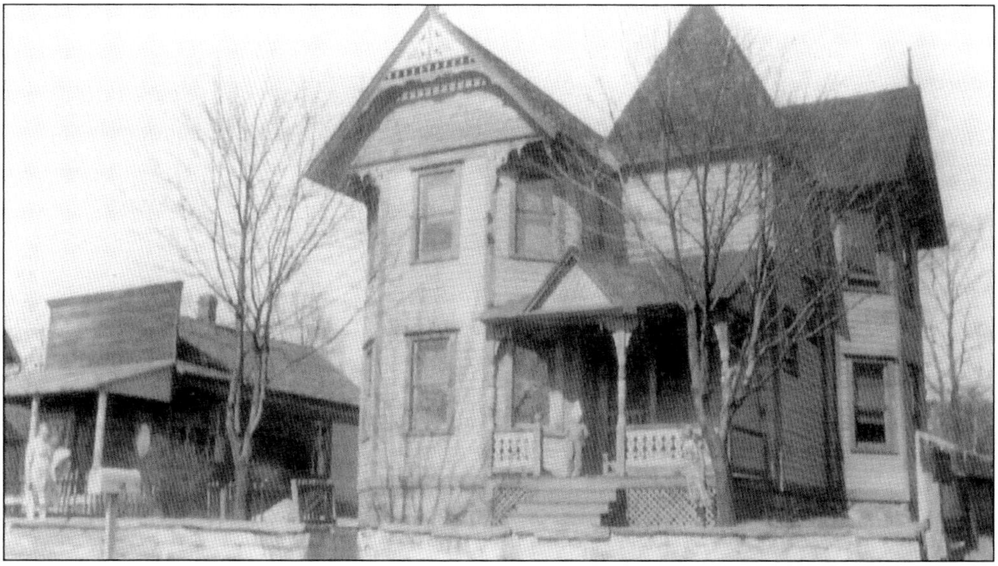

Bakery on Woodlawn Avenue. In the 1940s, a small bakery was located at Woodlawn Avenue in Penobscot. (Courtesy of Redmond Lines.)

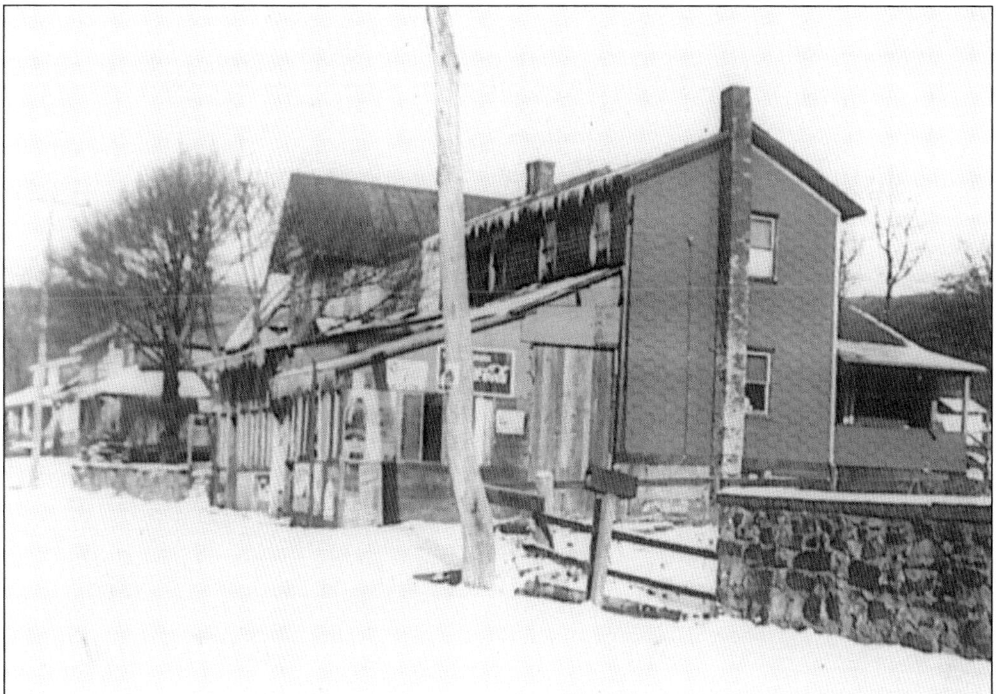

Wetzel's Store. Wetzel's Store and Gas, located along Woodlawn Avenue in Penobscot, served local railroaders in the 1940s. (Courtesy of Redmond Lines.)

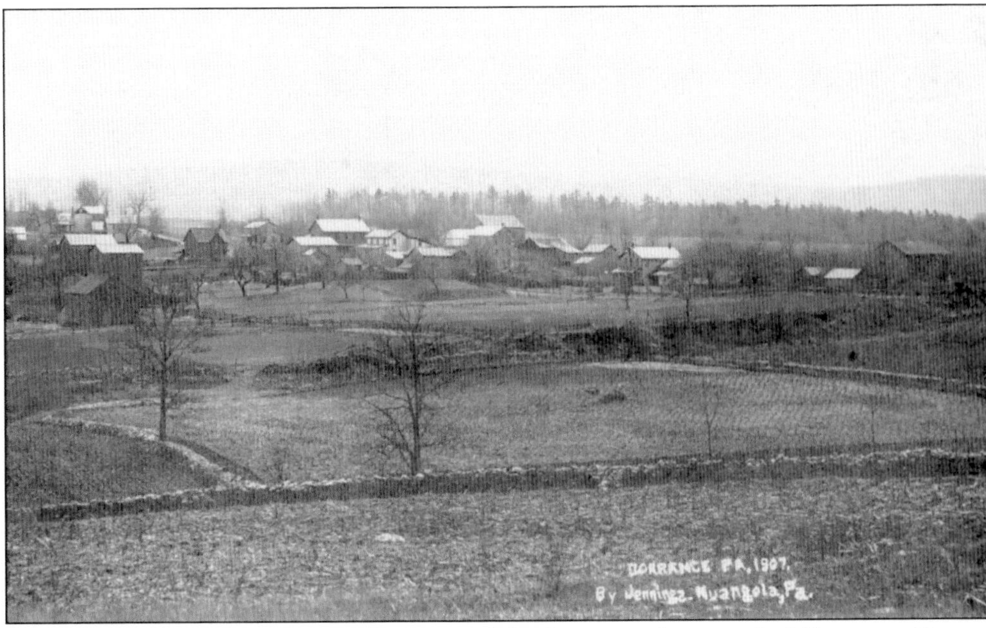

DORRANCE CORNERS, DORRANCE TOWNSHIP. John Jennings photographed Dorrance Corners in 1907. Visible at the center along the road now known as the Blue Ridge Trail was the local tavern, today called the Dorrance Inn. (Courtesy of Robert Hatcher.)

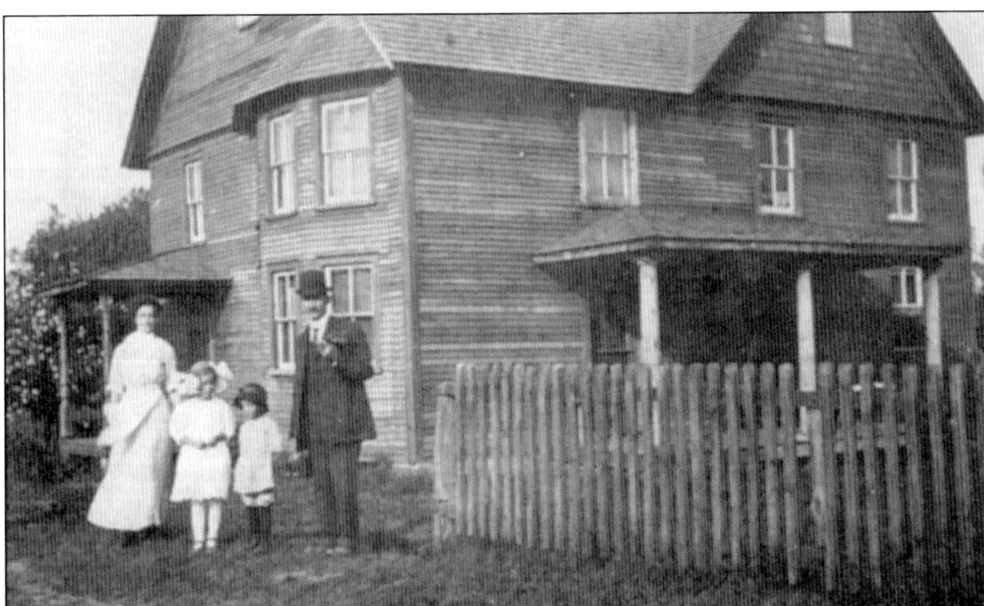

HART HOUSE. As listed on the federal census of 1910, Dr. David Hart was a physician residing at Dorrance Corners. He maintained his country practice there for many years. (Courtesy of the Mountain Top Historical Society: *Pieces of the Past.*)

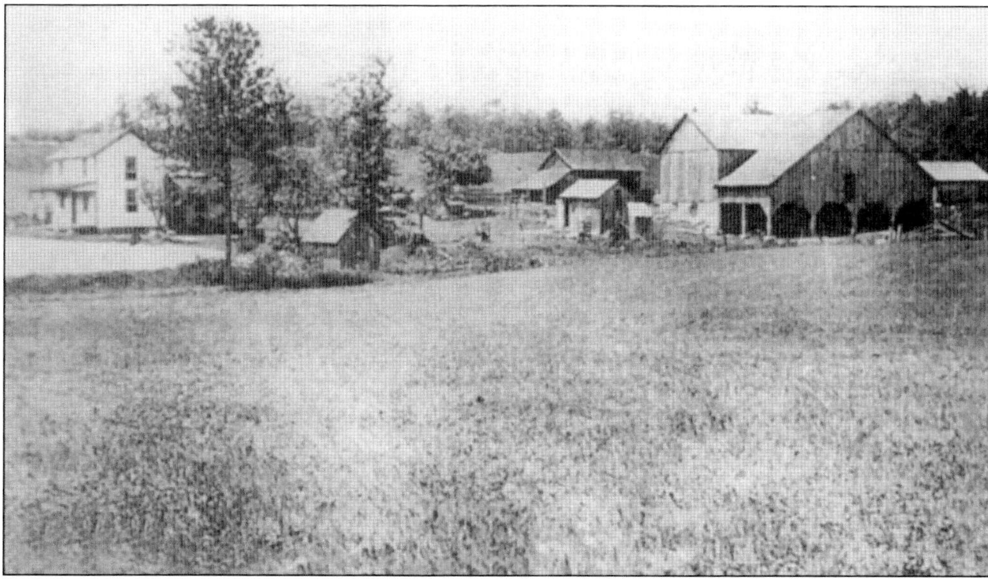

Hartswigen Farm. The Hartswigen family maintained this farm on Alberdeen Road in the early decades of the 20th century. Typical of many farms in the area, it included a house, barn, and numerous outbuildings. (Courtesy of the Mountain Top Historical Society: *Pieces of the Past.*)

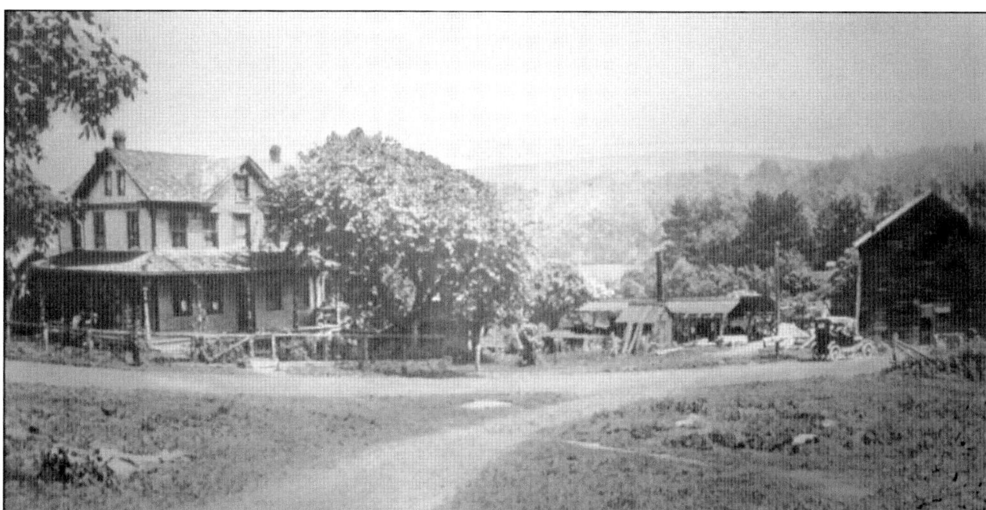

Heller's Mill. Water-powered sawmills and gristmills operated by William Heller along the Big Wapwallopen Creek were photographed in 1916. Also shown were his daughter Amelia, standing on the porch of a home located on present-day St. John's Road, and the Model T Ford owned by William Hart, postman. (Courtesy of Hilda Lewis.)

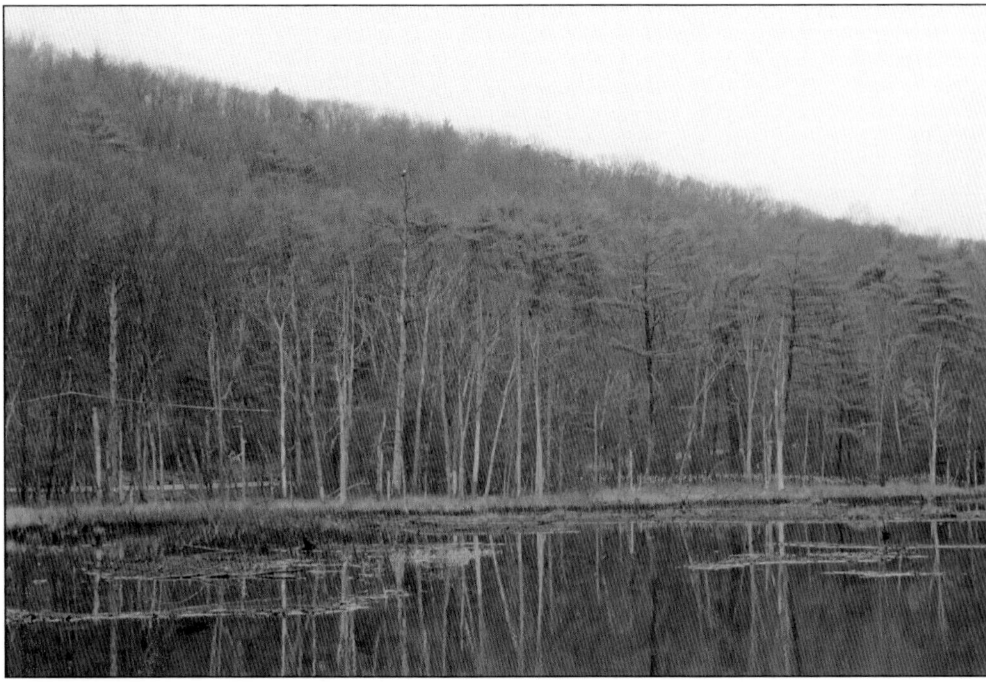

Mud Pond. For centuries, the mountains, lakes, and forests now recognized as Slocum Township have provided important habitats for wildlife. Native Americans and colonial settlers fished and hunted in the region. A dugout canoe, discovered at the Mud Pond in 1932, is in the collection of the Pennsylvania Historical and Museum Commission in Harrisburg. (Courtesy of Darlene Miller-Lanning.)

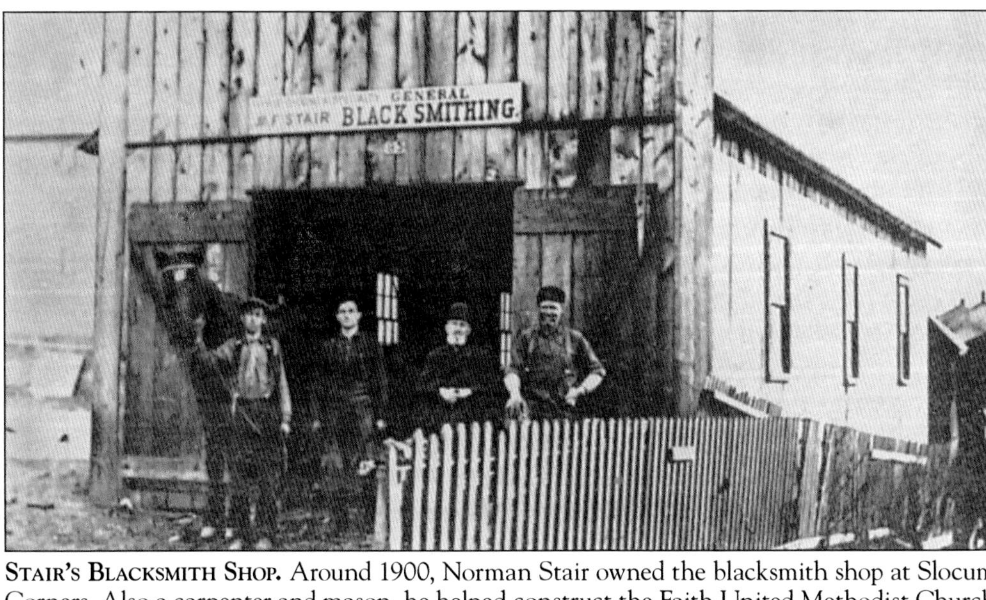

Stair's Blacksmith Shop. Around 1900, Norman Stair owned the blacksmith shop at Slocum Corners. Also a carpenter and mason, he helped construct the Faith United Methodist Church in 1890. (Courtesy of Mountain Top Photo: Whitebread, *History of Slocum Township*.)

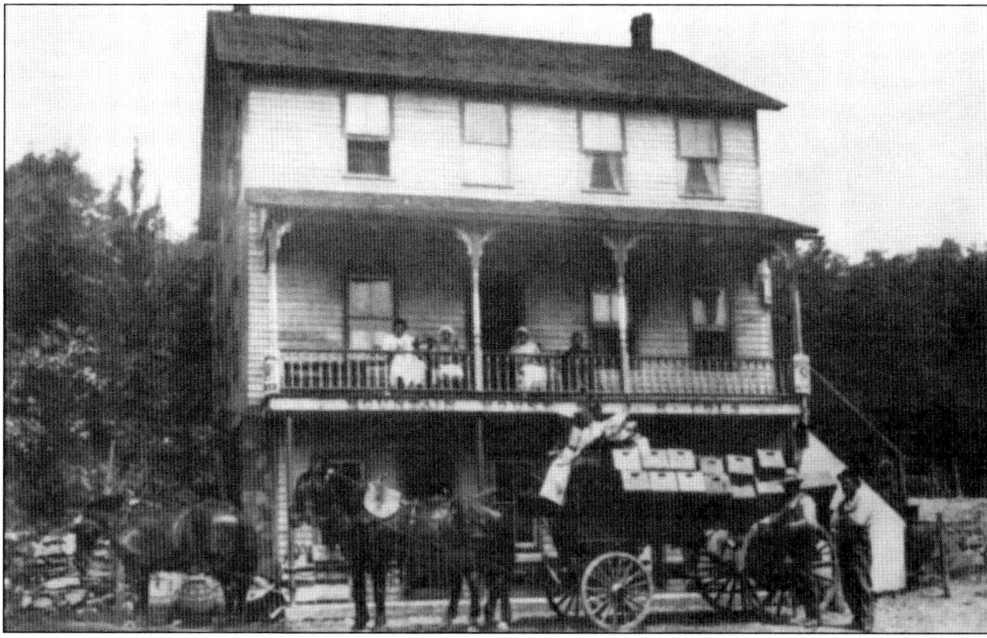

Fols Mountain House. In 1900, John Fols built a hotel, known as the Fols Mountain House, along present-day Nuangola Road. Beverages were brought to the tavern by wagon from the Bartels Brewery, Susquehanna Brewery, Class Nac Brewery, and Barrall's Soft Drink Company. (Courtesy of Mountain Top Photo: Whitebread, *History of Slocum Township*.)

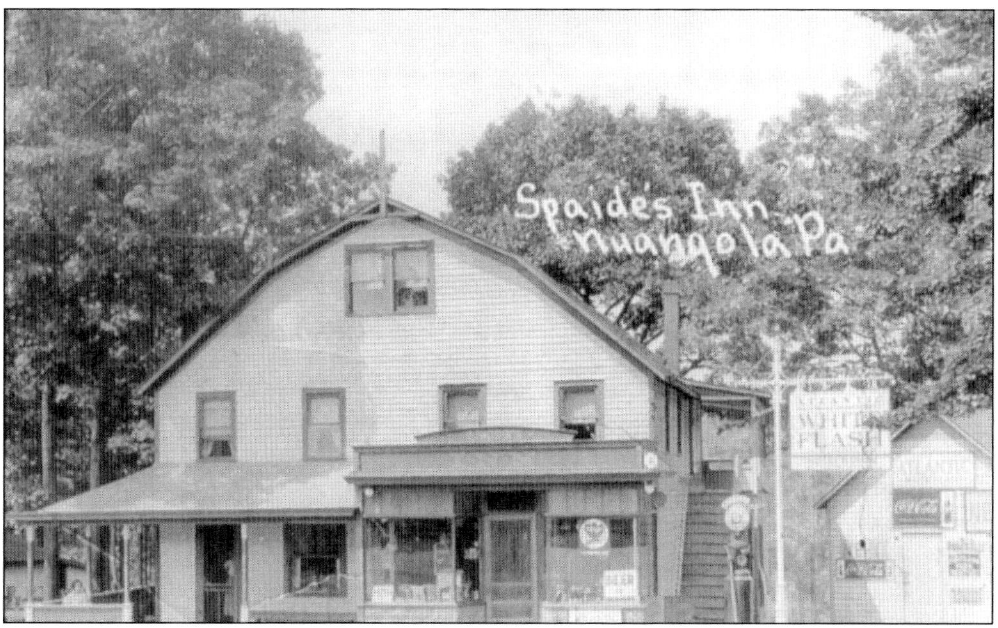

Spaide's Inn. Spaide's Inn and Gas Station was built on the property at the intersection of Blytheburn and Nuangola Roads formerly occupied by Peter Stair's General Store, which burned down. The inn was closed for several years but reopened in 2008 with a new owner. (Courtesy of the Mountain Top Historical Society: *Pieces of the Past*.)

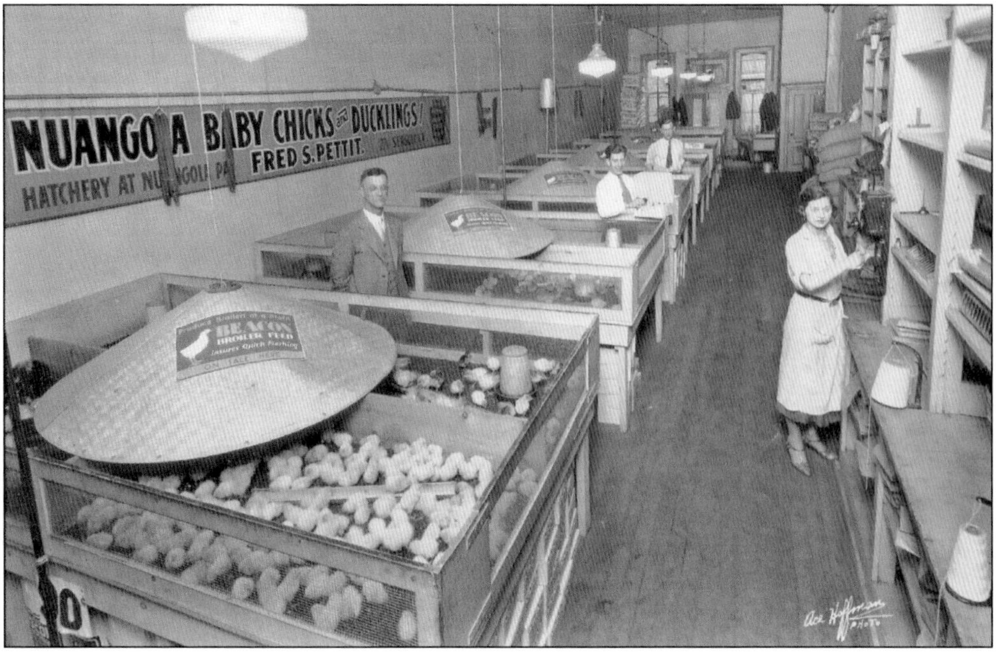

Baby Chicks at Pettit's Poultry Market. In 1904, Fred Pettit began raising baby chicks as a hobby. Soon, he opened a brood house at Nuangola Station where three large incubators could hold over 20,000 eggs. Pettit shipped his poultry on the Wilkes-Barre & Hazleton Railway to city stores. He was also in charge of the powerhouse for the electric railroad. (Courtesy of Donald Pettit.)

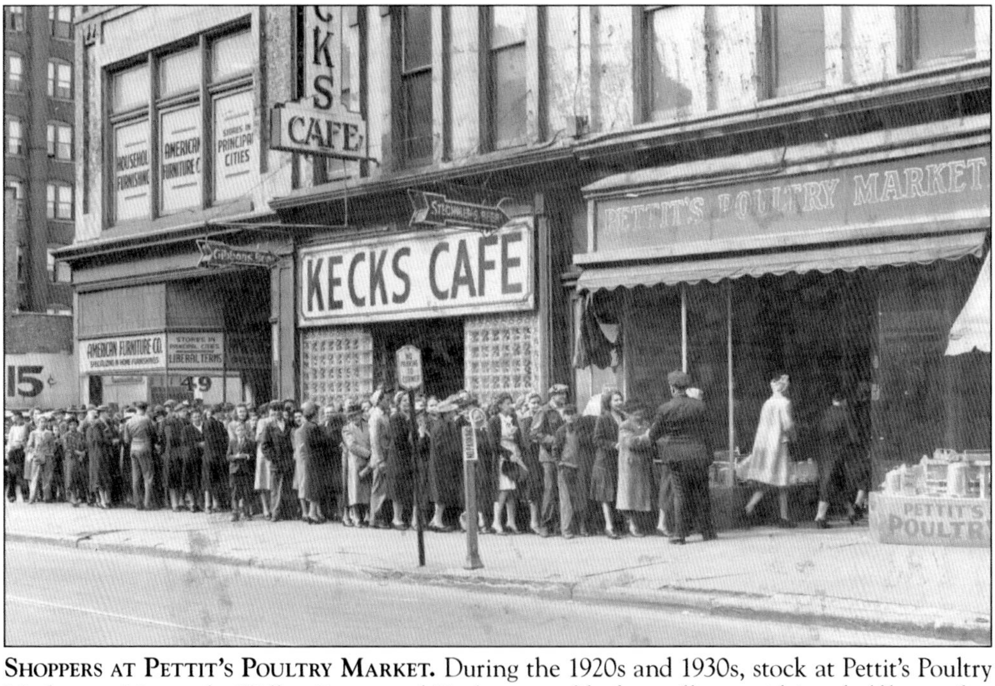

Shoppers at Pettit's Poultry Market. During the 1920s and 1930s, stock at Pettit's Poultry Markets in Nuangola, Wilkes-Barre, and Hazleton could often sell out within a half-hour after the store's opening. Pettit also wholesaled spring chicks to all parts of the country. (Courtesy of Donald Pettit.)

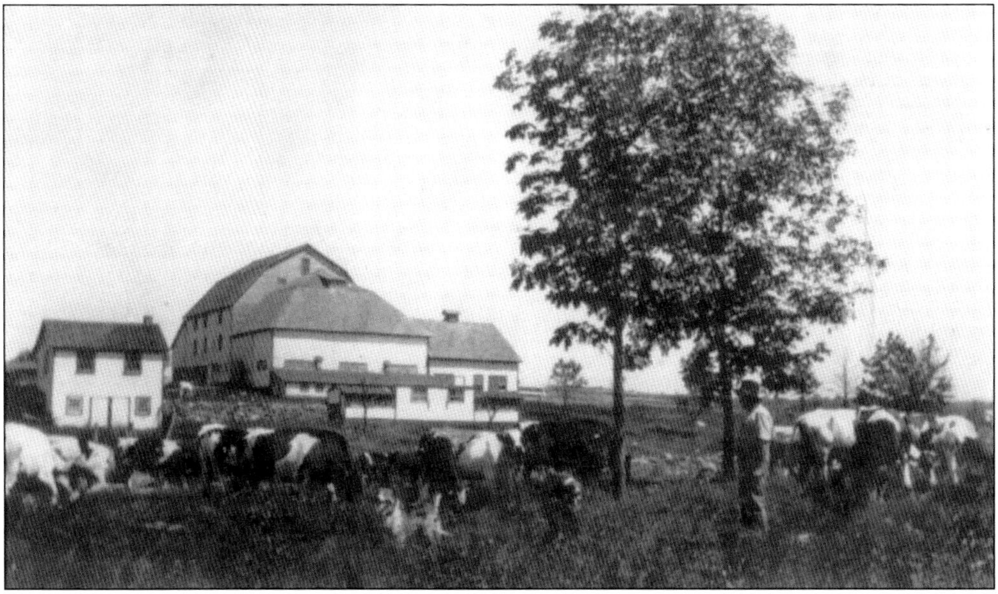

Smith's White Thorn Farm. Photographed in 1935, the White Thorn Stock Farm, located on South Main Road in Wright Township, was owned by the Smith brothers. The dairy farm pasteurized and distributed its own products, made from the milk of tubercular-tested cows. The farm closed in the 1950s. The Meadowbrook Riding Stables later rented and operated the property. (Courtesy of James and Edith Miller.)

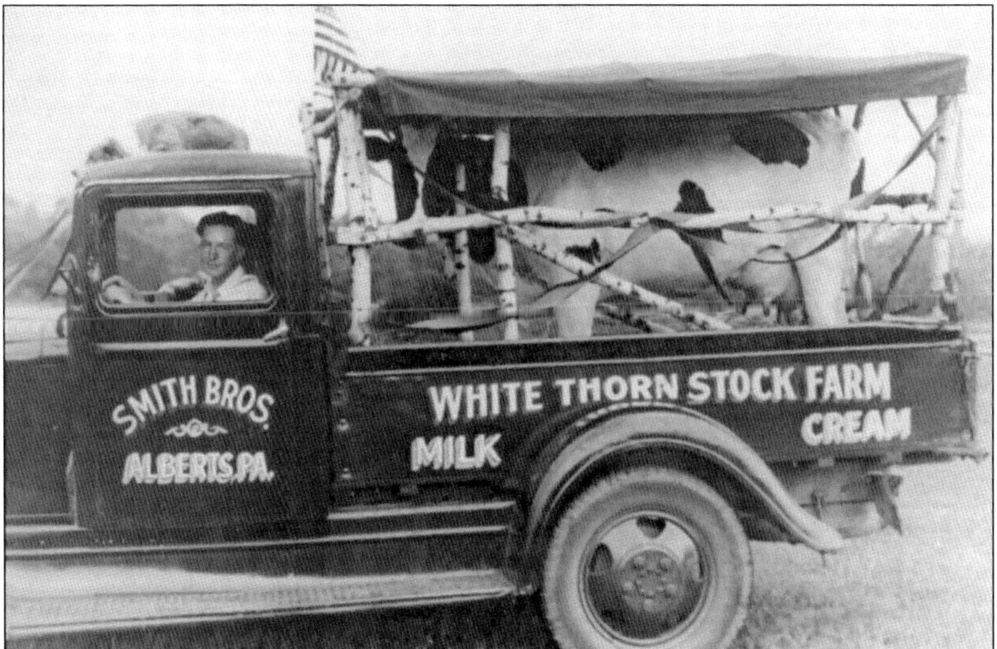

Smith's White Thorn Farm Truck. In 1935, Carl Smith drove this decorated White Thorn Stock Farm truck in the parade celebrating the opening of Route 309. He was accompanied by a milk cow in the back of the truck and a dog, shown resting on the roof of the cab. (Courtesy of Sam and Rachel Goyne.)

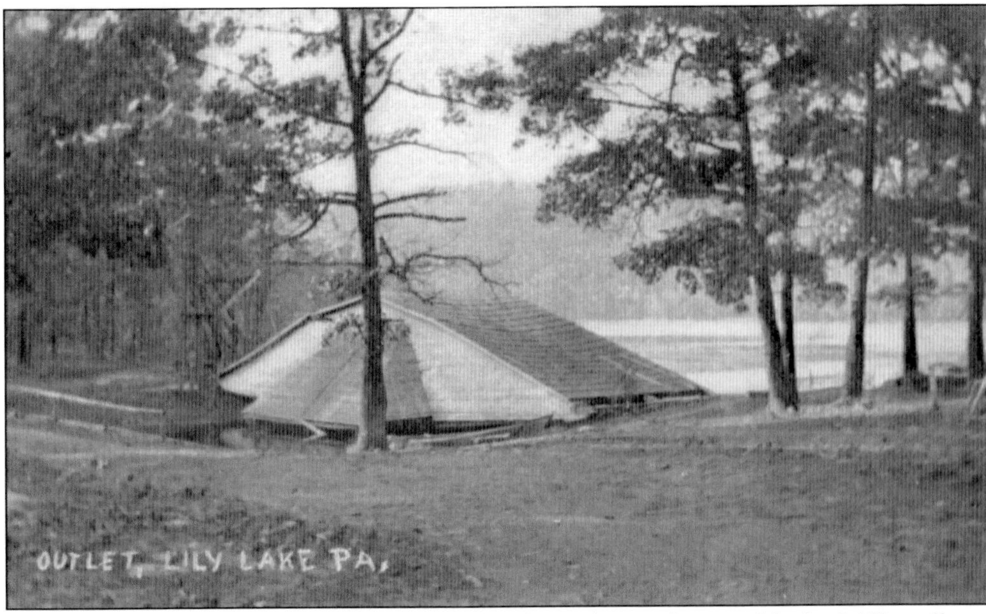

Lily Lake Outlet. Formerly Long Pond, Lily Lake is located on a tributary of the Little Wapwallopen Creek in Slocum Township. During the 1920s, William Miller operated the Lily Lake Hotel and rented cottages. Joseph Schappert was proprietor of Ye Olde Lantern Hotel from 1937 to 1942. Today, the Pennsylvania Fish and Boat Commission manages the lake. (Courtesy of the Mountain Top Historical Society: *Pieces of the Past.*)

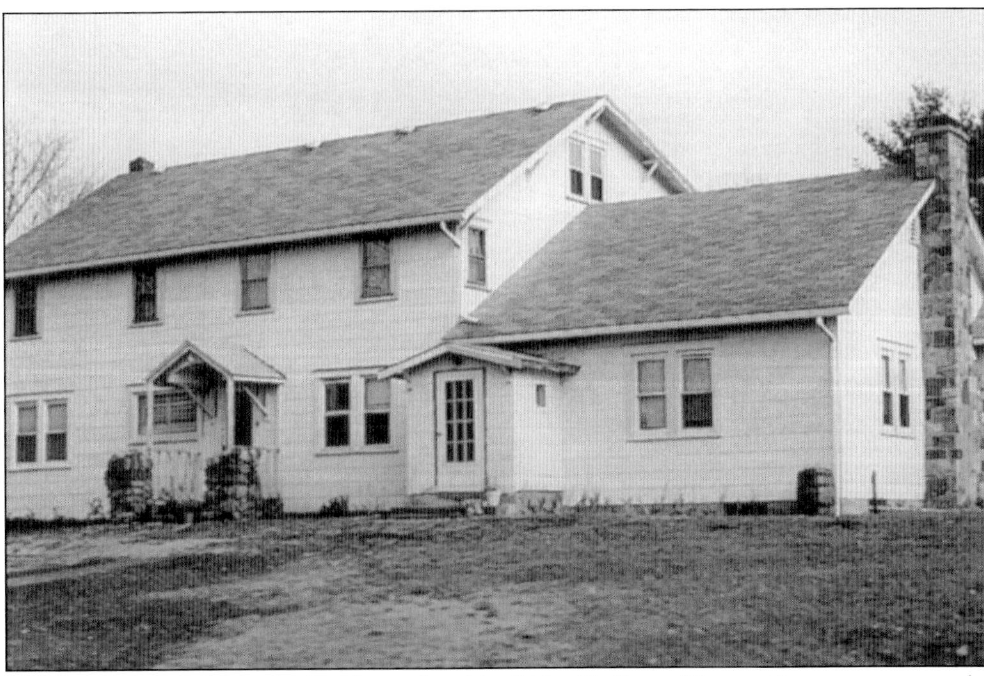

Makowski's Bar. Makowski's Bar, located on Blue Ridge Trail near Slocum Corners, was a popular local tavern. (Courtesy of Mountain Top Photo.)

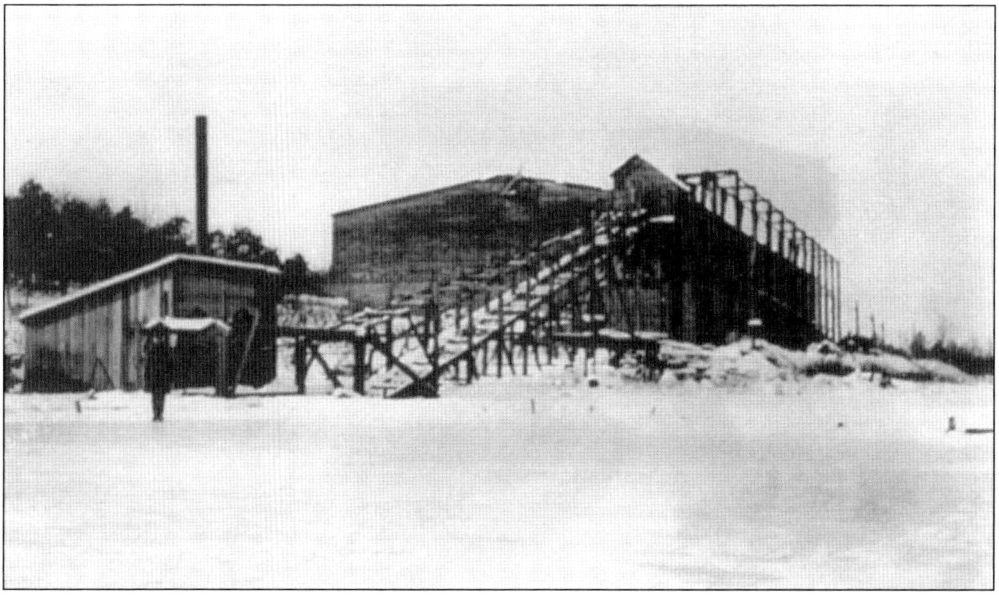

Icehouse at Upper Ice Lake in Winter. In 1912, the Crystal Lake Ice Company dammed the Little Wapwallopen Creek to form the Lower Ice Lake in what is now Rice Township. Nearby, the Wilkes-Barre and Hazleton Ice Company created the Upper Ice Lake in 1916. Blocks of ice were cut from the lake in winter and stored in an icehouse on its shore. (Courtesy of Joseph Tweedle Sr.)

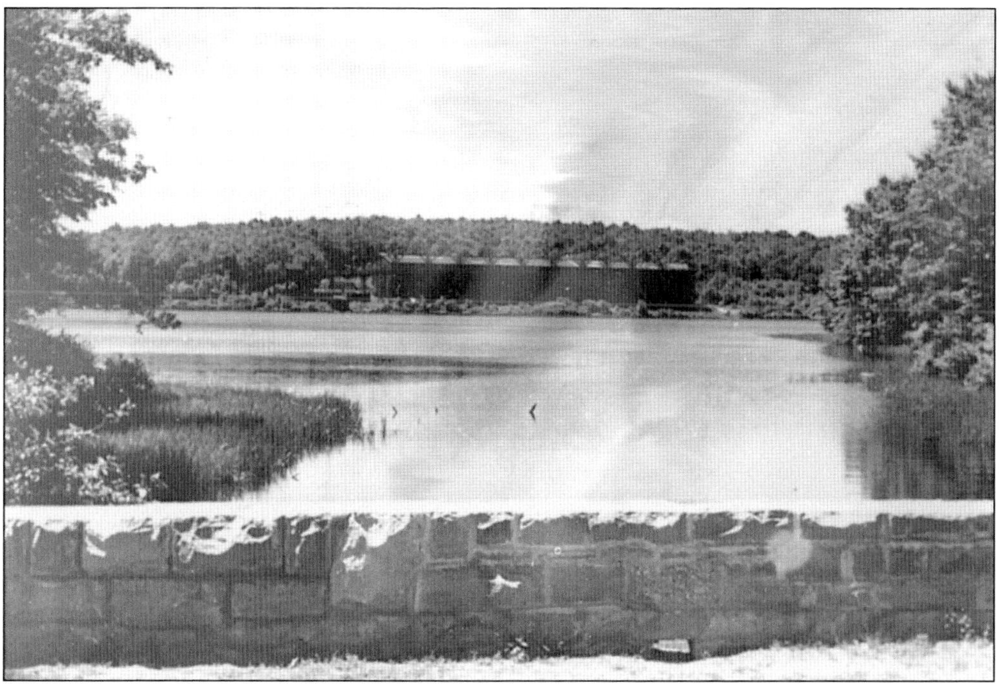

Icehouse at Upper Ice Lake in Summer. In the summer, ice that had been stored in the sawdust-insulated icehouse was shipped on the Wilkes-Barre & Hazleton Railway for distribution and use in private iceboxes, which predated refrigerators. Today, Rice Township maintains a recreational area near the Ice Lakes. (Courtesy of Joseph Tweedle Sr.)

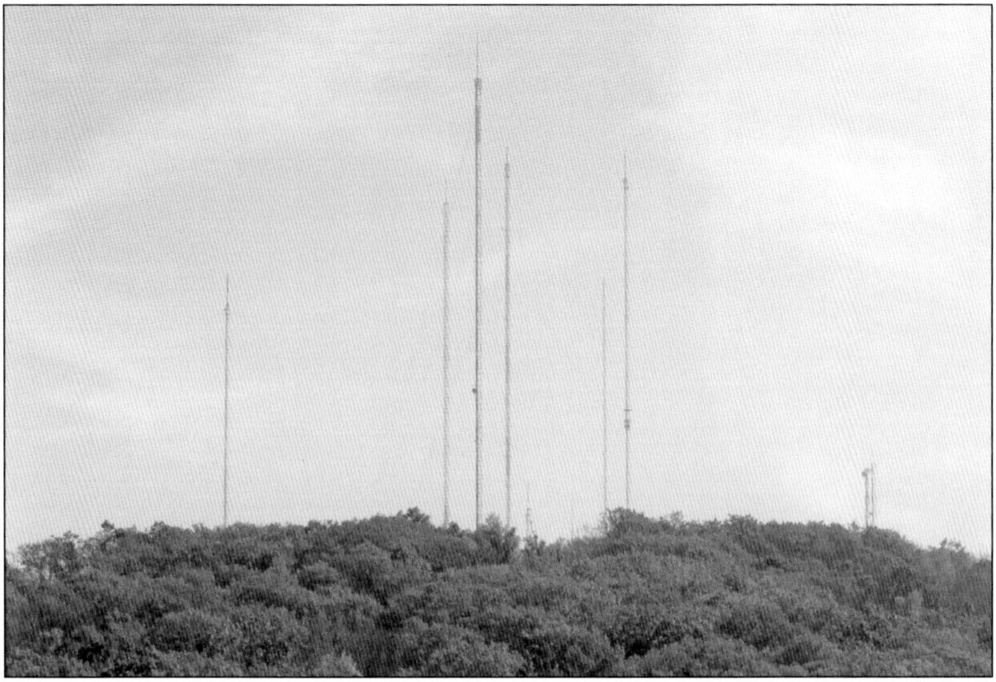

ELECTRONIC HEIGHTS. Many broadcasting towers are located at the summit of Penobscot Mountain in an area known as Electronic Heights. The towers are visible from a great distance and are local landmarks. (Courtesy of Darlene Miller-Lanning.)

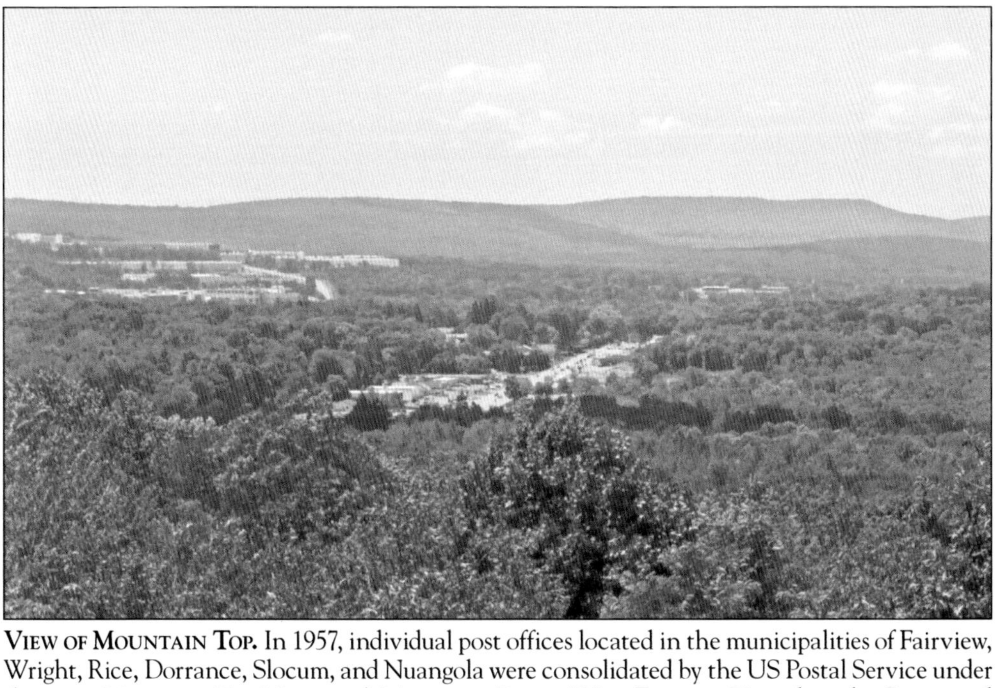

VIEW OF MOUNTAIN TOP. In 1957, individual post offices located in the municipalities of Fairview, Wright, Rice, Dorrance, Slocum, and Nuangola were consolidated by the US Postal Service under the name Mountain Top. Nescopeck Mountain, Route 309 in Fairview Township, the Crestwood Industrial Park, and Crestwood High School are visible in this view of Mountain Top looking south from Penobscot Mountain. (Courtesy of Darlene Miller-Lanning.)

Two

RAILS AND ENGINES

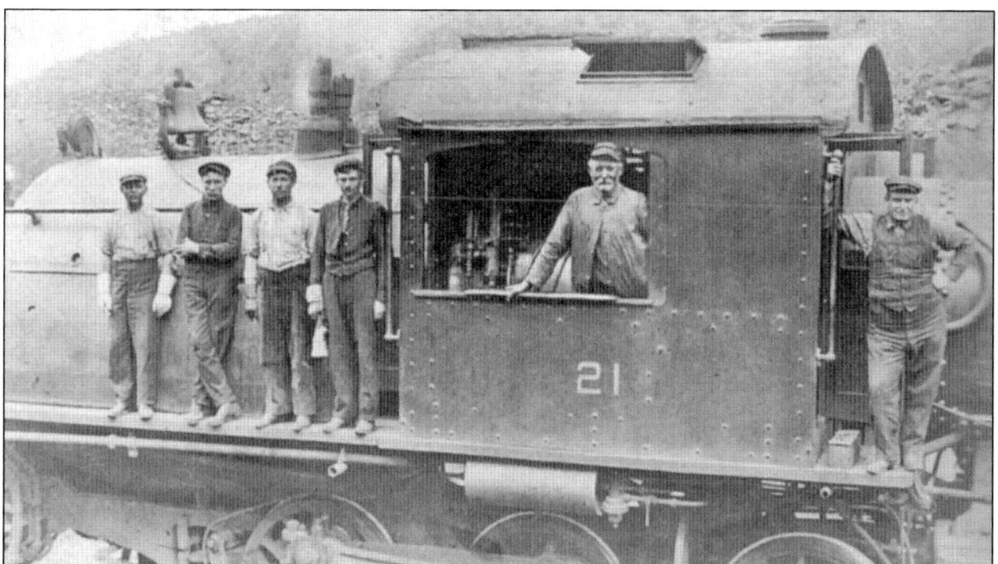

CENTRAL RAILROAD OF NEW JERSEY ENGINE NO. 21. The crew of the Central Railroad of New Jersey engine No. 21, including, from left to right, Lee Brown, Eddie McGinnis, Frank Dotter, Barnett Miller, engineer Norman Richard, and D. "Tucker" Swartwood, was photographed at the Penobscot Yard. (Courtesy of Leo Brookus.)

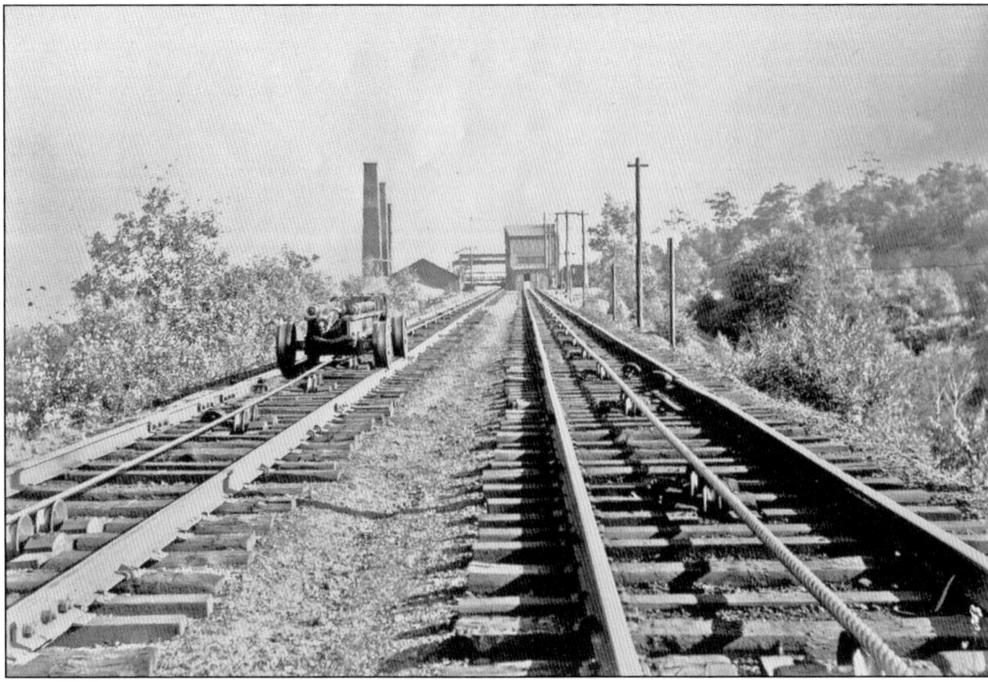

ASHLEY PLANES, PLANE NO. 1. Built by the Lehigh Coal and Navigation Company in 1843, the Ashley Planes were a series of three inclines crossing Penobscot Mountain. Cars loaded at Ashley were hauled up the planes on a cable pulled by stationary engines to Solomon's Gap at the summit. Plane No. 1, nearest Solomon's Gap, had a slope of three degrees per 15 feet. (Courtesy of the Mountain Top Historical Society: *Railroads*.)

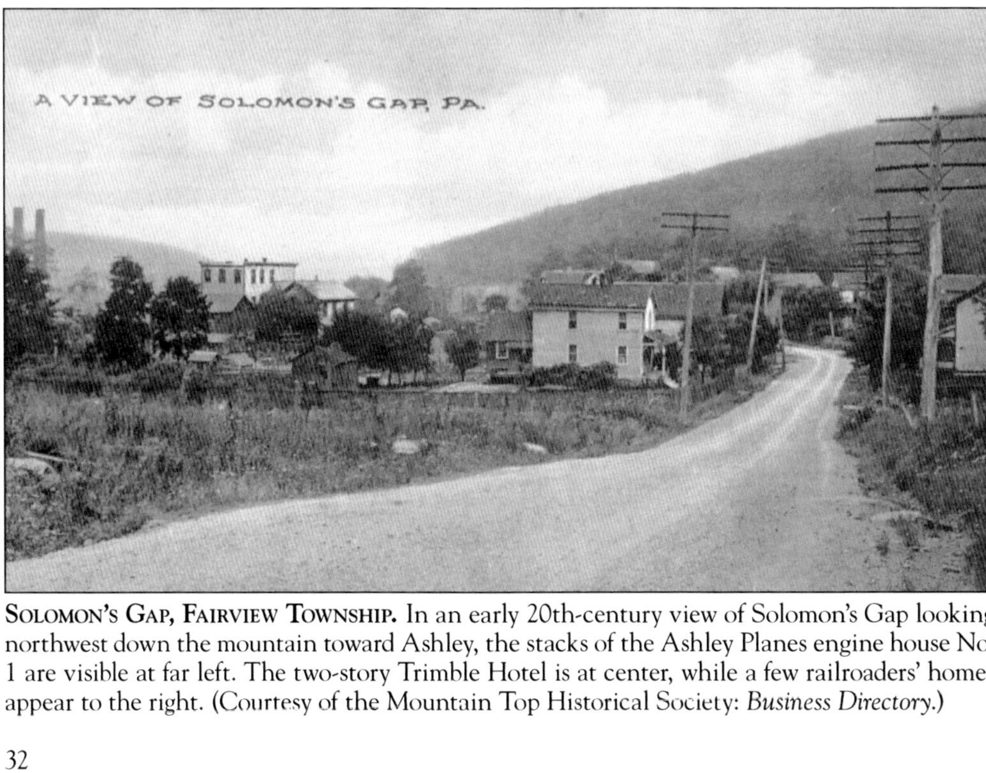

SOLOMON'S GAP, FAIRVIEW TOWNSHIP. In an early 20th-century view of Solomon's Gap looking northwest down the mountain toward Ashley, the stacks of the Ashley Planes engine house No. 1 are visible at far left. The two-story Trimble Hotel is at center, while a few railroaders' homes appear to the right. (Courtesy of the Mountain Top Historical Society: *Business Directory*.)

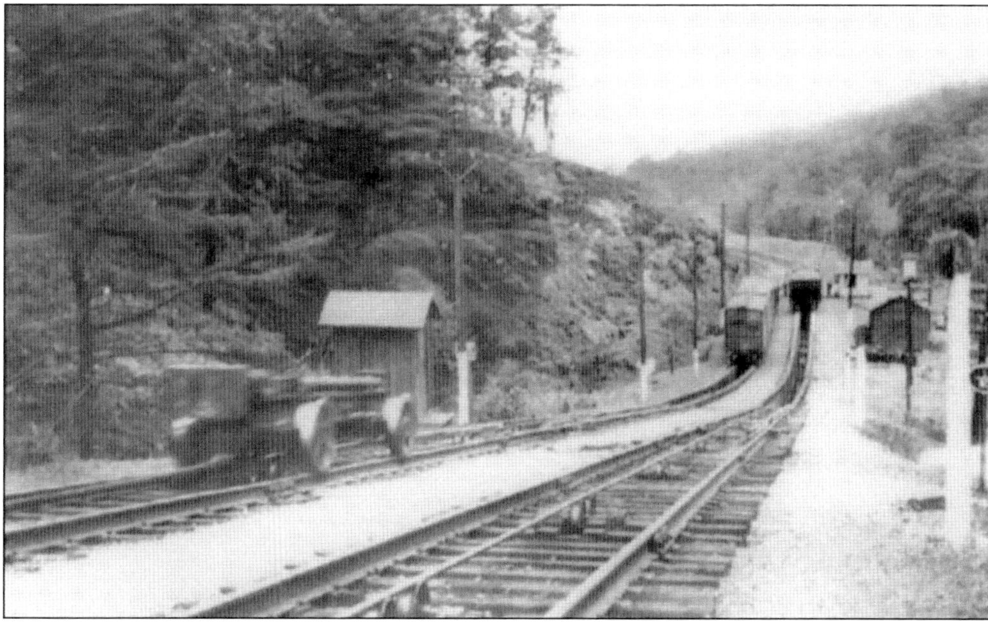

Ashley Planes, Plane No. 2. Plane No. 2 was located on Penobscot Mountain midway between Ashley and Solomon's Gap. Cars ascended the planes with help from a "barney car," shown to the left. Attached to a cable wound onto a drum at the top of the plane, the barney car pushed loaded cars before it as it was hauled up the incline. (Courtesy of the Mountain Top Historical Society: *Railroads.*)

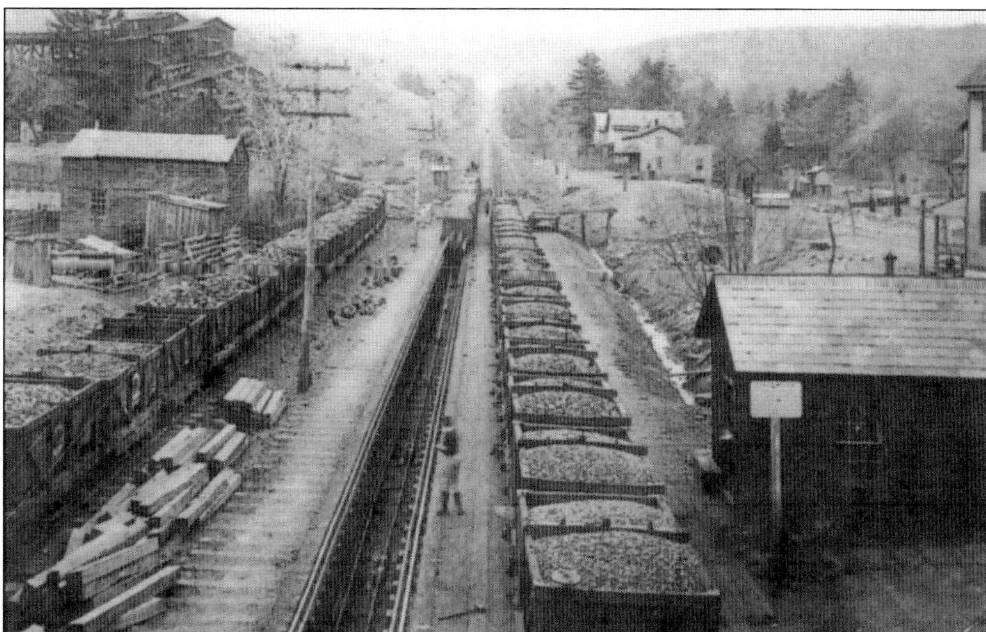

Ashley Planes, Plane No. 3. Plane No. 3 was located in Ashley, where loaded cars were gathered for transport on the planes. In this view south up the mountain, a set of cars was hoisted on the left track, while a second set awaited hoisting on the right. A coal breaker appeared on the left. (Courtesy of the Mountain Top Historical Society: *Railroads.*)

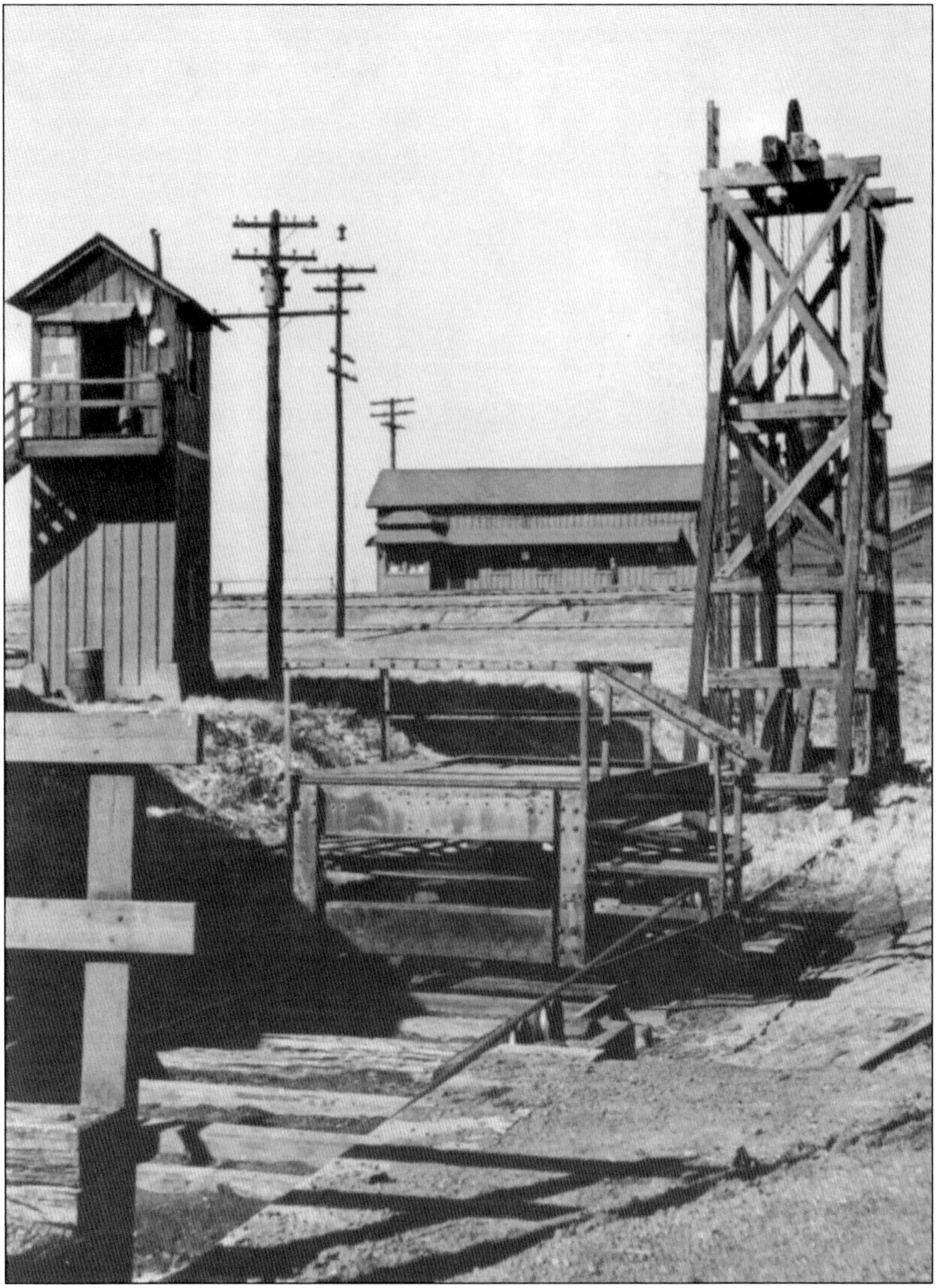

Ashley Planes Counterweight Tower. A counterweight tower and tail-rope anchoring mechanism at the bottom of plane No. 3 were photographed in 1944. (Courtesy of Annie Bohlin and William T. Greenberg: *History of the Ashley Planes.*)

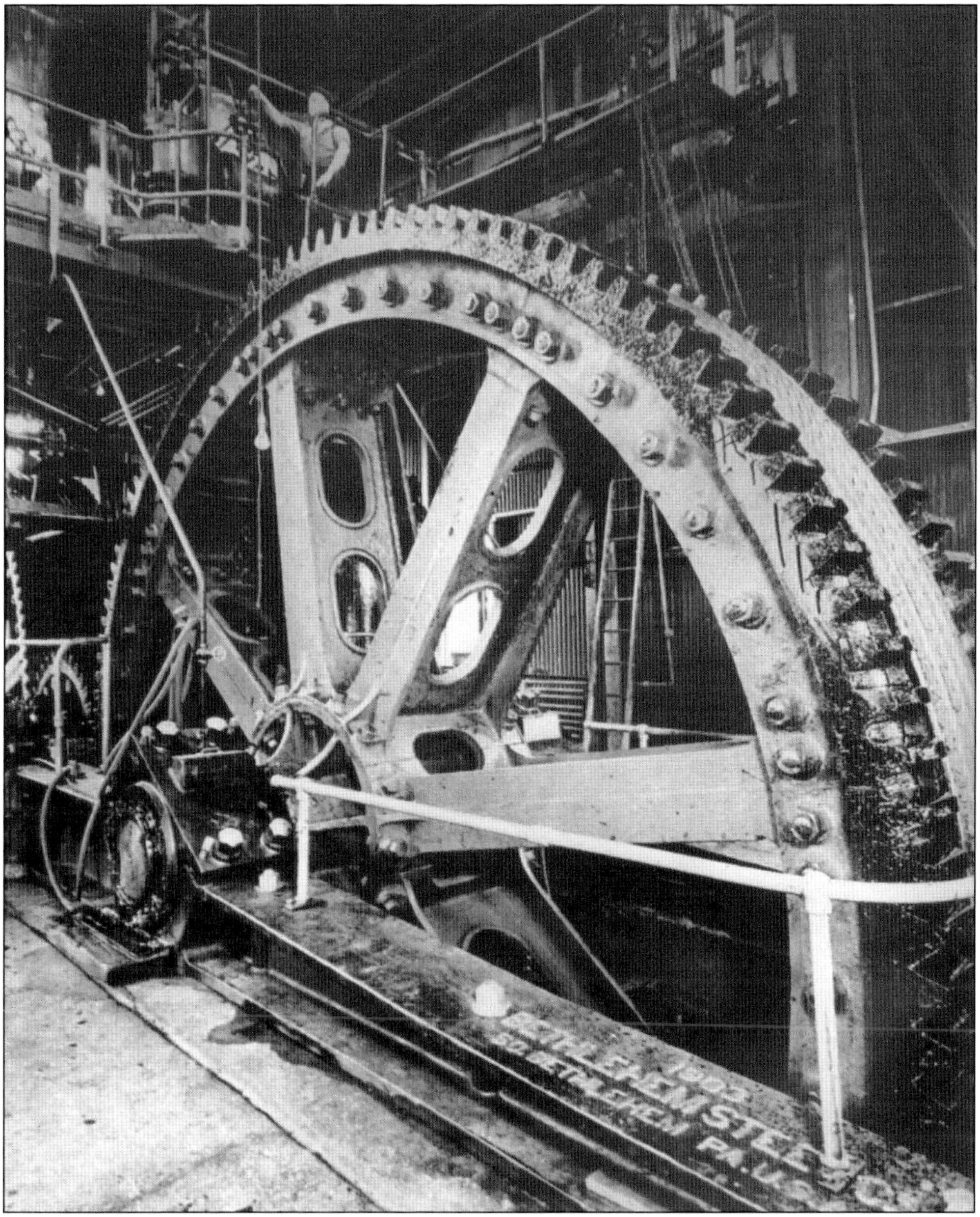

Ashley Planes Winding Drum. A cable drum and hoisting machinery were photographed inside an engine house on the Ashley Planes. The operator's location above the drum on the left provided him with a view of the plane. (Courtesy of Annie Bohlin and George Leilich: *History of the Ashley Planes.*)

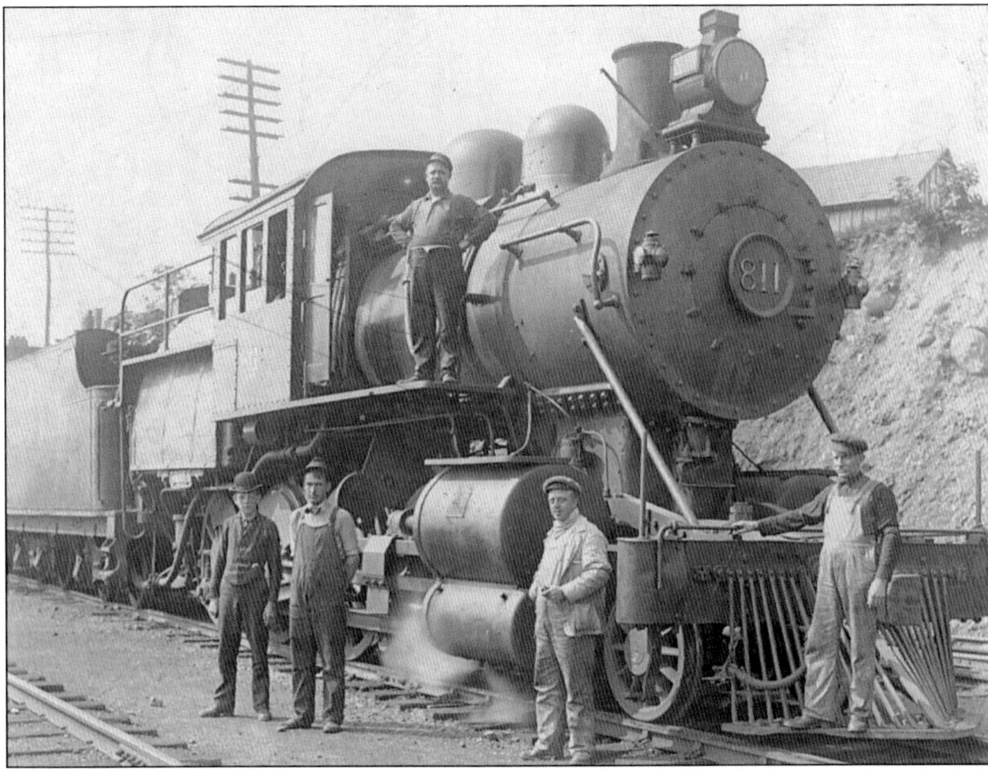

Lehigh Valley Railroad Engine No. 811. In 1867, the Lehigh Valley Railroad extended its line through the Mountain Top area. First used on the line were steam locomotives. Crew members could include engineers, conductors, firemen, and brakemen. This early photograph of the crew of engine No. 811 included Donald Koons Sr. (Courtesy of Russell Koons.)

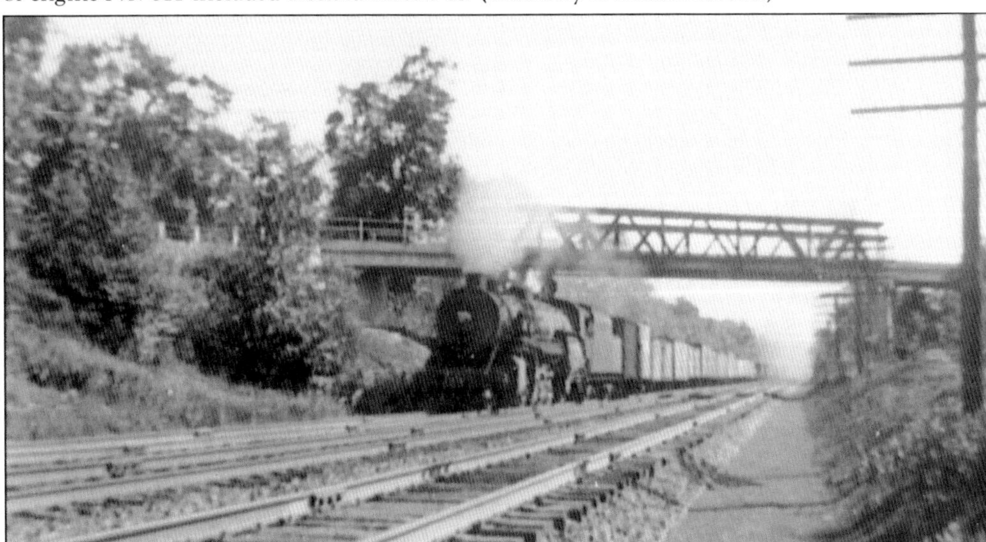

Lehigh Valley Railroad Bridge at Glen Summit. A steam locomotive was photographed in the 1950s on the Lehigh Valley Railroad line near the bridge at Glen Summit. (Courtesy of Leo Brookus.)

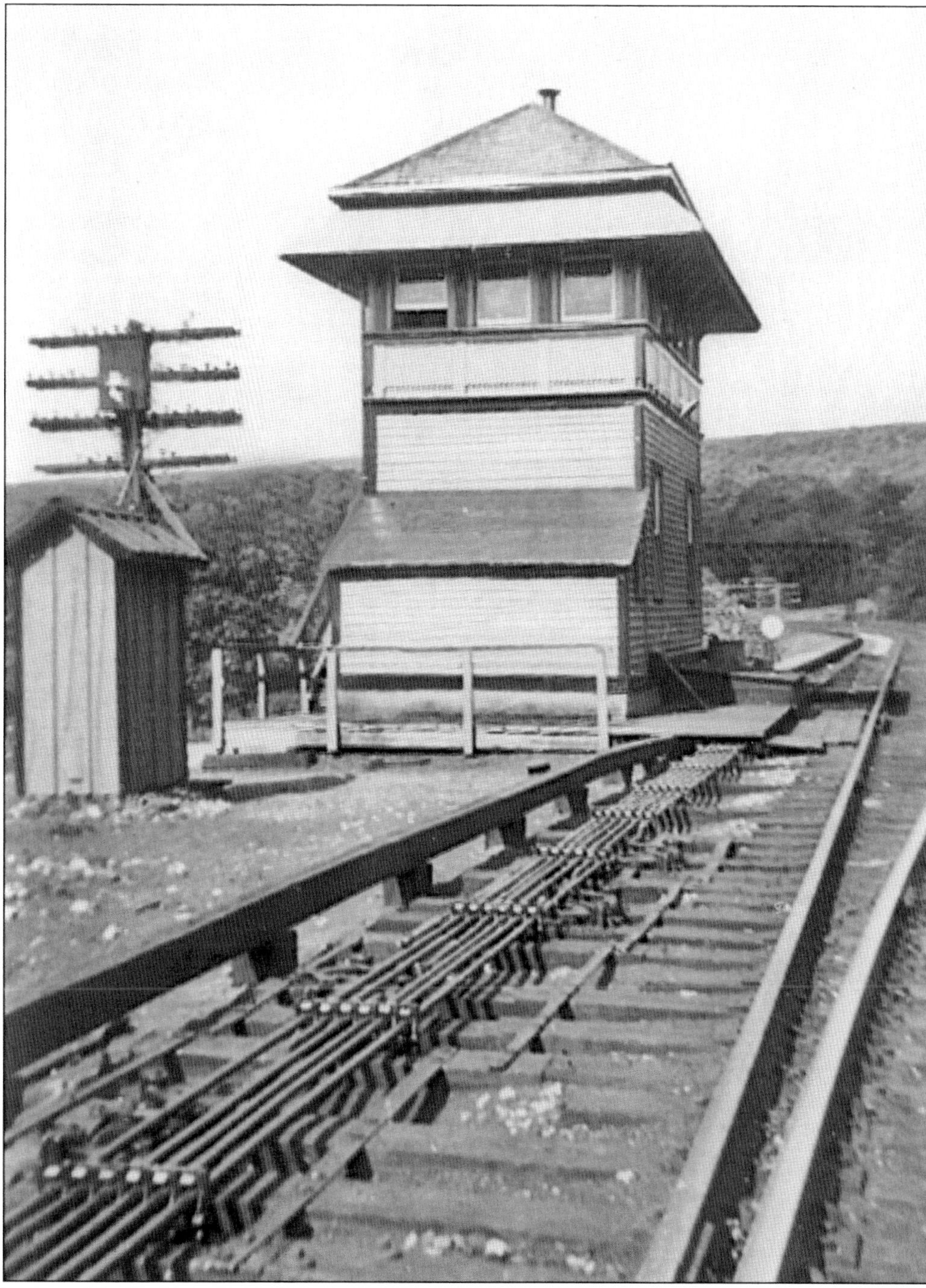

LEHIGH VALLEY RAILROAD GRACEDALE TOWER. Photographed in the 1960s, Gracedale Tower controlled train movements for the Lehigh Valley Railroad on five tracks through Mountain Top. Passenger trains went to Wilkes-Barre, while freight trains went to Pittston Junction. (Courtesy of Leo Brookus.)

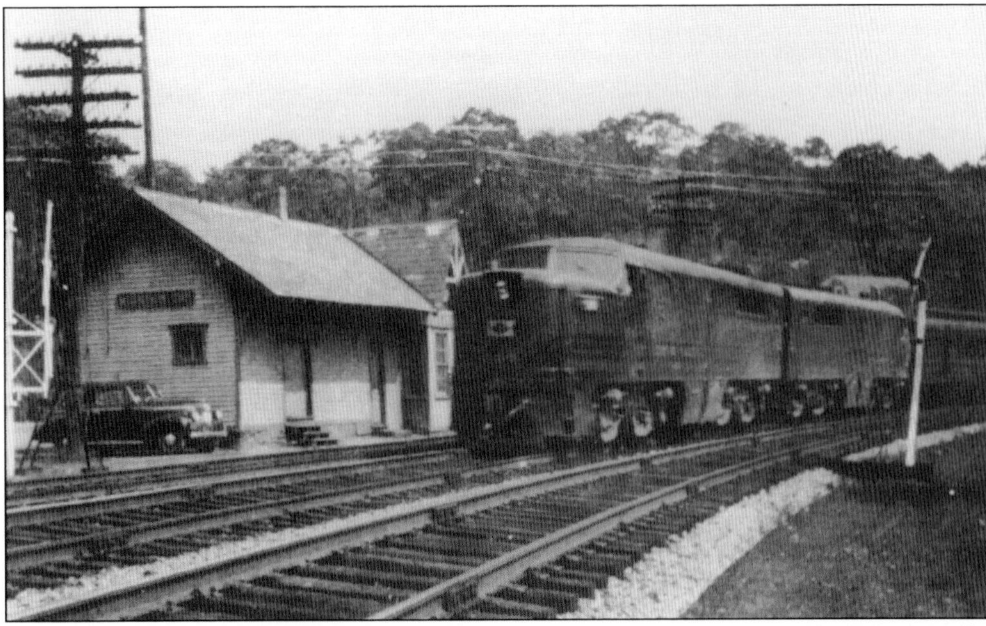

Lehigh Valley Railroad Fairview Station and the Black Diamond. The Lehigh Valley Railroad built Fairview Station for freight and passengers after 1867. The famous Black Diamond passenger train was photographed at Fairview around 1950. The station closed several years later, and the Mountain Top Hose Company No. 1 now occupies its site. (Courtesy of the Mountain Top Historical Society: *Railroads*.)

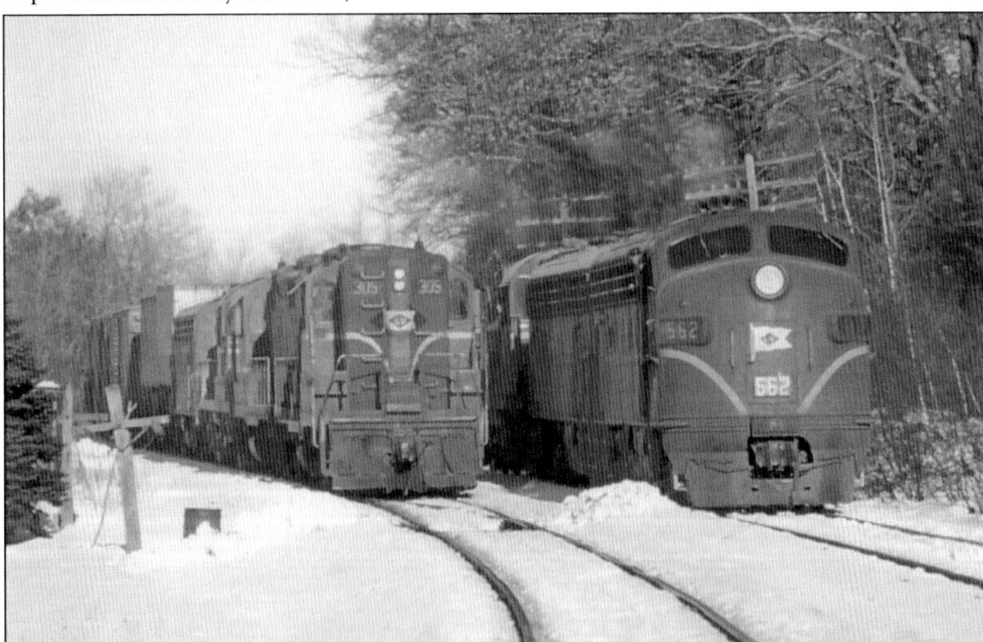

Lehigh Valley Railroad Engines Nos. 305 and 562. Built by General Motors during the diesel era of the 1950s and 1960s, Lehigh Valley Railroad engines Nos. 305 and 562 were photographed at the Kirby Avenue crossing. Engine No. 305 was an EMD GP18, while engine No. 562 was an EMD F7A. (Courtesy of Mountain Top Photo.)

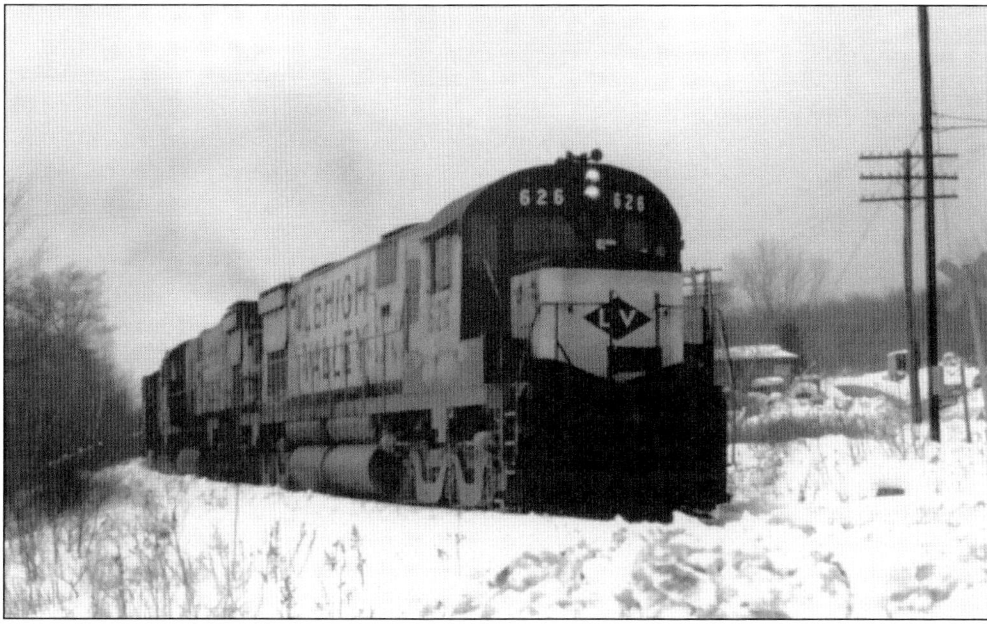

Lehigh Valley Railroad Engine No. 626. The Lehigh Valley Railroad operated several ALCO C628 engines, built by the American Locomotive Company in the 1960s, using its "Century" design. Engine No. 626, painted in the white-and-black "Snowbird" color scheme, was photographed near the Church Road crossing at Rita. Engine No. 628 was located at the back of the eastbound train. (Courtesy of Mountain Top Photo.)

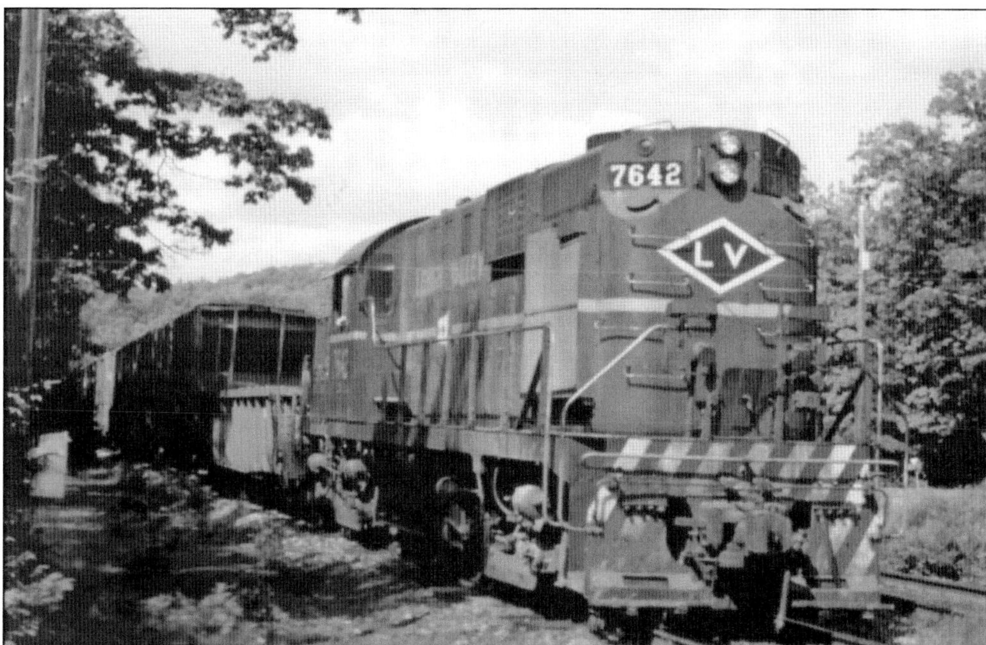

Lehigh Valley Railroad Engine No. 7642. The Lehigh Valley Railroad engine No. 7642 was photographed at the Glen Summit Water Company crossing. Engine No. 7642 was an ALCO RS11 built by the American Locomotive Company in the 1950s. (Courtesy of Mountain Top Photo.)

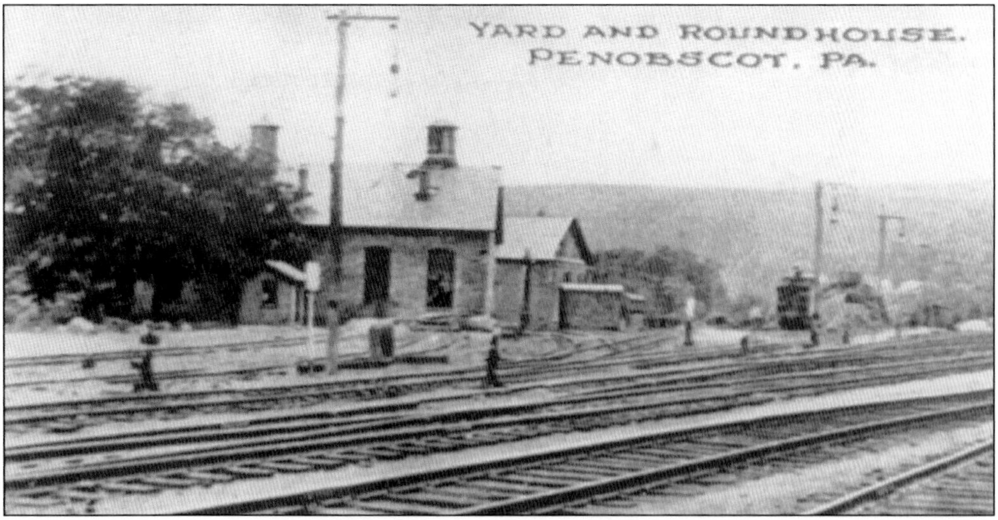

Central Railroad of New Jersey Yard and Roundhouse. The Central Railroad of New Jersey began operating in the Mountain Top area when it leased the properties of the Lehigh & Susquehanna Railroad in 1871. Its roundhouse, photographed in the early 1900s, was located at Penobscot Yards near Gracedale Avenue. Steam engines were serviced there and moved on a turntable. A station was located across the tracks. (Courtesy of Russell Koons.)

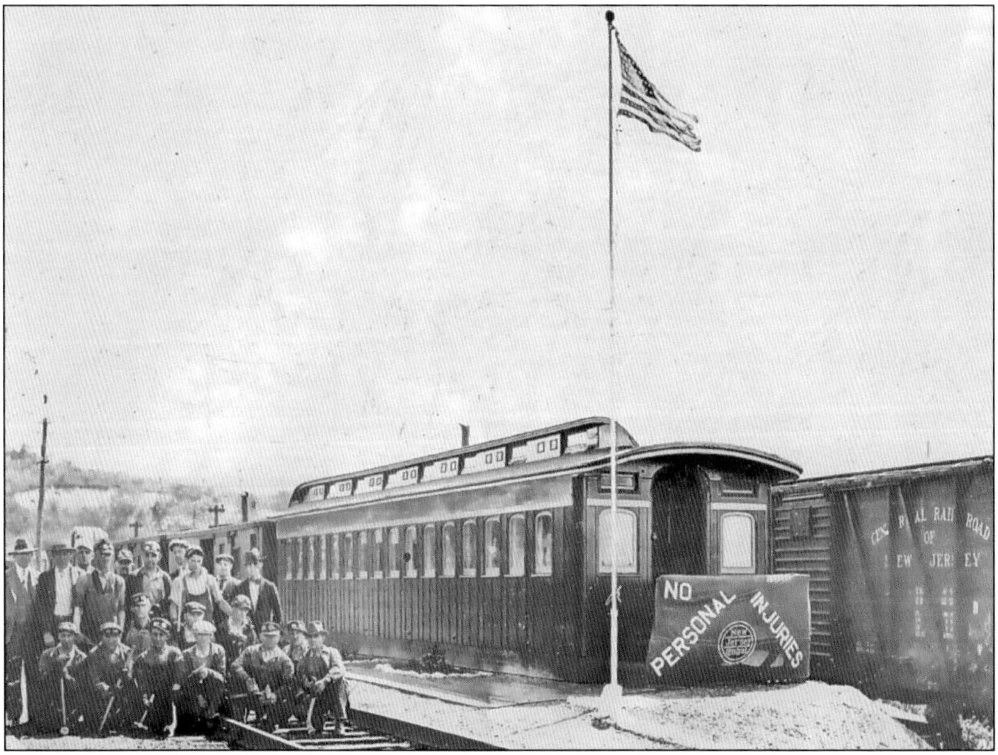

Central Railroad of New Jersey Penobscot Shops. The Penobscot Car Shop was located on the south side of the train yard, which included 11 tracks. Workers photographed there included Al Maiers, Paul Fillman, Leo Petrosky, Arthur Davis, Ray Richards, Fishy Maiers, Stanley Sincavage, John Paulick, Andy Fingner, Dominic Pasky, and Ray Hugh. (Courtesy of Hubert McGovern.)

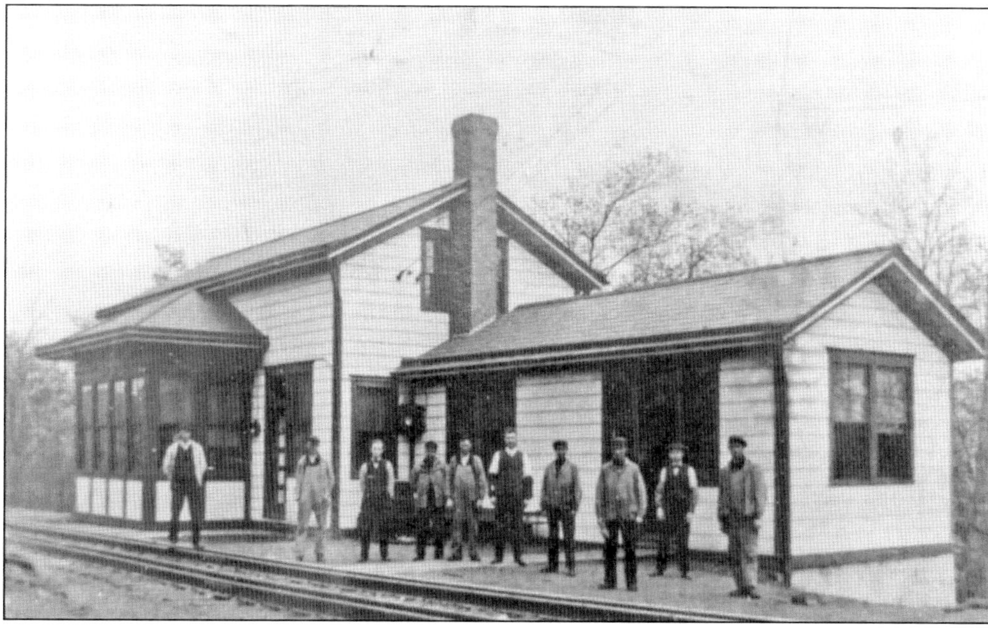

CENTRAL RAILROAD OF NEW JERSEY SCALE HOUSE. Coal hoppers and boxcars that had been lifted on the Ashley Planes were weighed at the Central Railroad of New Jersey's scale house at Penobscot. Destination waybills were written, and the cars were sent over the hump to be made into trains headed for the east coast. (Courtesy of the Mountain Top Historical Society: *Railroads.*)

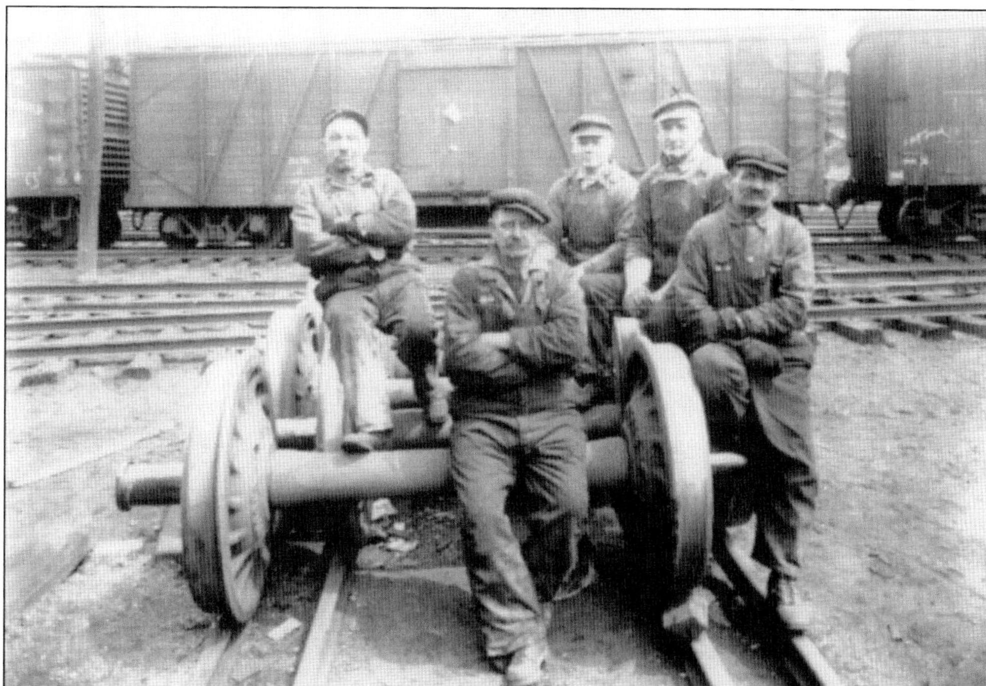

CENTRAL RAILROAD OF NEW JERSEY WORKERS. Central Railroad of New Jersey employees, including Redmond Philip Lines, second from right, were photographed at the Penobscot Yards in the early 20th century. (Courtesy of Redmond Lines.)

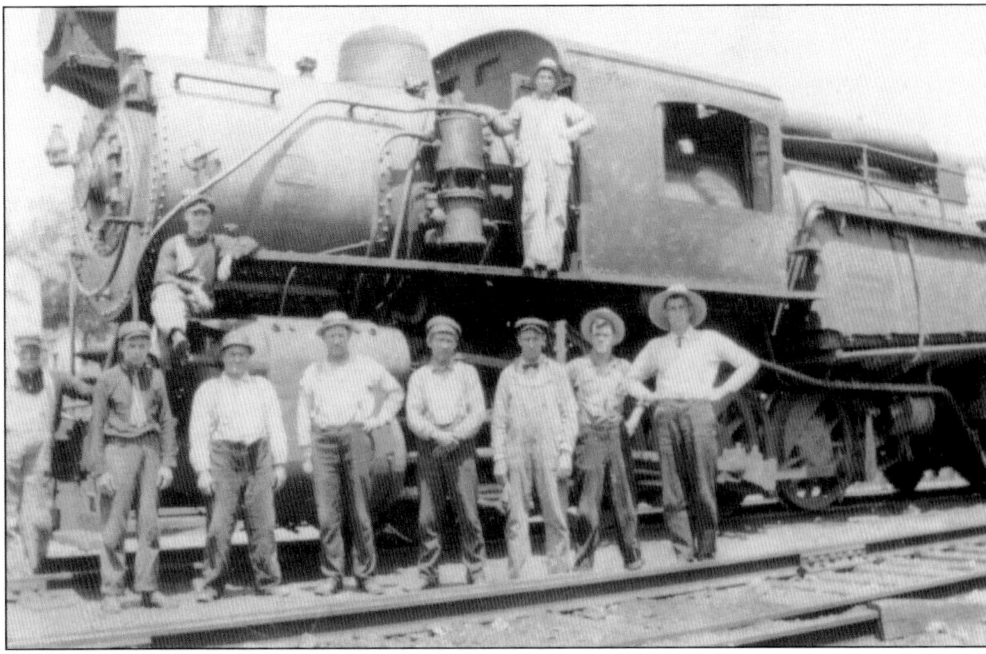

Central Railroad of New Jersey Engine No. 273. During the late 19th century and early 20th century, the Central Railroad of New Jersey ran steam locomotives fueled by coal. The crew of engine No. 273, including Norman Richards, posed for a photograph at Penobscot Yards. (Courtesy of the Mountain Top Historical Society: *Railroads*.)

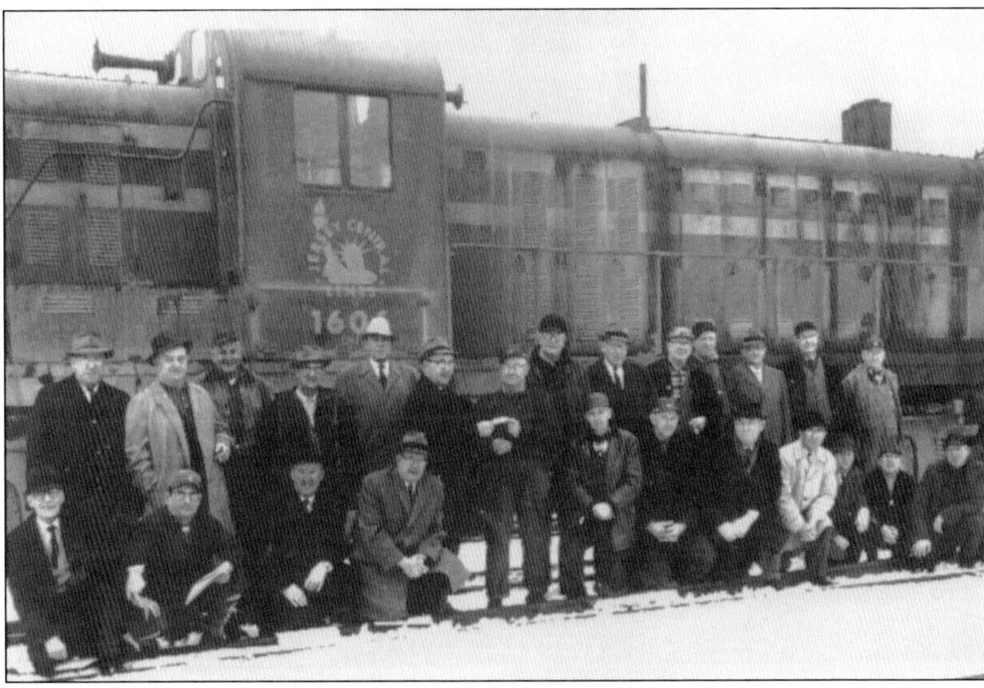

Central Railroad of New Jersey Engine No. 1606. Diesel engines were in use on the Central Railroad of New Jersey by the 1930s. Photographed by engine No. 1606 were Edward Shea, James Searfoss, Harry Fey, and John Curran Jr., among others. (Courtesy of Hubert McGovern.)

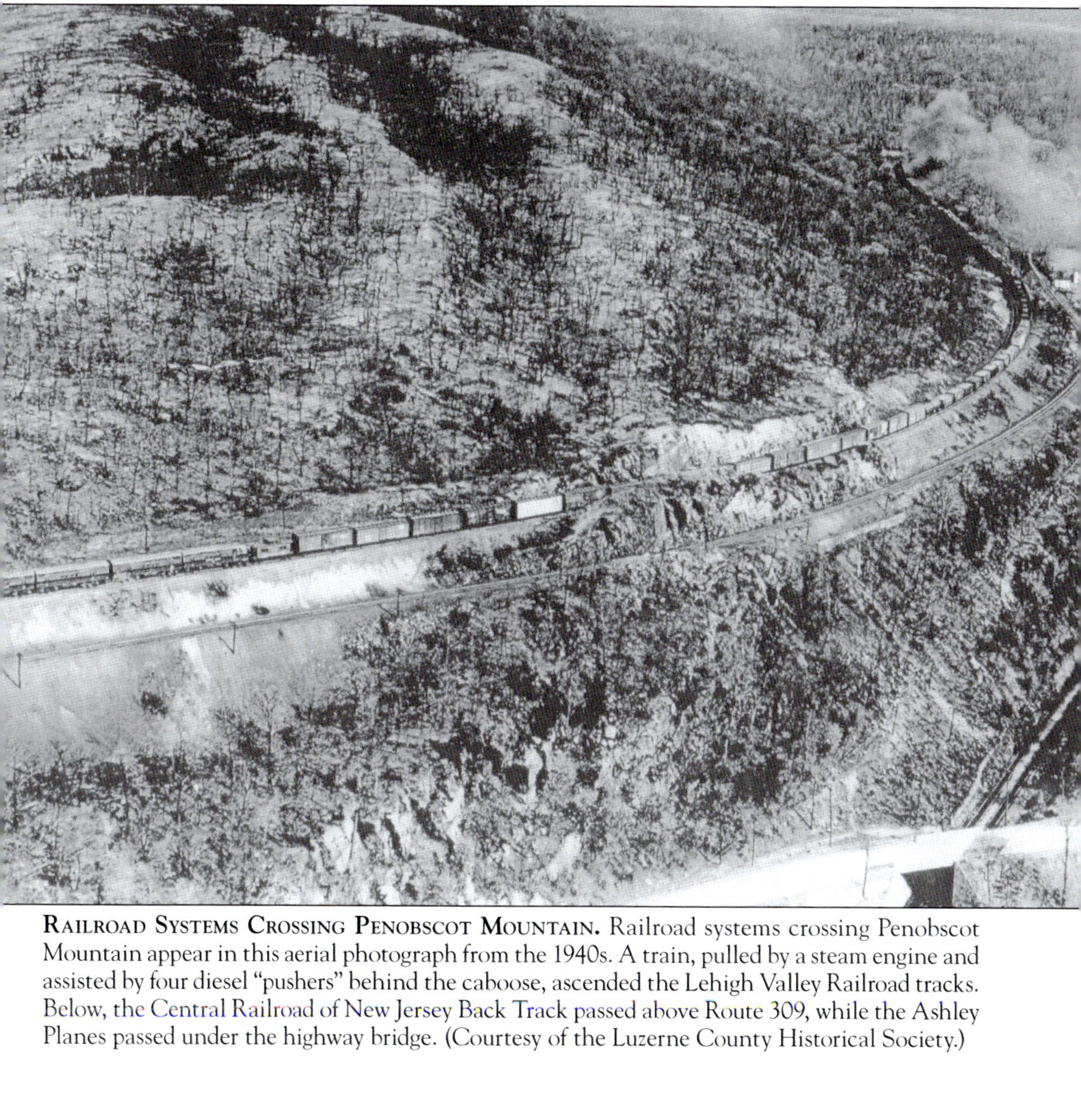

Railroad Systems Crossing Penobscot Mountain. Railroad systems crossing Penobscot Mountain appear in this aerial photograph from the 1940s. A train, pulled by a steam engine and assisted by four diesel "pushers" behind the caboose, ascended the Lehigh Valley Railroad tracks. Below, the Central Railroad of New Jersey Back Track passed above Route 309, while the Ashley Planes passed under the highway bridge. (Courtesy of the Luzerne County Historical Society.)

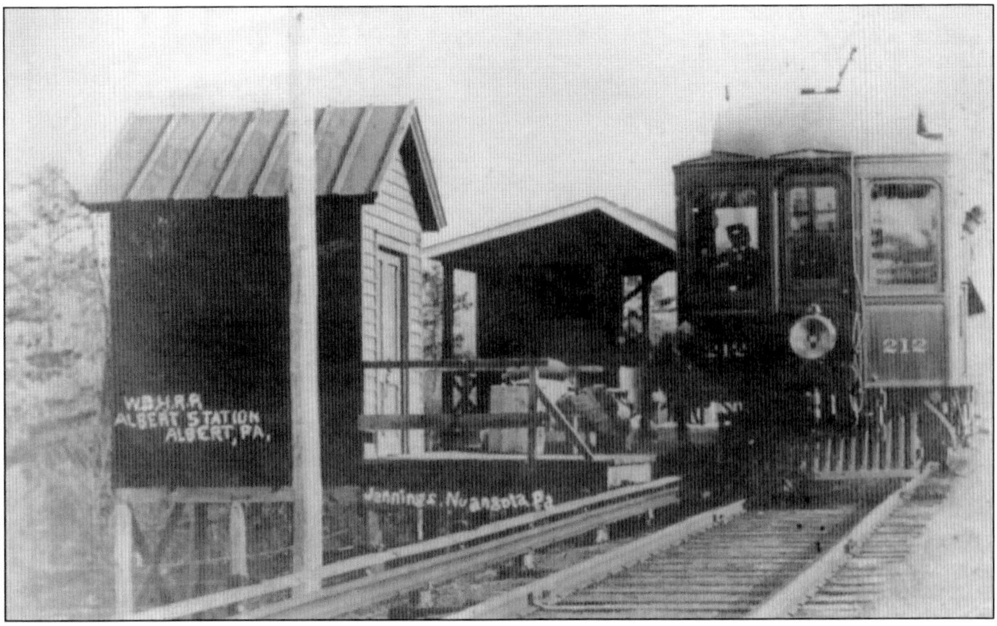

Wilkes-Barre & Hazleton Railway at Albert Station. From 1903 through 1933, the electric Wilkes-Barre & Hazleton Railway operated a line through Mountain Top with stations at Albert, Blytheburn, Pine View, and Nuangola. John Jennings photographed car No. 212 at Albert Station in 1907. The shot was taken looking east toward Hazleton. The electrified third rail was located on the left side of the tracks. (Courtesy of Sam and Rachel Goyne.)

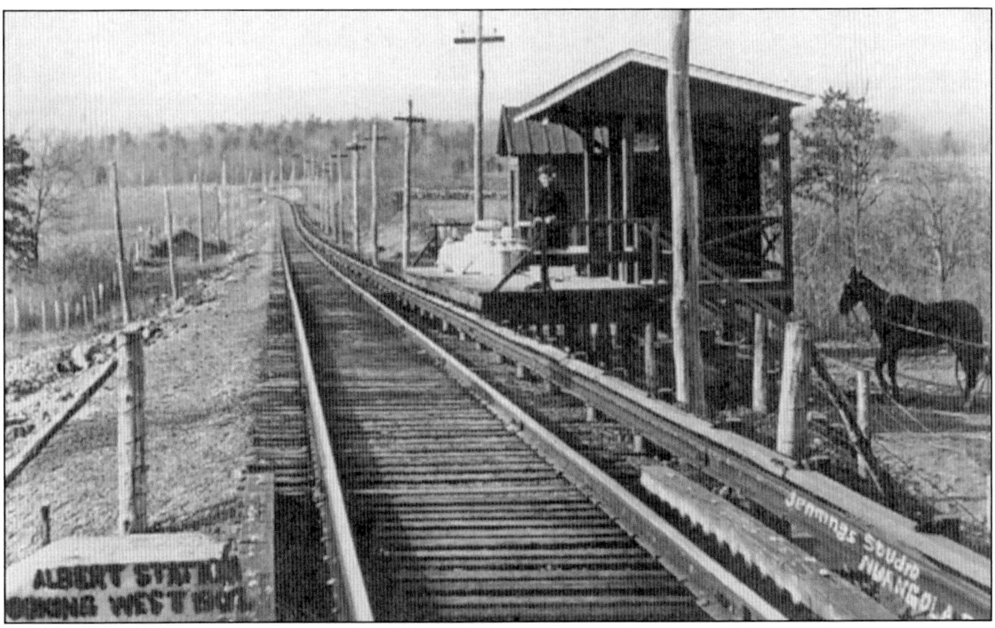

Wilkes-Barre & Hazleton Railway at Albert Station. A second Jennings photograph of Albert Station from 1907 was taken looking west toward Wilkes-Barre. A woman and several milk cans are shown waiting on the platform; the Wilkes-Barre & Hazleton Railway carried both passengers and freight. The Albert Station was located at the Laude farm on Alberdeen Road. (Courtesy of Sam and Rachel Goyne.)

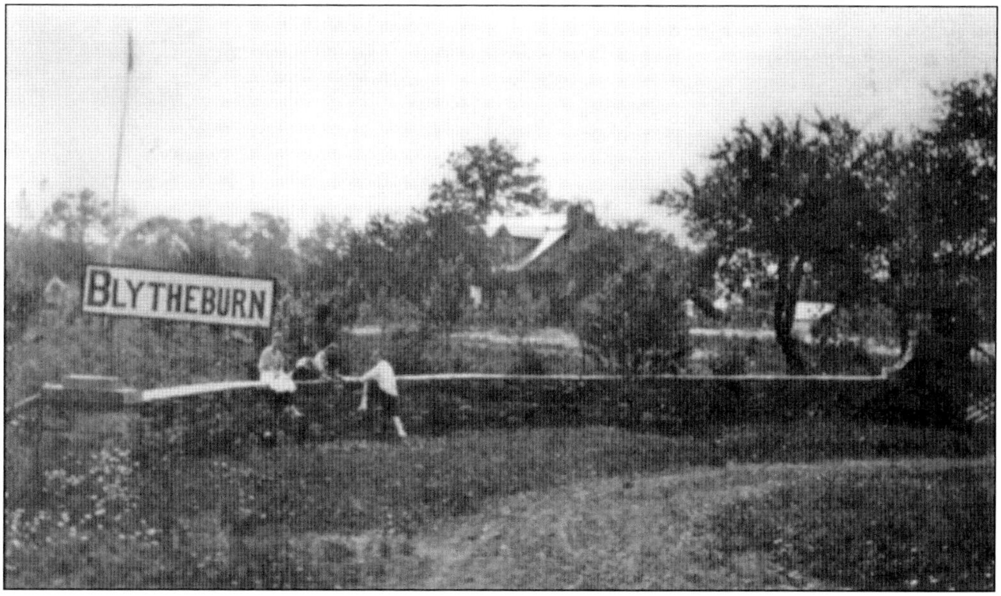

WILKES-BARRE & HAZLETON RAILWAY AT BLYTHEBURN STATION. The Wilkes-Barre & Hazleton Railway's Blytheburn Station, located in the area between present-day Blytheburn Road and Henry Drive near Blytheburn Lake, served the resort community there. A large stone wall near the station was photographed in 1916. (Courtesy of the Mountain Top Historical Society: *Railroads*.)

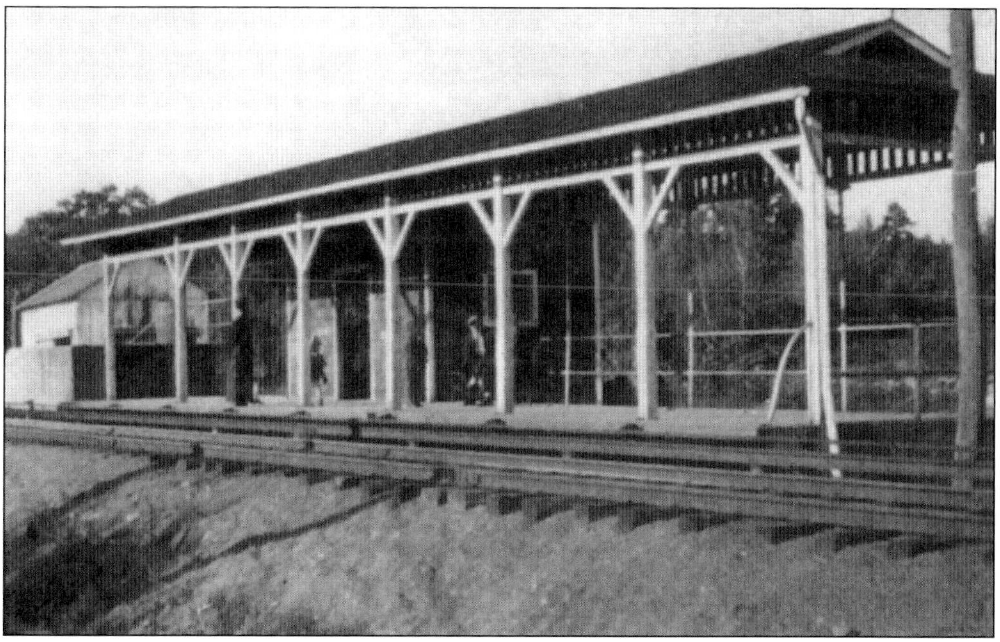

WILKES-BARRE & HAZLETON RAILWAY AT NUANGOLA STATION. The Nuangola Station of the Wilkes-Barre & Hazleton Railway, located near the present-day Rice Township Fire Hall on Nuangola Road, was photographed in 1916. The protected third rail carried 600 volts DC to power the interurban cars' traction motors. The station's concrete platform is still visible today. (Courtesy of the Mountain Top Historical Society: *Railroads*.)

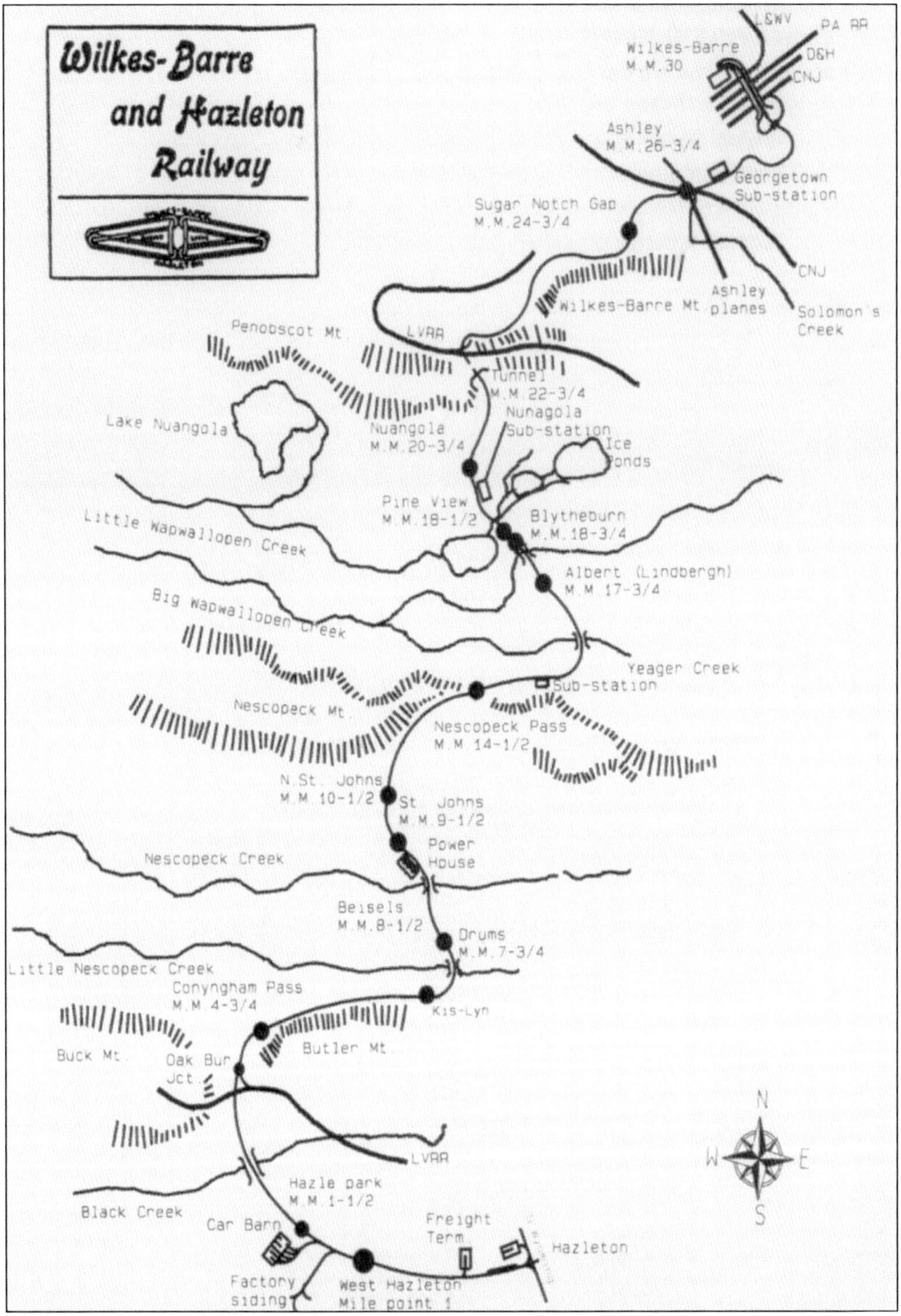

MAP OF THE WILKES-BARRE & HAZLETON RAILWAY. A map of the Wilkes-Barre & Hazleton Railway shows the location of towns, stations, and interchange points with other rail lines along its right-of-way. (Courtesy of Mountain Top Photo.)

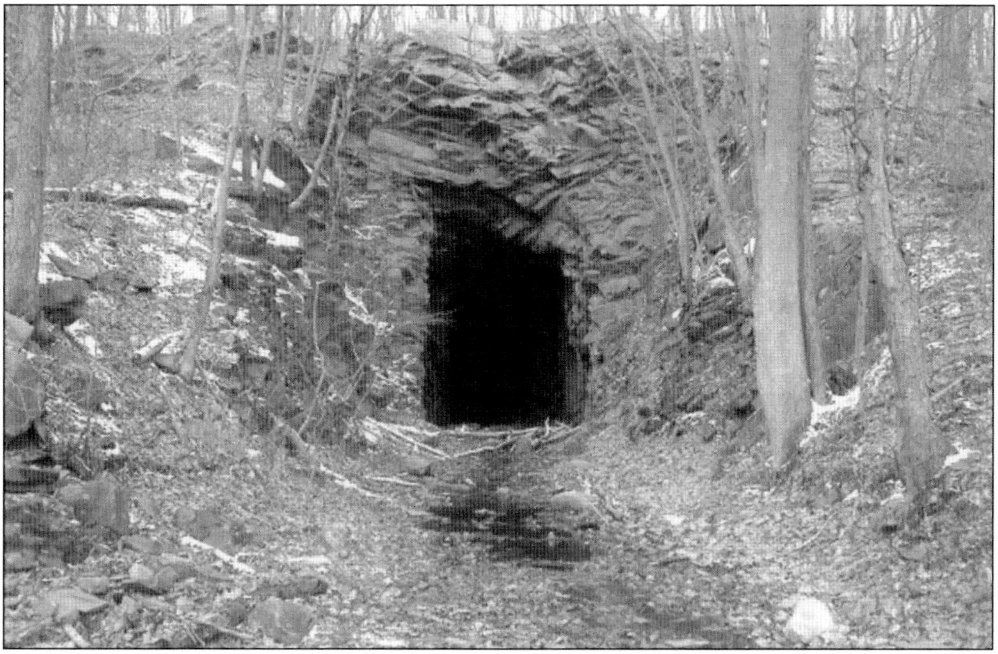

Wilkes-Barre & Hazleton Railway Tunnel at Penobscot Mountain. A significant feature of the Wilkes-Barre & Hazleton Railway was a half-mile tunnel carved through the Penobscot Mountain. The tunnel was located near present-day rock cuts on Interstate 81. (Courtesy of Mountain Top Photo.)

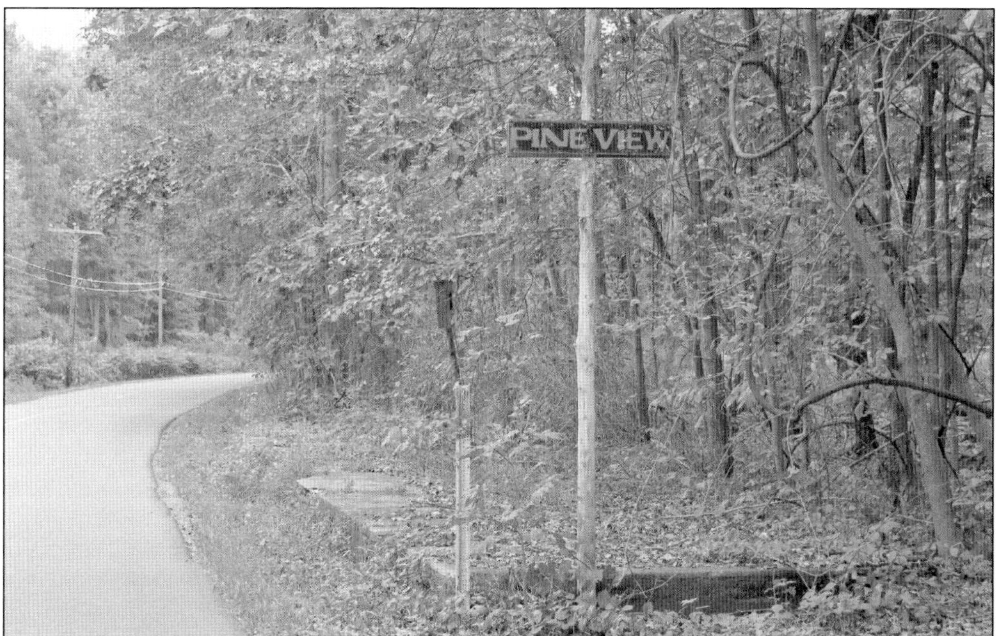

Wilkes-Barre & Hazleton Railway Station at Pine View. The remains of the Wilkes-Barre & Hazleton Railway's concrete platform at Pine View Station still exist on Henry Drive. The road was built on the rail bed of the interurban transit system after it closed. (Courtesy of Darlene Miller-Lanning.)

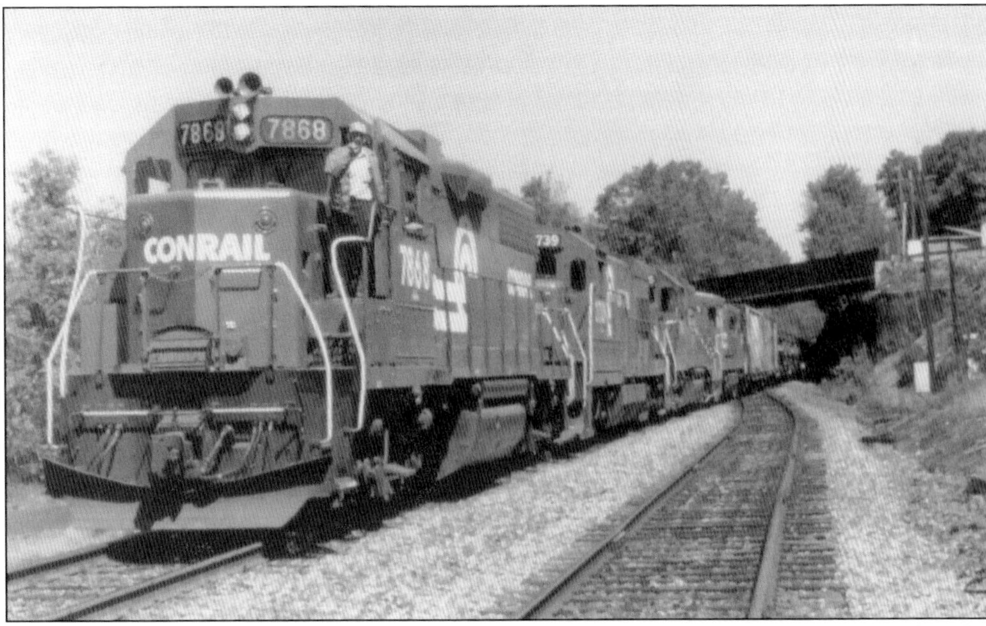

CONRAIL ENGINE NO. 7868. In the 1970s, the Lehigh Valley Railroad and Central Railroad of New Jersey, like many independent railroads, faced severe financial difficulties. As a result, they became part of the Consolidated Rail System, or Conrail, created by the federal government in 1976. Conrail engine No. 7868 was photographed emerging from the rock cut under the bridge on Woodlawn Avenue at Solomon's Gap. (Courtesy of Mountain Top Photo.)

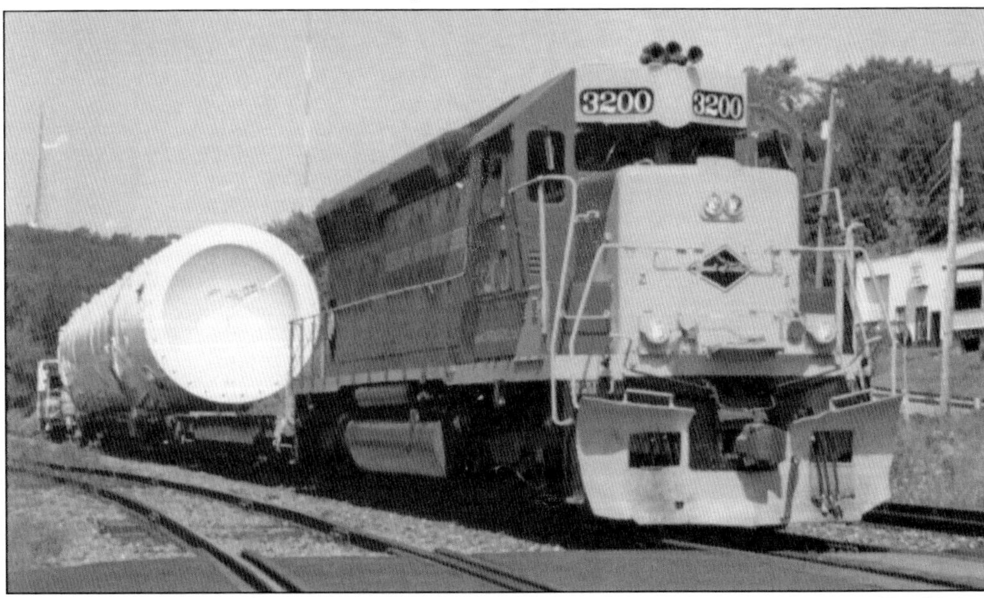

READING, BLUE MOUNTAIN & NORTHERN RAILROAD AIR PRODUCTS SPECIAL NO. 3200. Established in 1983, the Reading, Blue Mountain & Northern Railroad moved into Mountain Top in 1996 after acquiring Conrail's Lehigh Division, formerly part of the Lehigh Valley Railroad. Operating steam and diesel engines, the company provides passenger and freight services. Engine No. 3200 was photographed at Gracedale crossing on its "Air Products Special" run in 2003. (Courtesy of Mountain Top Photo.)

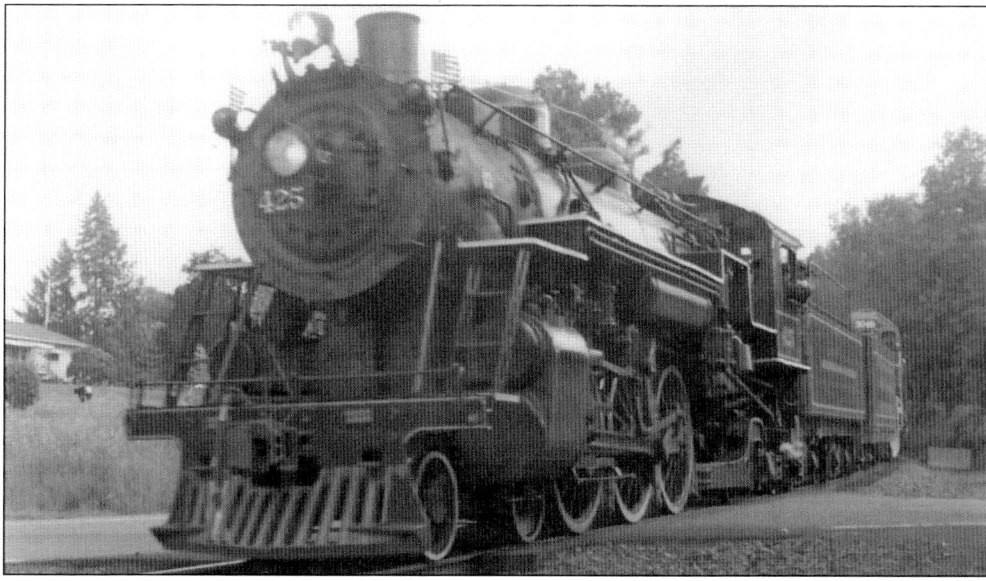

READING, BLUE MOUNTAIN & NORTHERN RAILROAD ENGINE NO. 425. In 2007, the Reading, Blue Mountain & Northern Railroad restored engine No. 425, photographed at Rita crossing in 2008. As a steam-powered 4-6-2 Pacific built in 1928, engine No. 425 previously served the Gulf, Mobile & Northern Railroad as engine No. 425; the Gulf, Mobile & Ohio Railroad as engine No. 580; and the Valley Forge Scenic Railroad as engine No. 425. (Courtesy of Mountain Top Photo.)

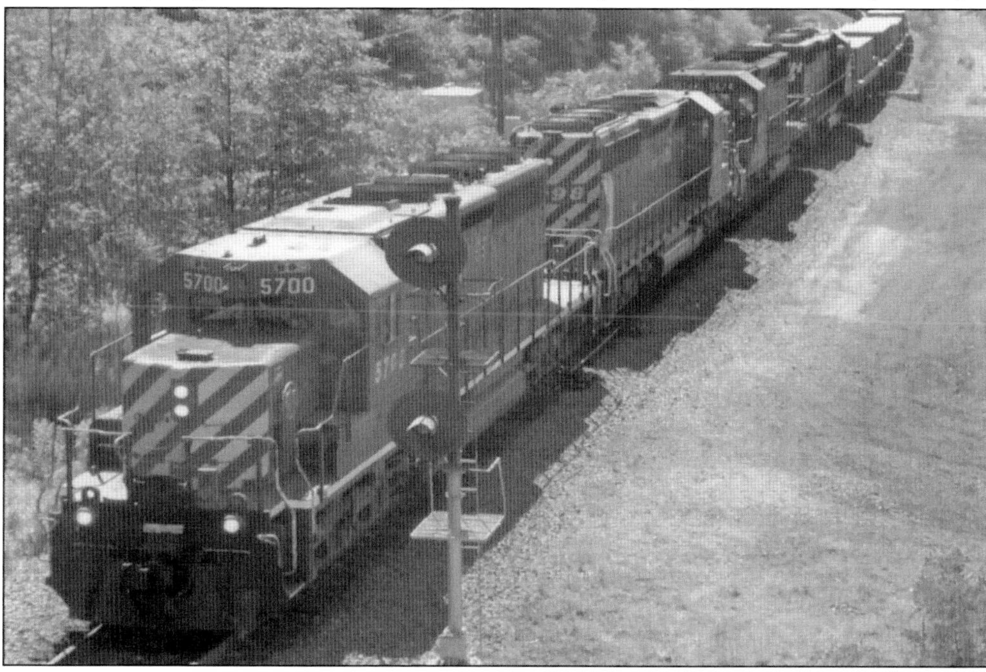

CANADIAN PACIFIC RAILROAD ENGINE NO. 5700. In 2000, both the Canadian Pacific Railroad and the Norfolk Southern Railroad entered into trackage agreements with the Reading, Blue Mountain & Northern Railroad, allowing them to operate through Mountain Top on the company's line. The Canadian Pacific Railroad's engine No. 5700 was photographed at Solomon's Gap in 2004 as it headed a four-power lash-up on a container train. (Courtesy of Mountain Top Photo.)

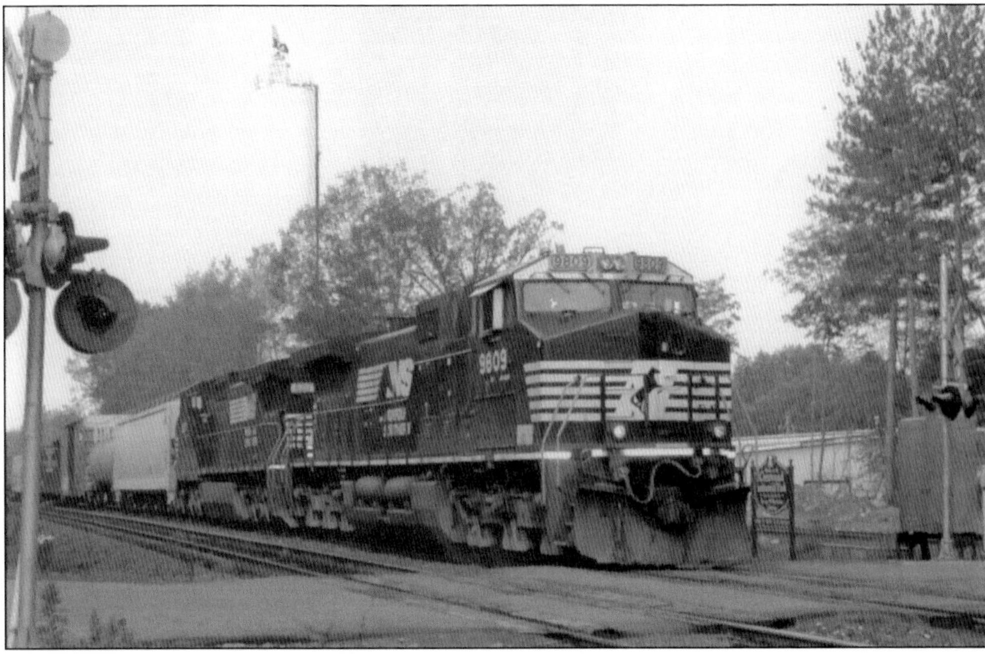

NORFOLK SOUTHERN RAILROAD ENGINE NO. 9809. The Norfolk Southern Railroad engine No. 9808 was photographed at the Glen Summit Water Company crossing in 2006. Norfolk Southern Railroad trains are a common sight on the line as they move through Mountain Top on a daily basis. (Courtesy of Mountain Top Photo.)

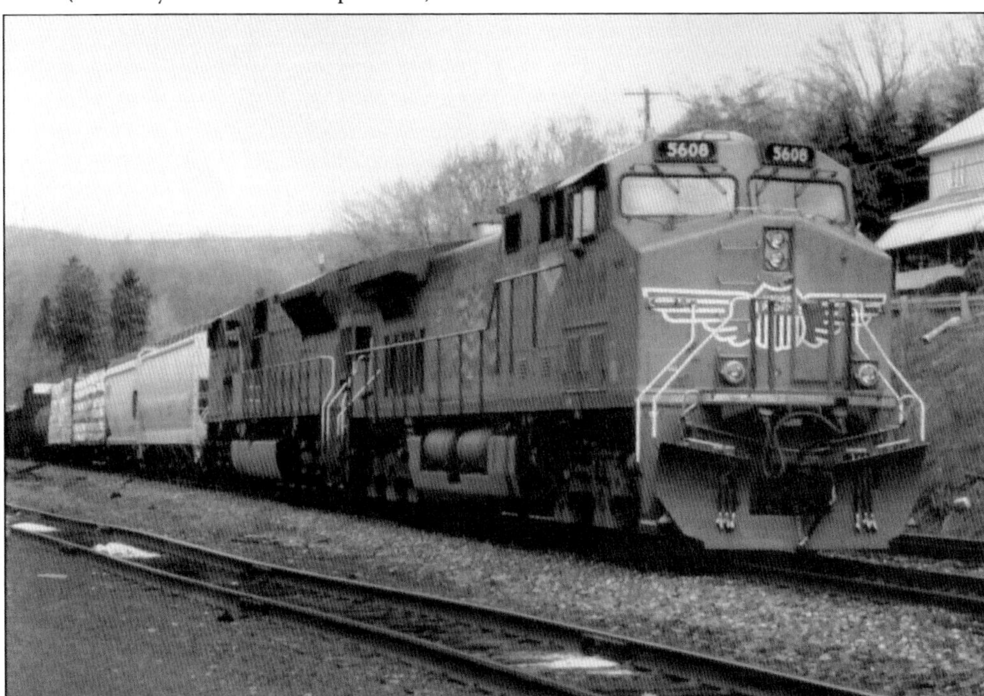

UNION PACIFIC RAILROAD ENGINE NO. 5608. The Union Pacific Railroad engine No. 5608 was photographed at the Gracedale crossing in 2005. (Courtesy of Mountain Top Photo.)

Three

Resorts and Recreation

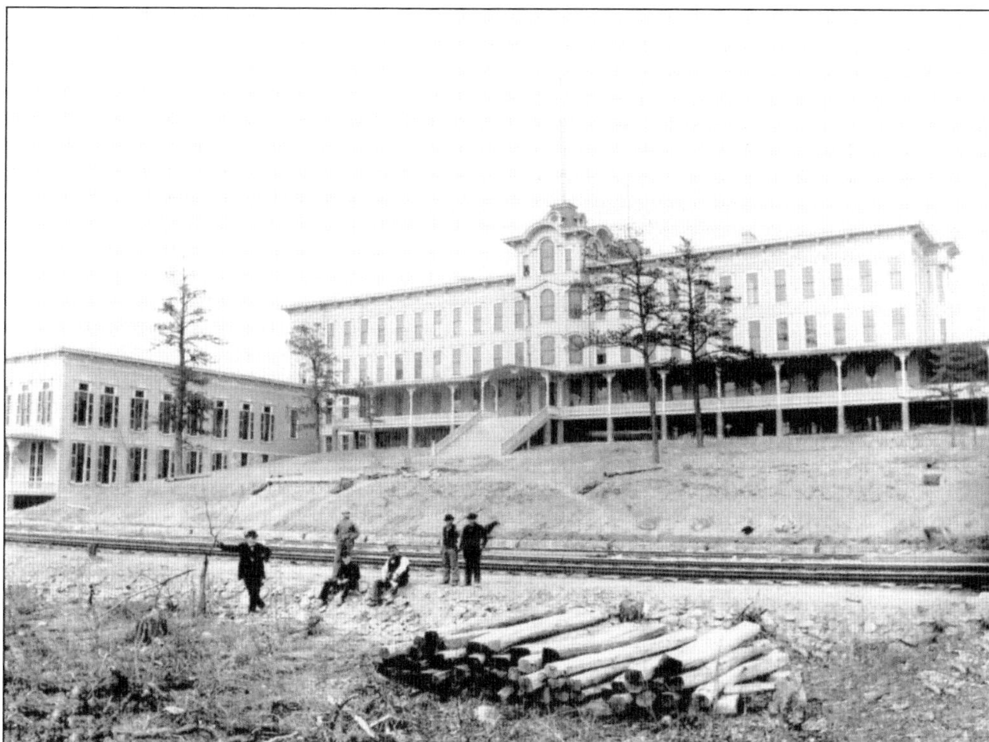

Glen Summit Springs Hotel Under Construction. In 1882, the Lehigh Valley Railroad established the Glen Summit Hotel and Land Company for the purpose of developing resort properties near its line on the Nescopeck Mountain. The Glen Summit Springs Hotel was constructed in 1883 and opened for business in 1884. The three-story building, which offered accommodations for some 250 guests, was conveniently accessed from the rail line via broad staircases. (Courtesy of the Edward Welles family.)

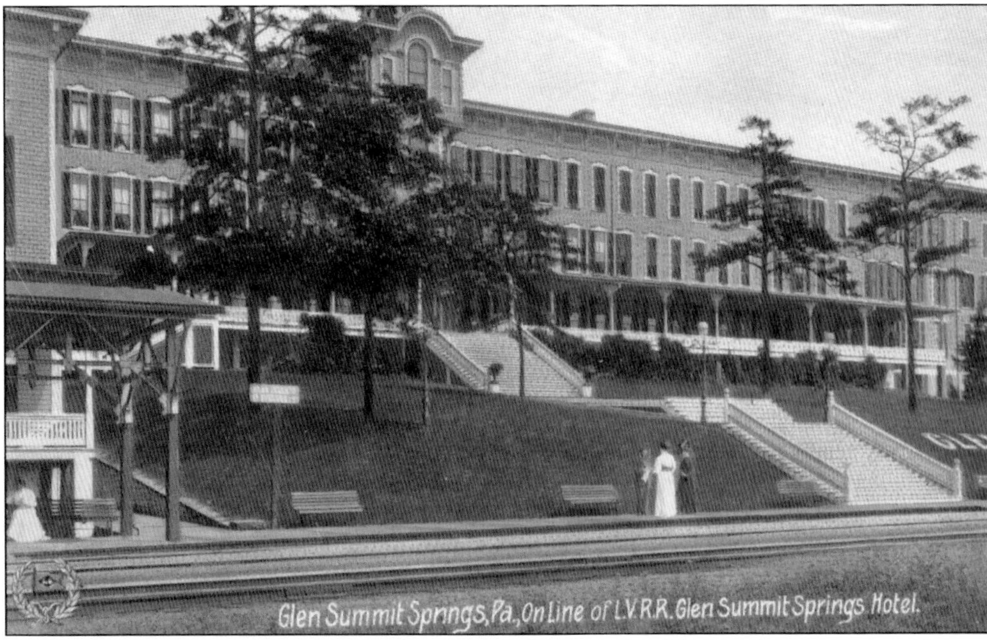

Glen Summit Springs Hotel. The Glen Summit Springs Hotel featured guest rooms and suites with brass bedsteads; hot and cold water; private bathrooms; steam heat and electric lights; reading, writing, and reception rooms; telephone, telegraph, and mail service; dining rooms and a café; and a dance hall. Following its heyday at the turn of the 20th century, the hotel closed in 1915 and was torn down. (Courtesy of Thomas Hollock.)

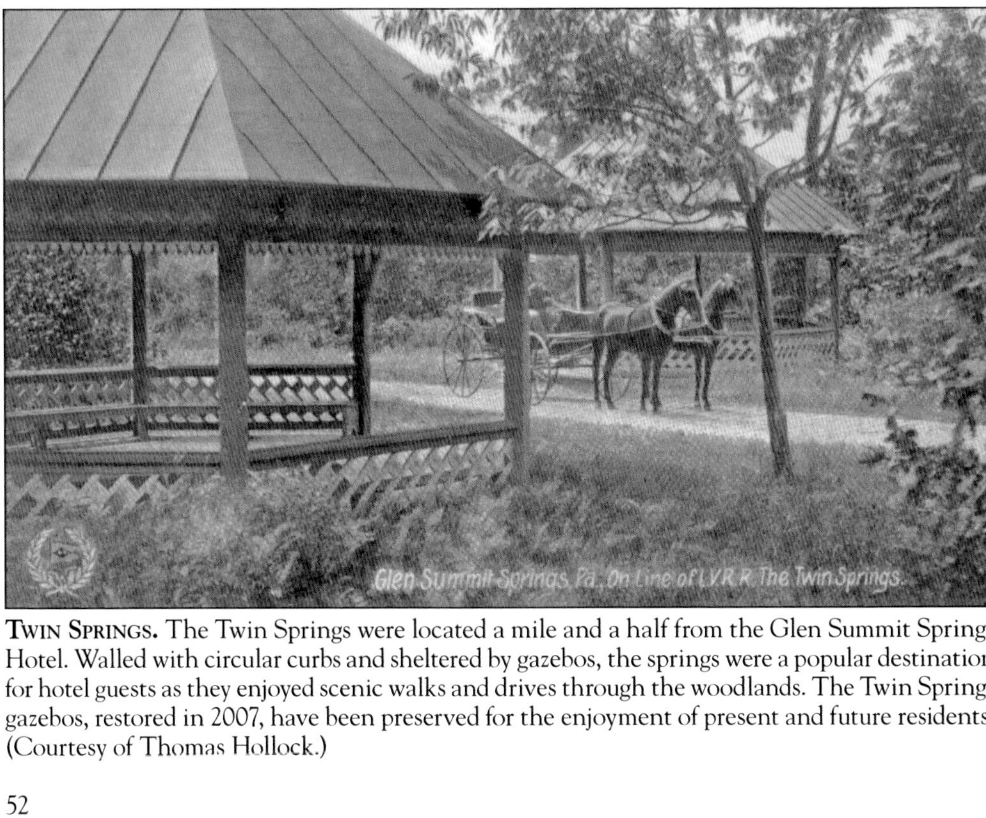

Twin Springs. The Twin Springs were located a mile and a half from the Glen Summit Springs Hotel. Walled with circular curbs and sheltered by gazebos, the springs were a popular destination for hotel guests as they enjoyed scenic walks and drives through the woodlands. The Twin Springs gazebos, restored in 2007, have been preserved for the enjoyment of present and future residents. (Courtesy of Thomas Hollock.)

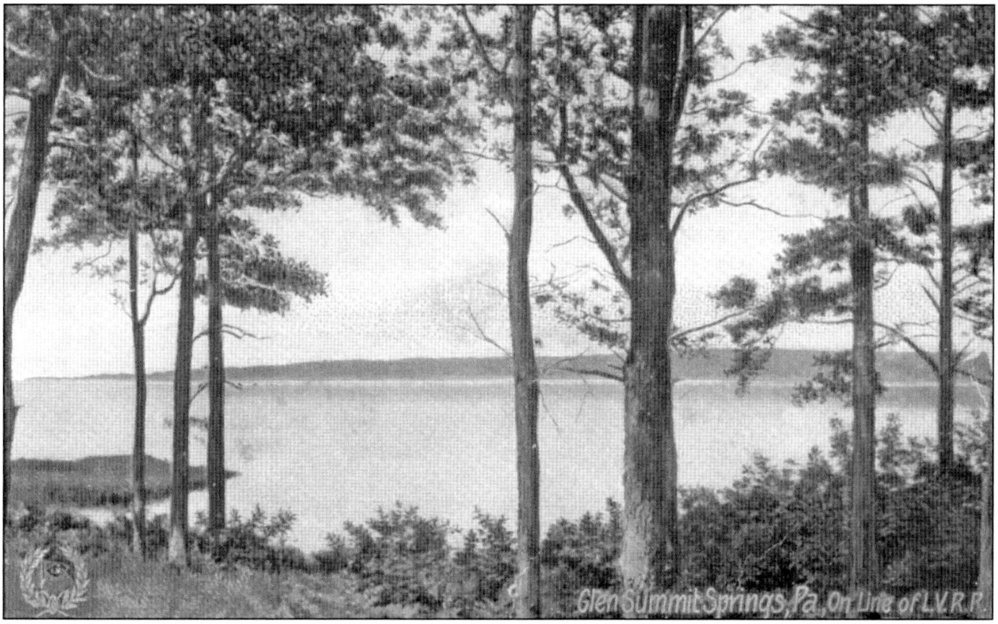

CRYSTAL LAKE. The Crystal Springs Water Company built a reservoir near Penobscot in 1873. Situated in the mountains northeast of Glen Summit, Crystal Lake is nine miles in circumference. The reservoir, now operated by the Pennsylvania American Water Company, provides drinking water for Mountain Top. The territory surrounding Crystal Lake has been designated part of the Lackawanna State Forest. (Courtesy of Thomas Hollock.)

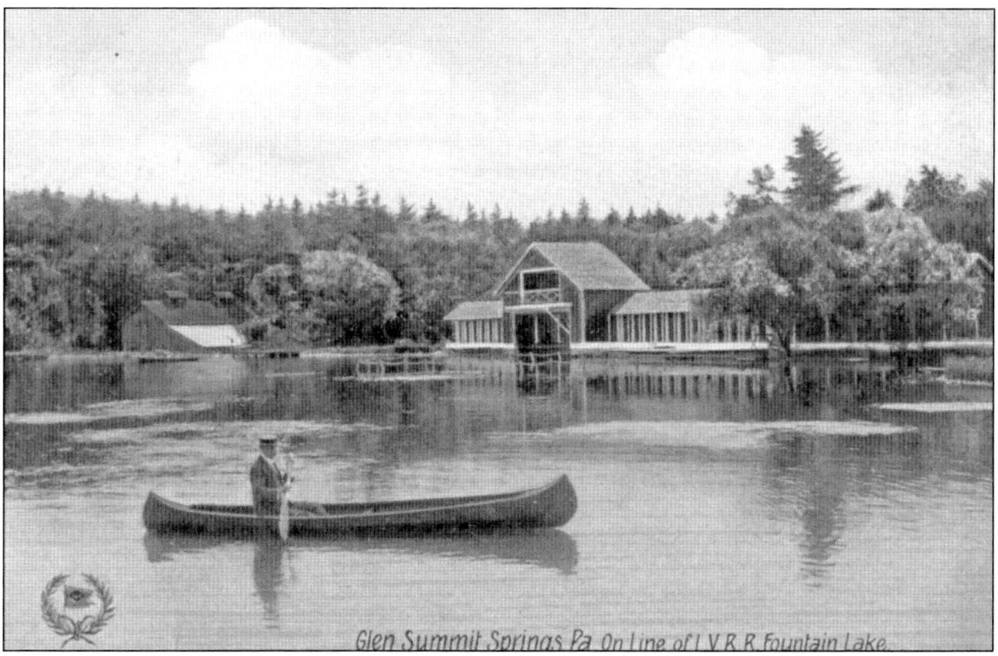

FOUNTAIN LAKE. In 1888, the Glen Summit Hotel and Land Company directed water from Indian Springs and the Twin Springs into a reservoir at Fountain Lake. The lake was later used for boating and swimming, and a dock, bath houses, and diving boards were added. A fountain that was once installed in the center of the lake no longer exists. (Courtesy of Thomas Hollock.)

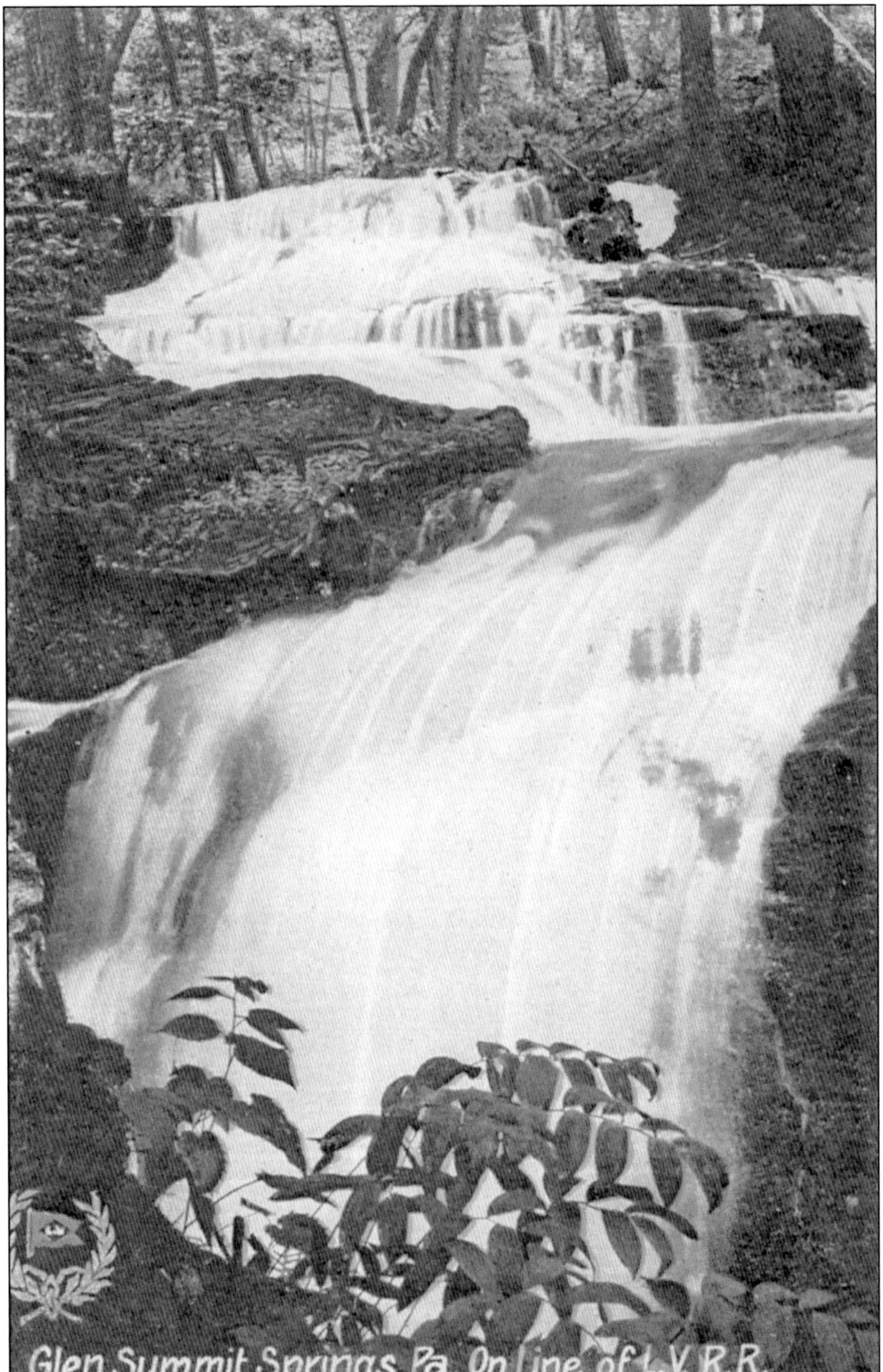

GLEN SUMMIT SPRINGS. The Glen Summit Hotel and Land Company emphasized the benefits of clear waters and wooded glens when advertising its resort properties. Nescopeck Springs, later called Indian Springs, is located 1,900 feet above sea level. Between 93,000 and 110,000 gallons of water flow from the spring every 24 hours in dry and normal seasons, respectively. (Courtesy of Clare Myers.)

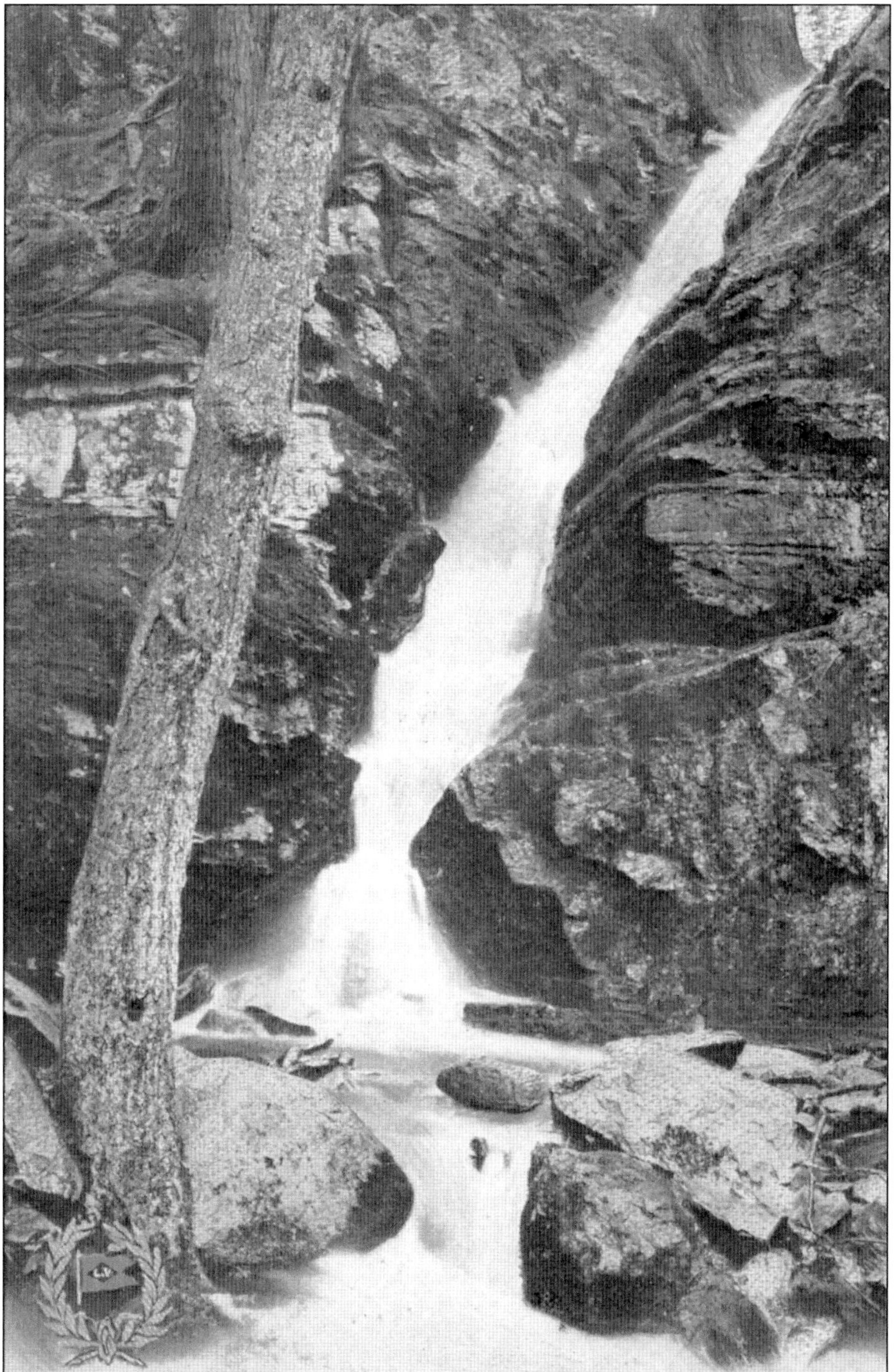

In the Glen. Two small streams originate in Glen Summit. Conety Run flows south into the Nescopeck Creek, while Bow Creek flows west into the Big Wapwallopen Creek. (Courtesy of Clare Myers.)

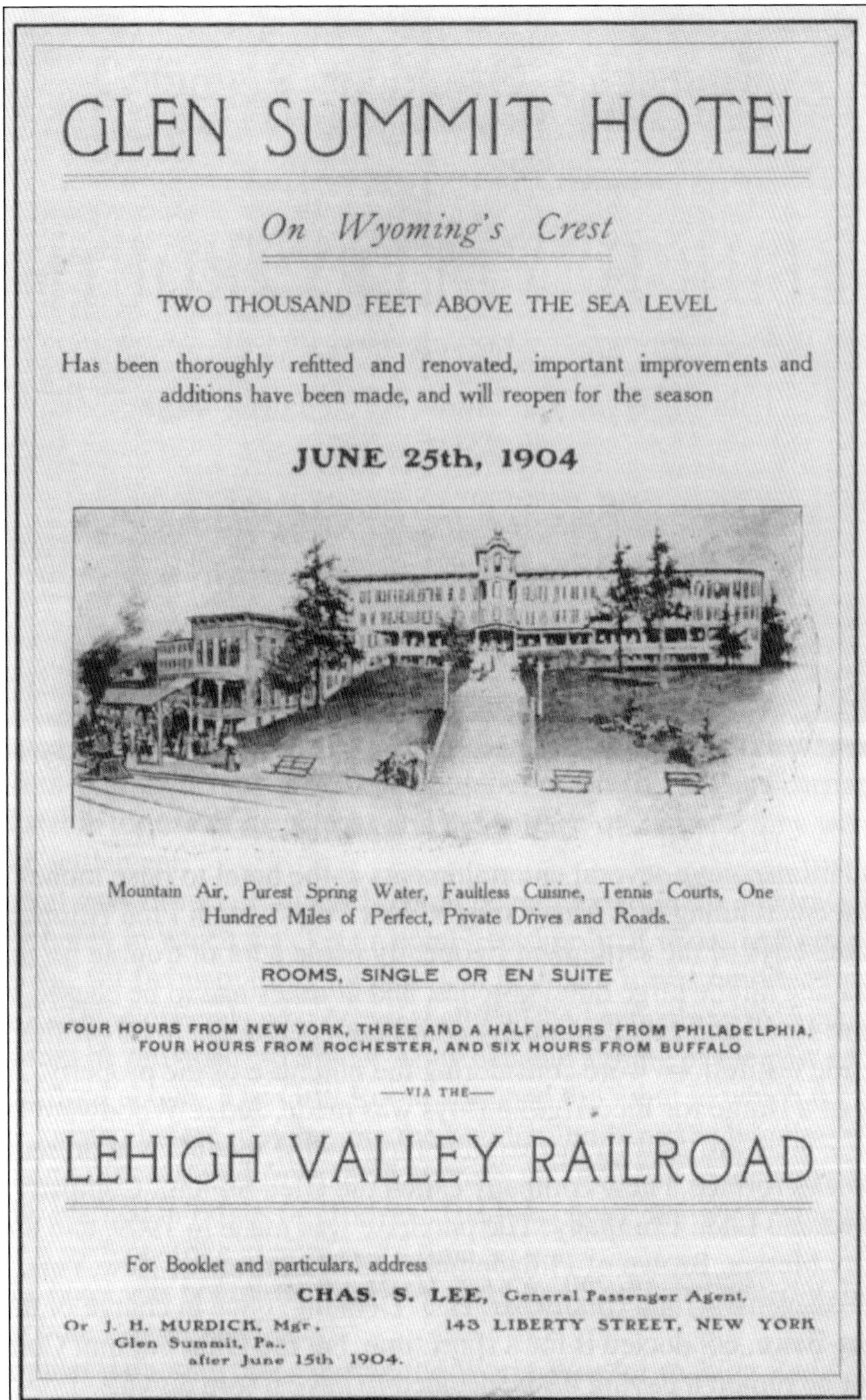

Glen Summit Hotel Advertisement. An advertisement for the Glen Summit Hotel published in 1904 highlighted the elegant hotel's improved amenities, the surrounding area's natural beauty, and the nearby railroad's convenient connections to metropolitan centers. (Courtesy of the Mountain Top Historical Society: *Glen Summit Springs*.)

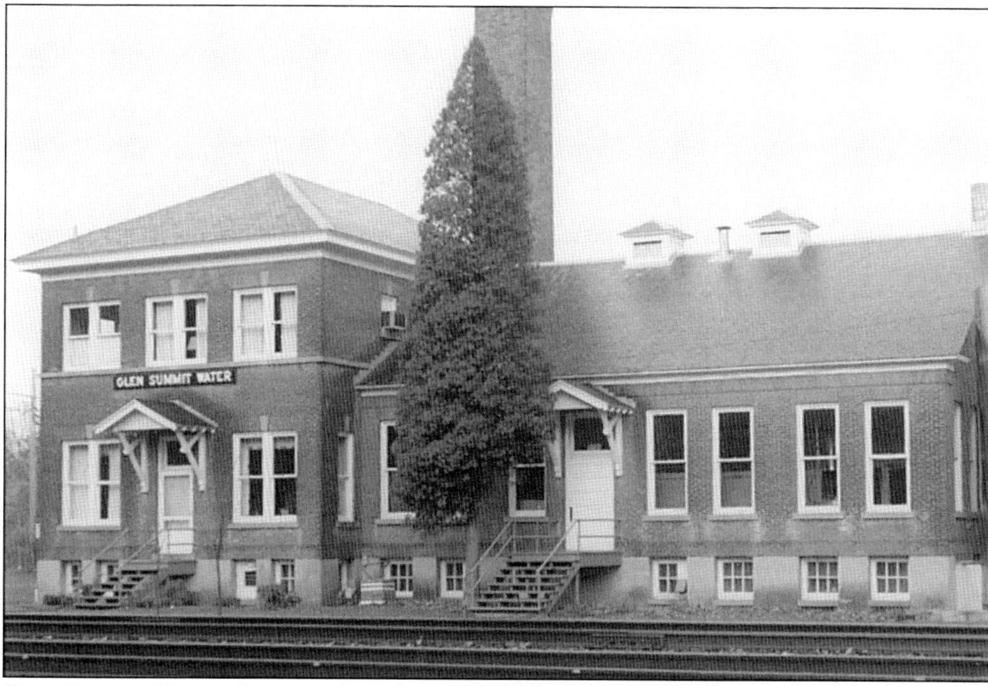

GLEN SUMMIT WATER COMPANY. Joseph Patterson, the first manager of the Glen Summit Springs Hotel, established the Glen Summit Water Company in 1884. Water from springs in the Glen Summit area was bottled in a building located along Woodlawn Avenue. The Glen Summit Water Company still operates at this location today. (Courtesy of the Mountain Top Historical Society: *Glen Summit Springs*.)

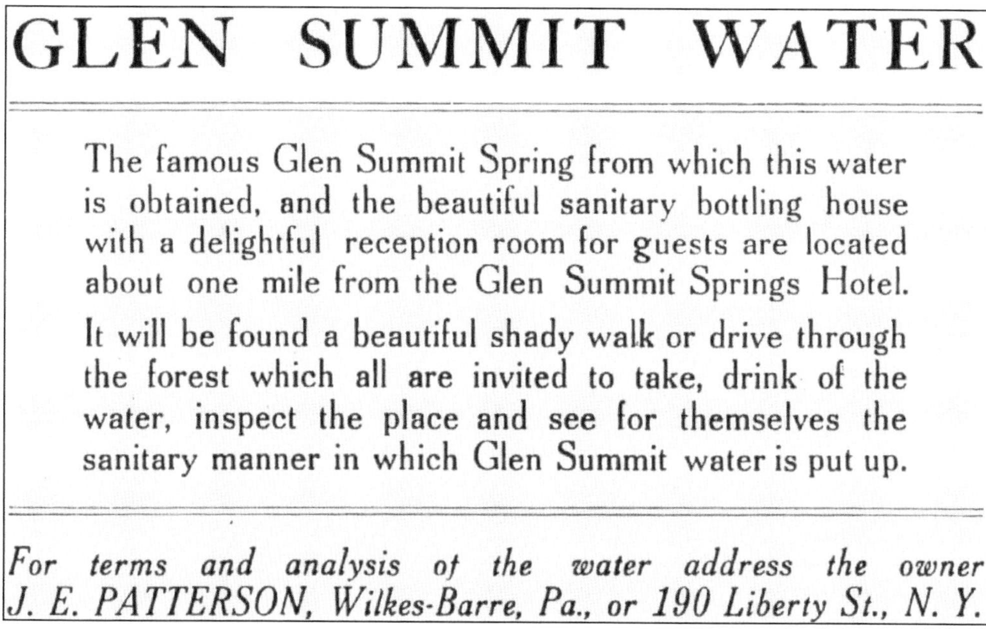

GLEN SUMMIT WATER

The famous Glen Summit Spring from which this water is obtained, and the beautiful sanitary bottling house with a delightful reception room for guests are located about one mile from the Glen Summit Springs Hotel.

It will be found a beautiful shady walk or drive through the forest which all are invited to take, drink of the water, inspect the place and see for themselves the sanitary manner in which Glen Summit water is put up.

For terms and analysis of the water address the owner J. E. PATTERSON, Wilkes-Barre, Pa., or 190 Liberty St., N. Y.

GLEN SUMMIT WATER COMPANY ADVERTISEMENT. In this advertisement, the Glen Summit Water Company highlighted the "beautiful" and "sanitary" characteristics of its product. (Courtesy of the Mountain Top Historical Society: *Glen Summit Springs*.)

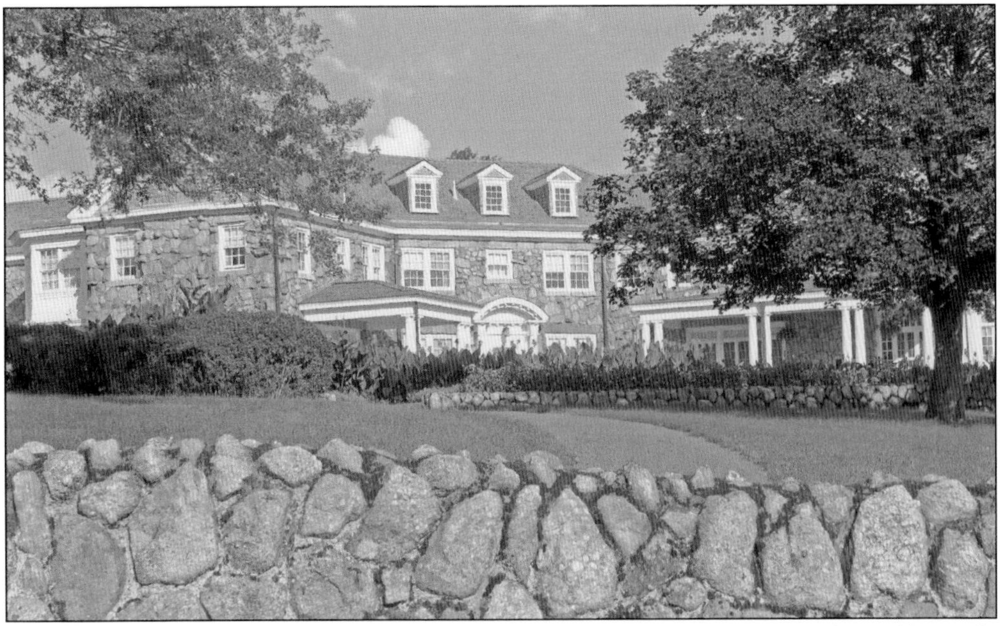

KIRBY EPISCOPAL HOUSE. In 1914, five-and-dime store founder Fred Morgan Kirby and his wife, Jessie, constructed Graystone Terrace as a summer home at Glen Summit. The grounds included Japanese gardens and a teahouse. In 1955, their son Allan Price Kirby gifted the home to the Episcopal Diocese of Bethlehem for use as a conference center for educational, charitable, and religious groups. (Courtesy of Darlene Miller-Lanning.)

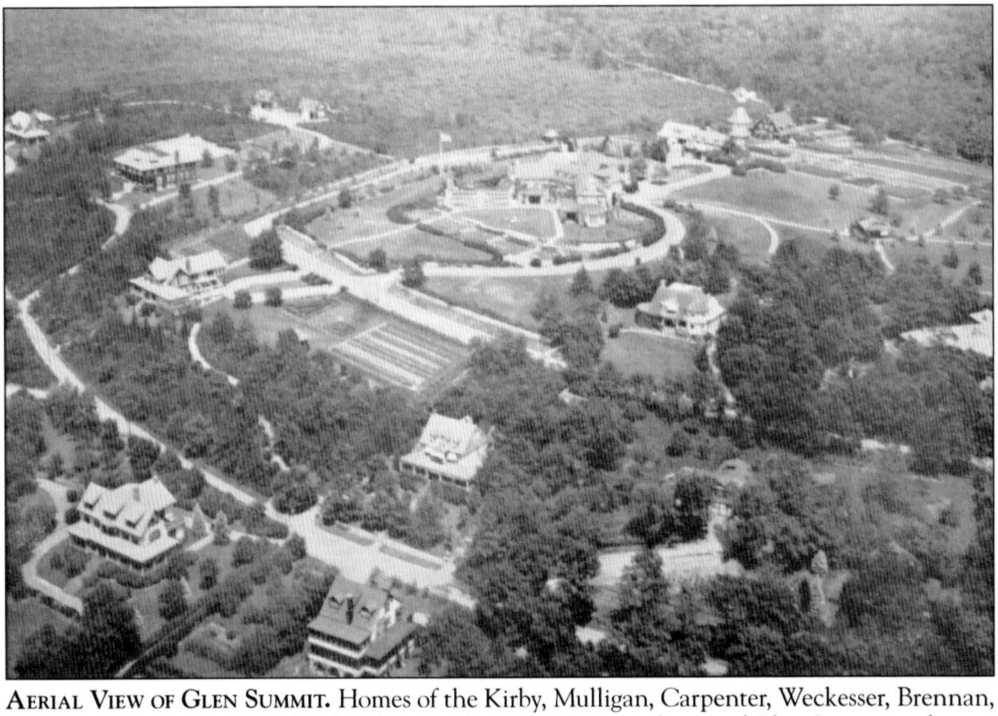

AERIAL VIEW OF GLEN SUMMIT. Homes of the Kirby, Mulligan, Carpenter, Weckesser, Brennan, Shoemaker, Taylor, and Welles families are shown in this aerial view of Glen Summit, taken in 1932. (Courtesy of Dave and Carol Lippincott: Atkins, *Wilkes-Barre and Vicinity*.)

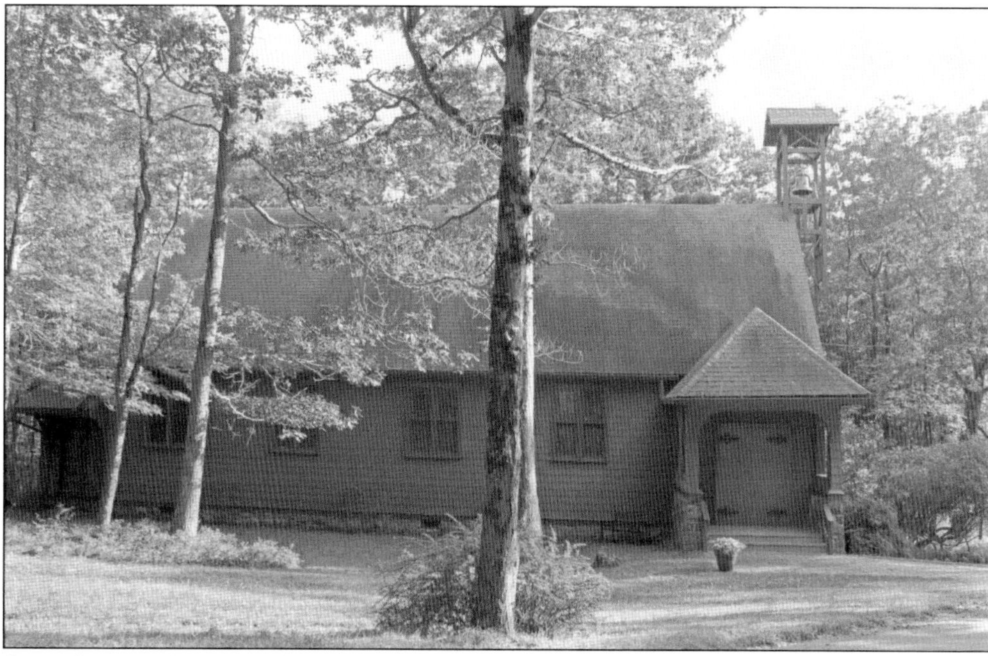

Glen Summit Chapel. The Glen Summit Chapel was constructed in 1888. For many years, Episcopalians, Methodists, and Presbyterians each held four summer services in the chapel for a total of 12 services during the season. In 1932, this number was reduced to nine. Today, the chapel conducts a yearly service and is a popular site for weddings. (Courtesy of Mountain Top Photo.)

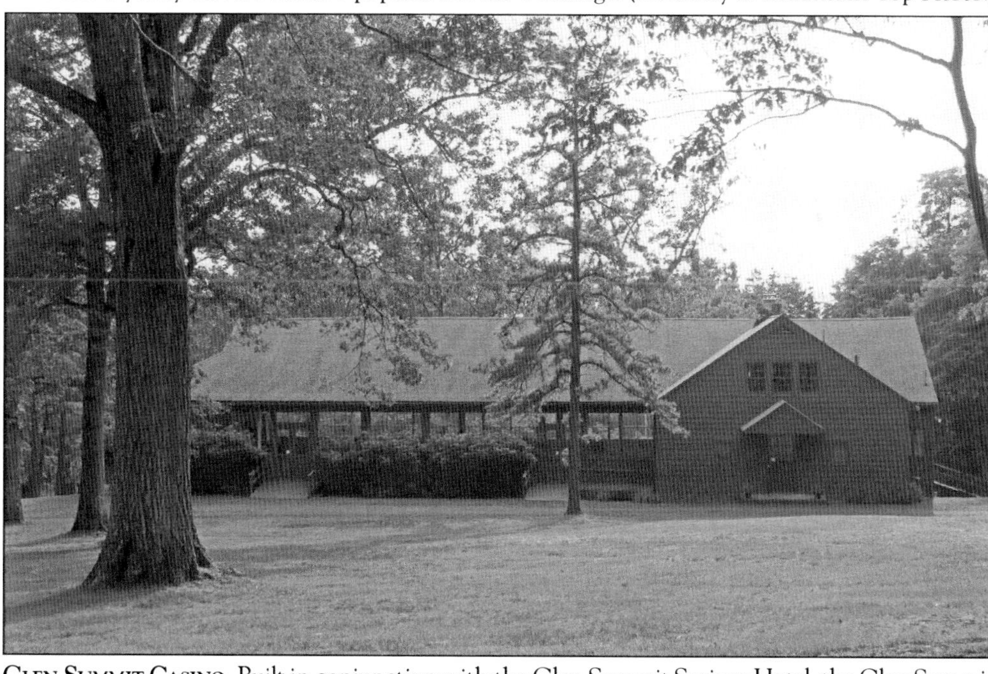

Glen Summit Casino. Built in conjunction with the Glen Summit Springs Hotel, the Glen Summit Casino provided entertainment for guests and residents. The Glen Summit Association later used the building as a community center. The original structure burned in 1939 but was replaced in 1940. This building is now used for special events. (Courtesy of Mountain Top Photo.)

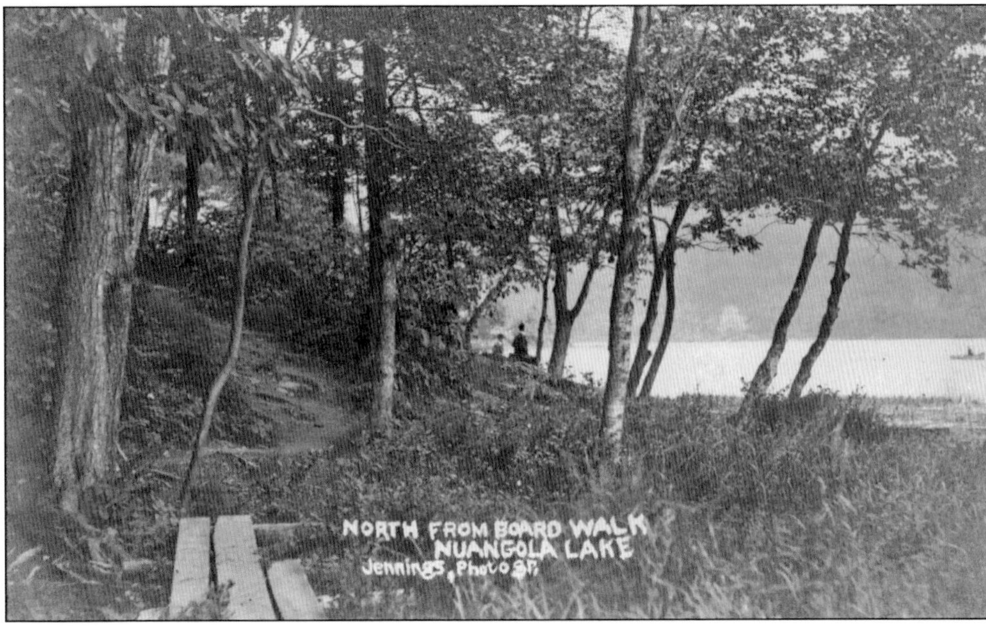

View North from Boardwalk at Nuangola Lake. First known as Triangular Lake or Three-cornered Pond, Nuangola Lake became a popular resort community during the early 20th century. John Jennings, whose family operated a boat rental at the lake, photographed this view looking north from the boardwalk in the early 1900s. (Courtesy of the Mountain Top Historical Society: *Past and Present.*)

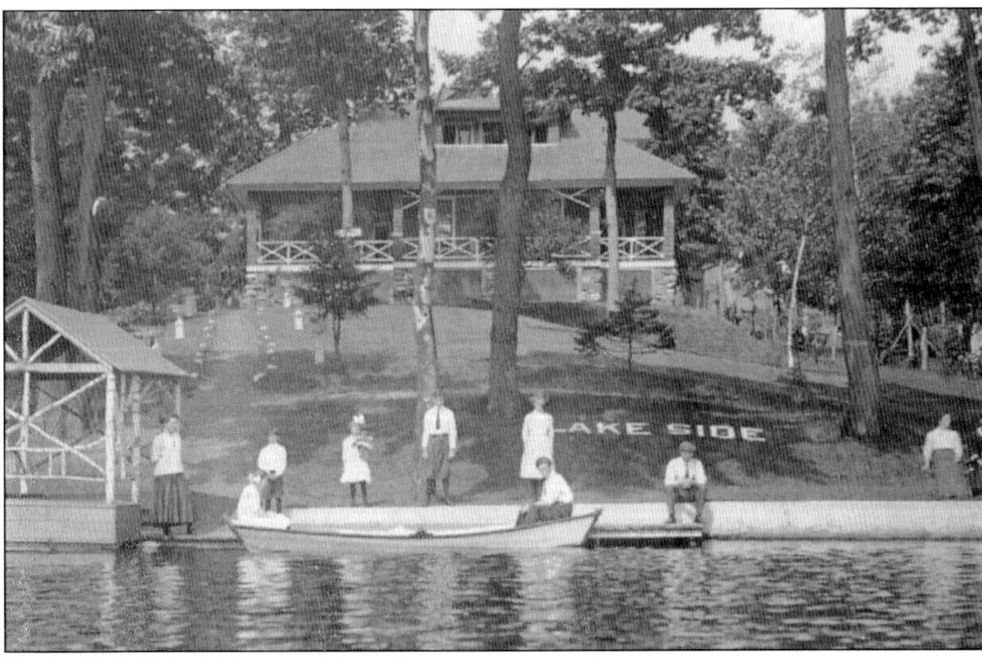

Keating Summer Home at Nuangola Lake. Families began constructing summer homes at Nuangola Lake in the 1880s. John Jennings photographed the Keating summer home, named Lakeside, in the early 20th century. By that time, the Wilkes-Barre & Hazleton Railway provided easy access to the area. (Courtesy of the Mountain Top Historical Society: *Pieces of the Past.*)

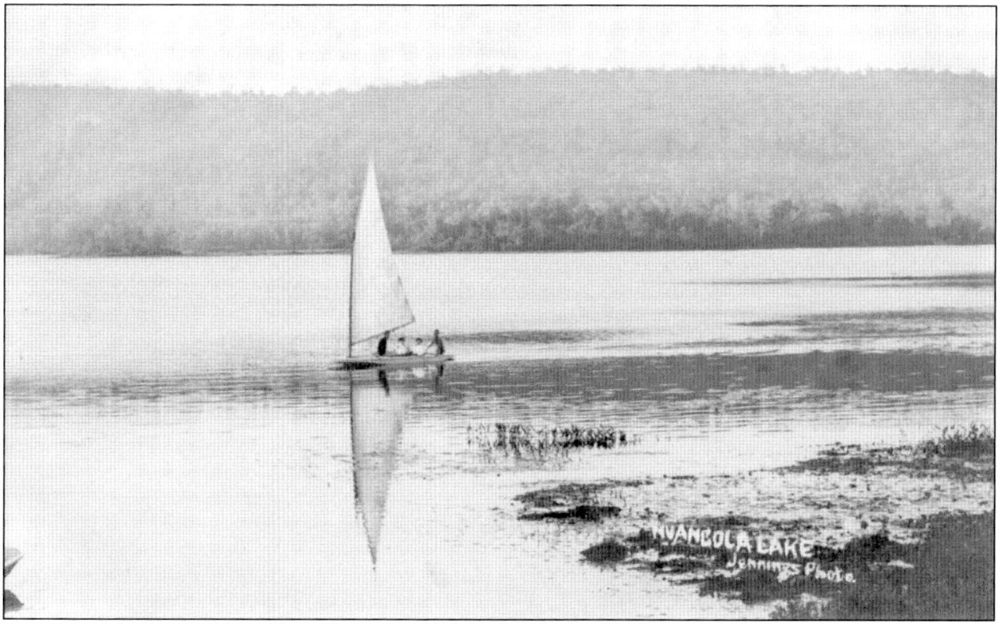

SAILBOAT ON NUANGOLA LAKE. In the early 1900s, John Jennings photographed this sailboat on Nuangola Lake. Sailing remains a popular activity at the lake today. (Courtesy of the Mountain Top Historical Society: *Past and Present*.)

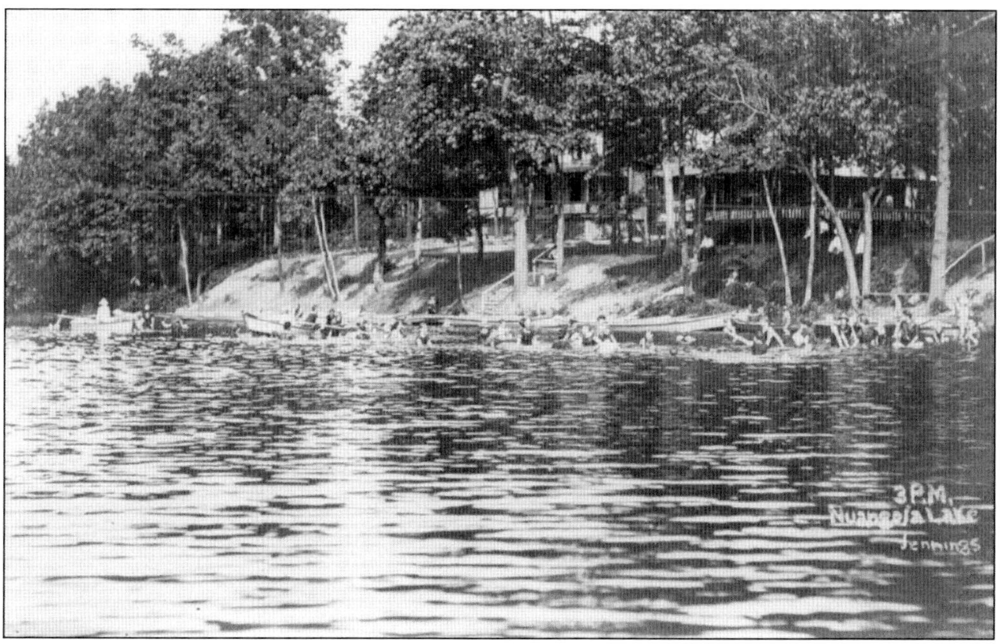

SWIMMING AT NUANGOLA LAKE, "3 P.M." Another photograph by John Jennings depicted residents bathing in Nuangola Lake at "3 p.m." (Courtesy of Mountain Top Photo.)

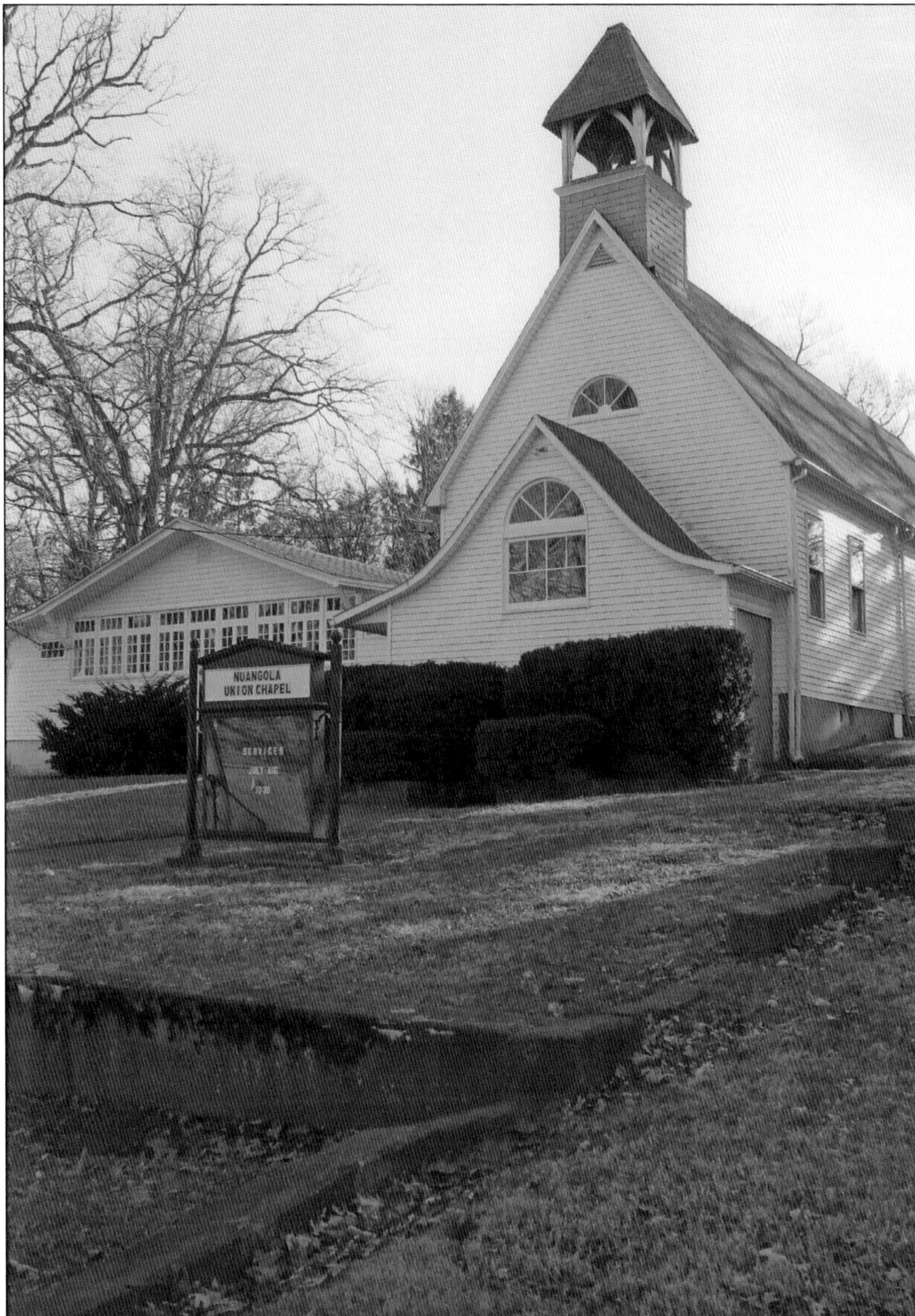

NUANGOLA UNION CHAPEL. The Nuangola Union Chapel was built by William Stair in 1900 and dedicated in 1904. Located on Vandermark Avenue, the chapel has served the lake community for over 100 years. (Courtesy of Darlene Miller-Lanning.)

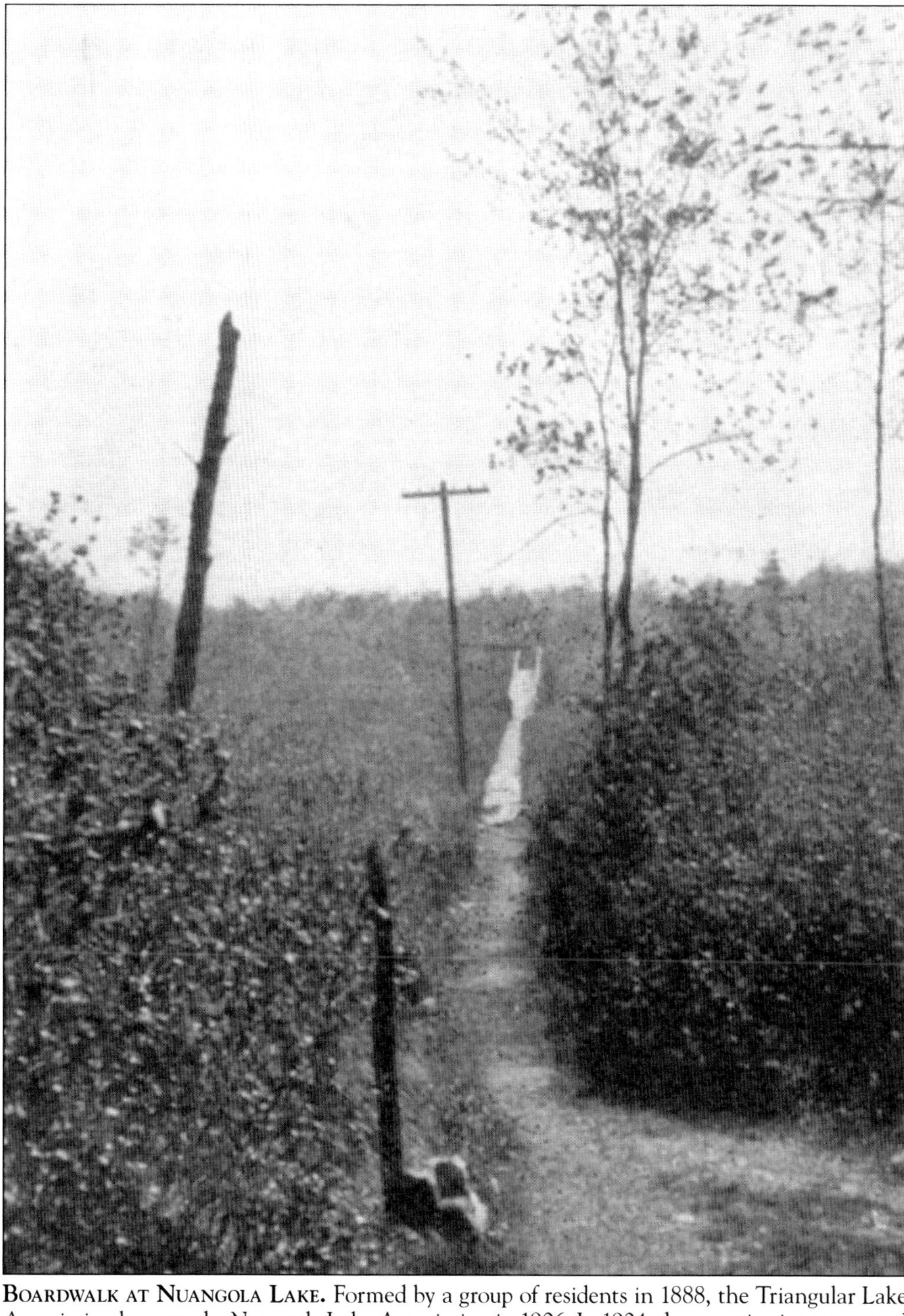

Boardwalk at Nuangola Lake. Formed by a group of residents in 1888, the Triangular Lake Association became the Nuangola Lake Association in 1906. In 1904, the organization sponsored construction of a boardwalk and bridge over the south marsh at the end of the lake. The boardwalk is currently maintained by the Nuangola Pines Association, founded in 1964. (Courtesy of the Mountain Top Historical Society: *Pieces of the Past.*)

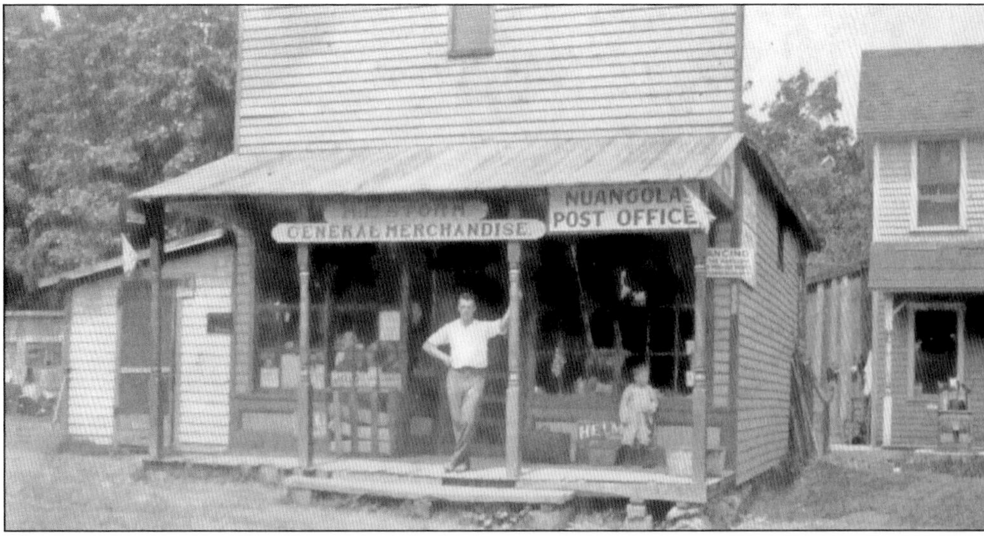

STORM'S STORE. Amos Storm served as postmaster at Nuangola Lake from 1908 into the 1930s. In 1910, he and his sons Edward and Perry opened a general store on Lake Avenue. Perry Storm later operated the store for many years. (Courtesy of the Mountain Top Historical Society: *Pieces of the Past.*)

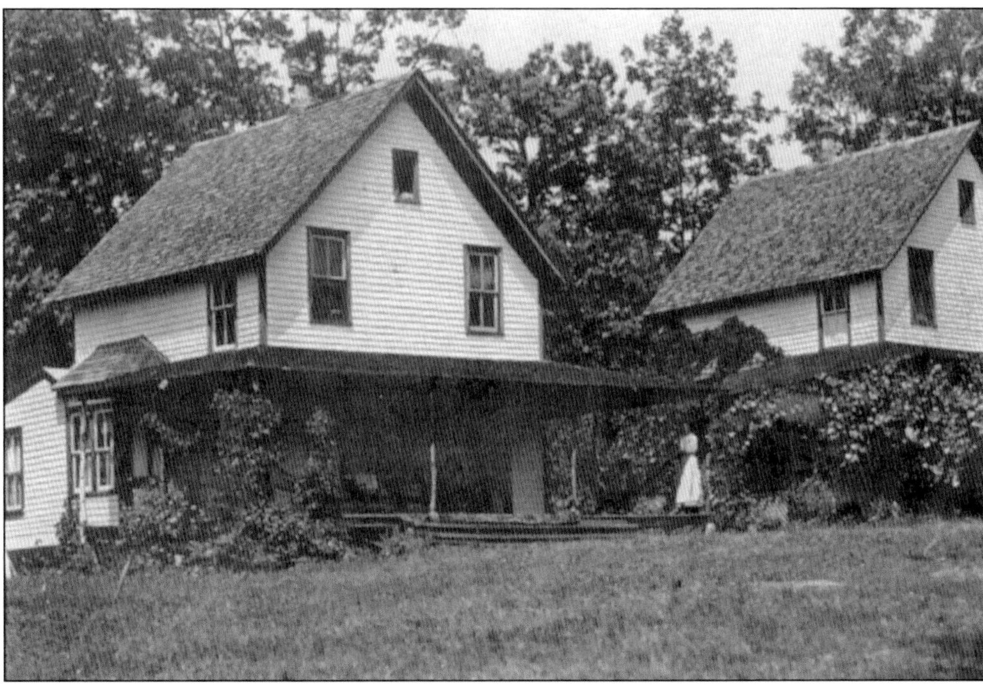

COTTAGES AT NUANGOLA LAKE. Archie Childs told his grandchildren that when he first saw Nuangola Lake, a 50-foot border of water lilies grew there, with a fragrance that was noticeable a mile away. Cottages owned by the Childs family, photographed around 1905, were constructed of lumber from trees cut to clear the building lots. (Courtesy of the Mountain Top Historical Society: *Pieces of the Past.*)

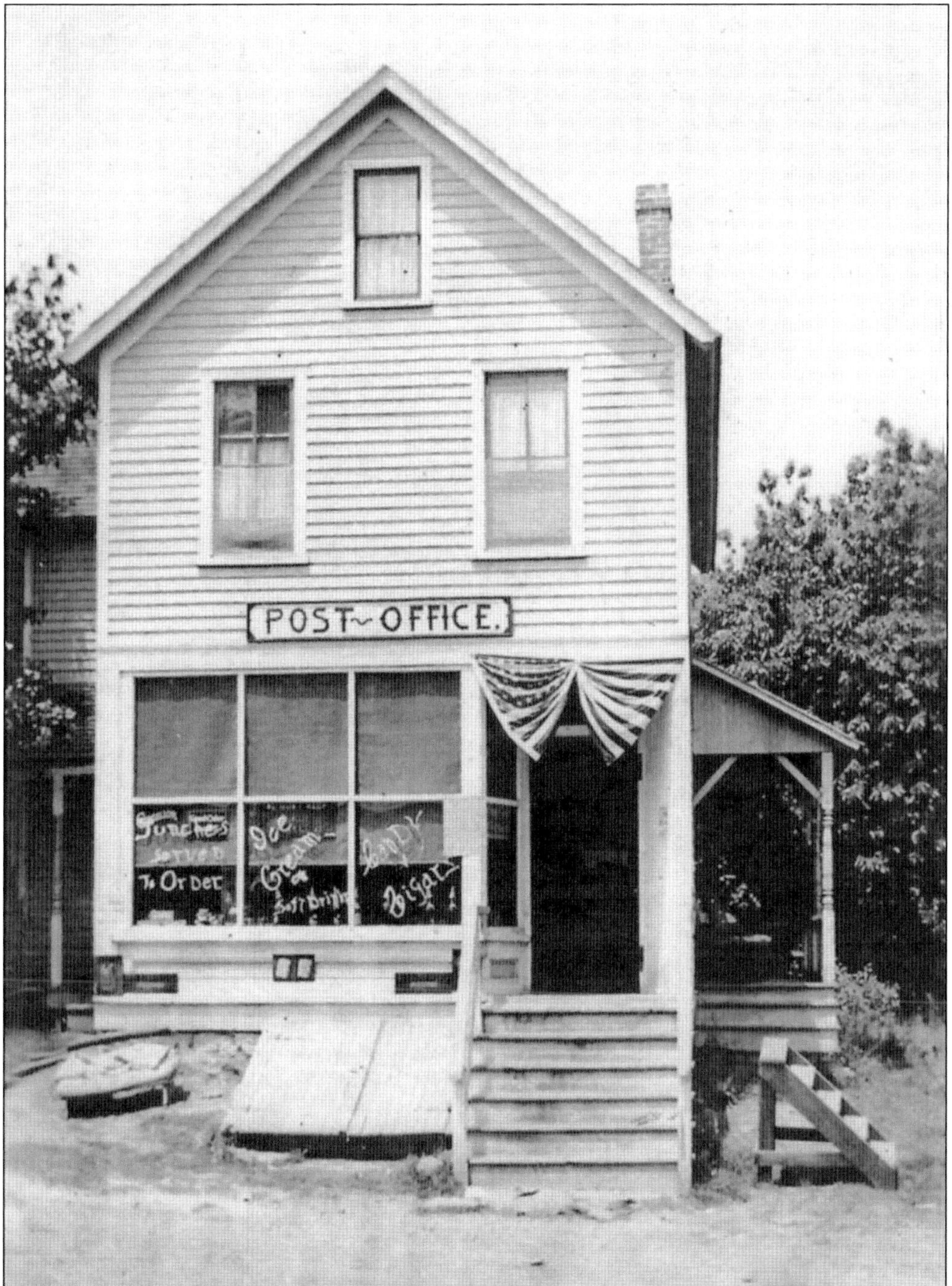

Nuangola Post Office. In 1898, Triangular Lake residents petitioned for a post office. The name Triangular Lake was already taken, so the US Postal Service named the lake and community Nuangola, translated from Algonquin as "people of the north" or the name of a drowned Indian maiden. In 1903, the post office was located in this building on the corner of Nuangola Road and Lake Avenue. (Courtesy of Mountain Top Photo.)

THE GROVE THEATRE

NUANGOLA, PA.

Foster and Perry Storm, Owners

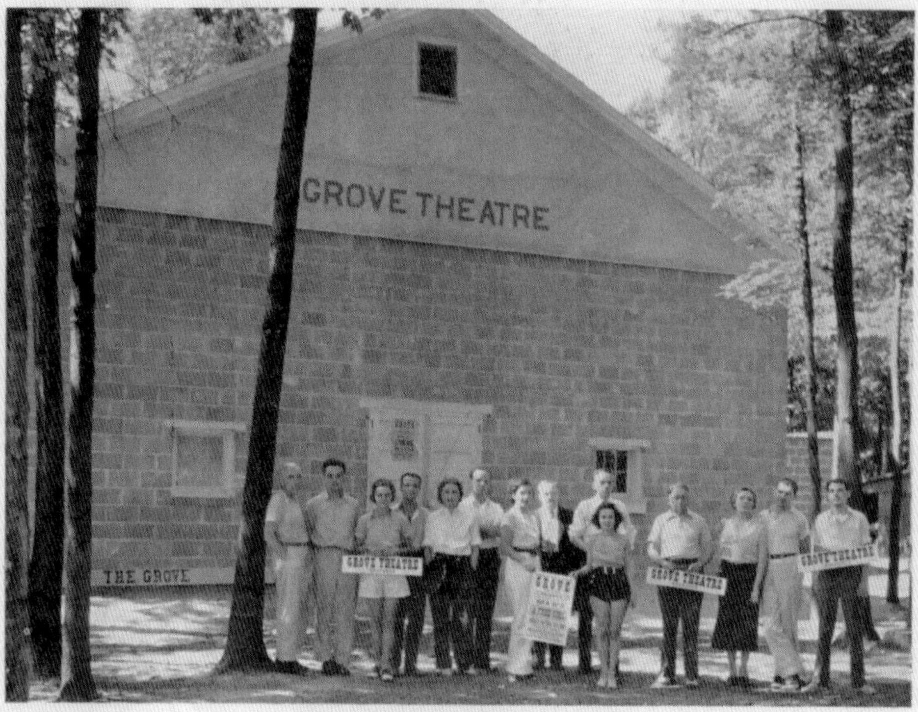

BROADWAY PLAYERS

A group of New York Professional Actors in a Festival of Broadway Plays which includes:
"Her Best Years" — "It's A Wise Child" — "Post Road"
"Arrow Strings" — "The Bishop Misbehaves"
"The Milky Way" — "Accent On Youth" — "Petticoat Fever"
"The Petrified Forest" — "Ceiling Zero" and a revival of "Romeo and Juliet"

Prices 35c to $1.00

For the Second Year Nuangola Has Gone Broadway

GROVE THEATER ADVERTISEMENT. In 1934, Perry Storm and his son Foster opened the Grove Theater at Nuangola Road and Lake Avenue. Managed by Royal Stout, whose wife, Nellie Kennedy Stout, was a Broadway actress, it was home to the Broadway Players summer stock troupe. Well-known performers appeared at the theater, including Buster Keaton, Florence Henderson, and Kirk Douglas, who debuted there in 1941. (Courtesy of James and Edith Miller.)

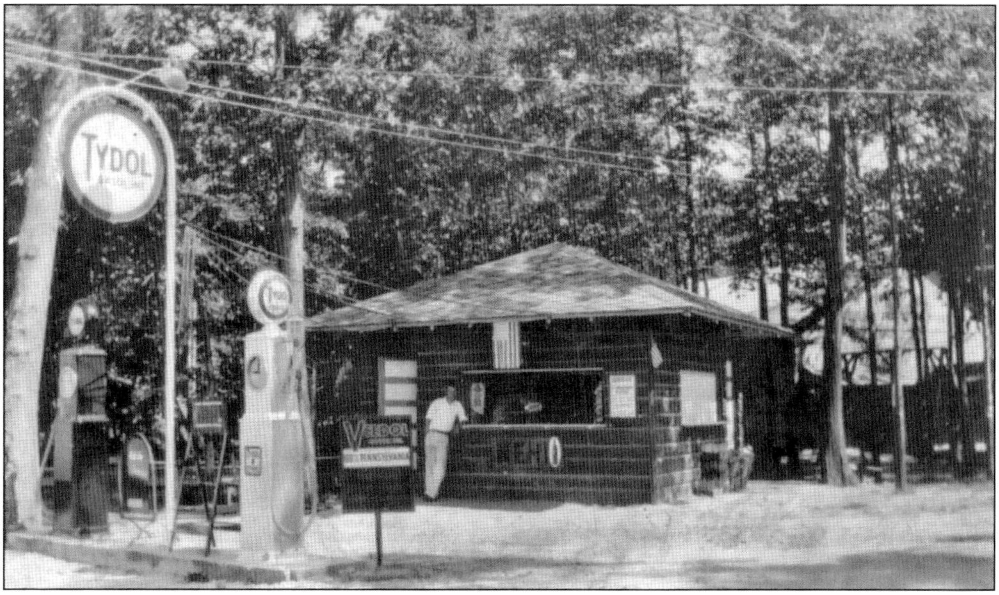

STAND AT THE GROVE THEATER. A hot dog stand near the Grove Theater was open all summer until Labor Day. (Courtesy of James and Edith Miller.)

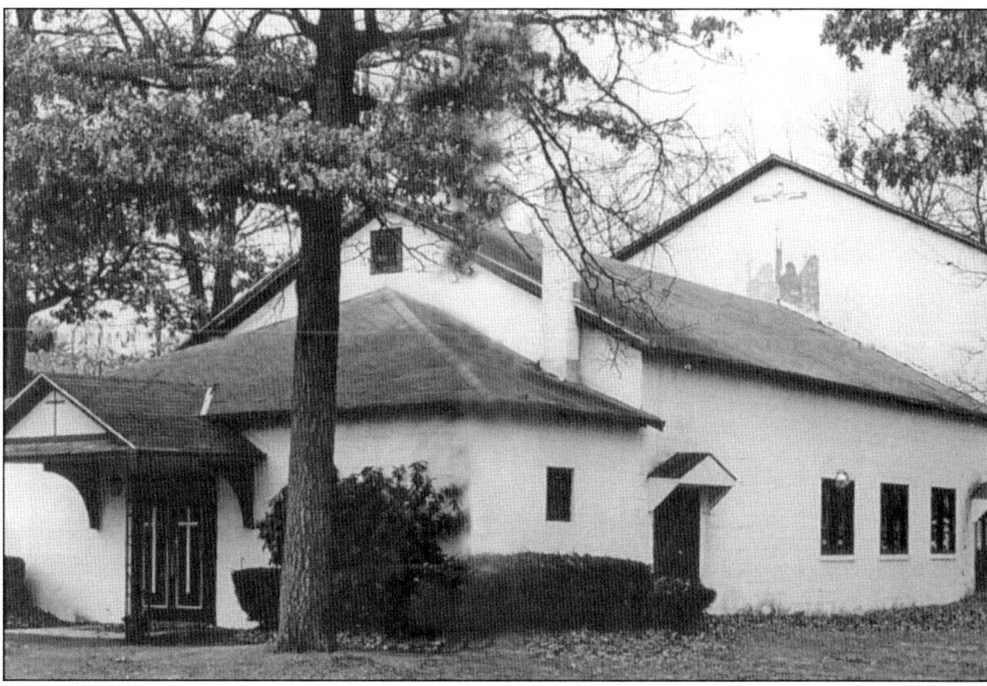

ST. ANNE'S CHAPEL. In 1959, the former Grove Theater closed and was purchased by the Diocese of Scranton, which converted the building for use as St. Anne's Chapel. After the chapel closed in 2000, the building was purchased by the Nuangola Lake Association and Nuangola Fire Company. It is once again used as a summer-theater facility. (Courtesy of the Mountain Top Historical Society: *Pieces of the Past.*)

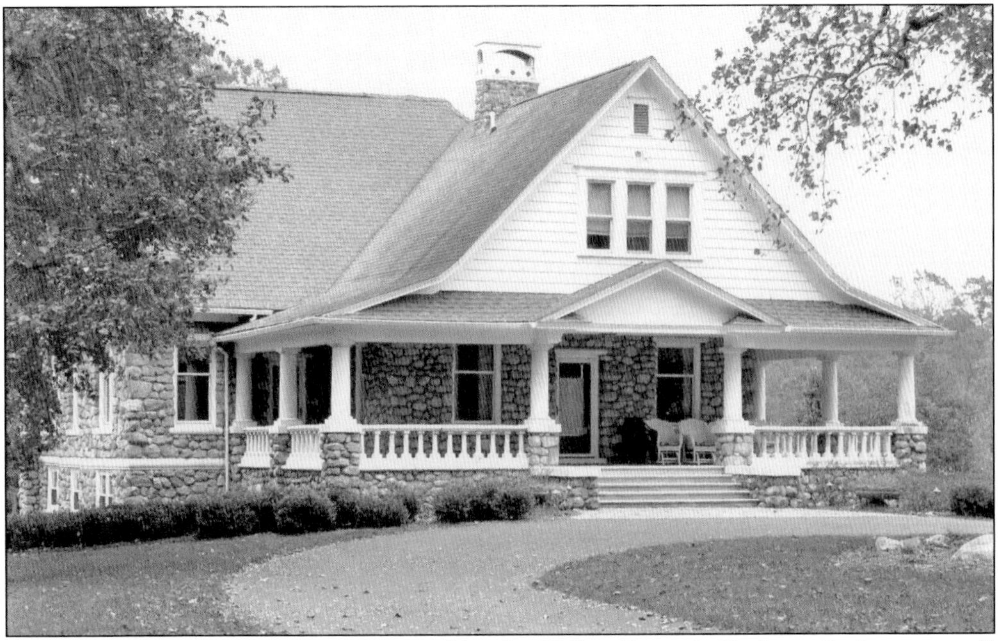

Schaeffer House at Pine View. Served by the Wilkes-Barre & Hazleton Railway, a small summer colony grew up at the hamlet of Pine View, located on Church Road near the Ice Lakes. William Schaeffer, president of the Wyoming Valley Trust Company, resided there by the 1920s. (Courtesy of Mountain Top Photo.)

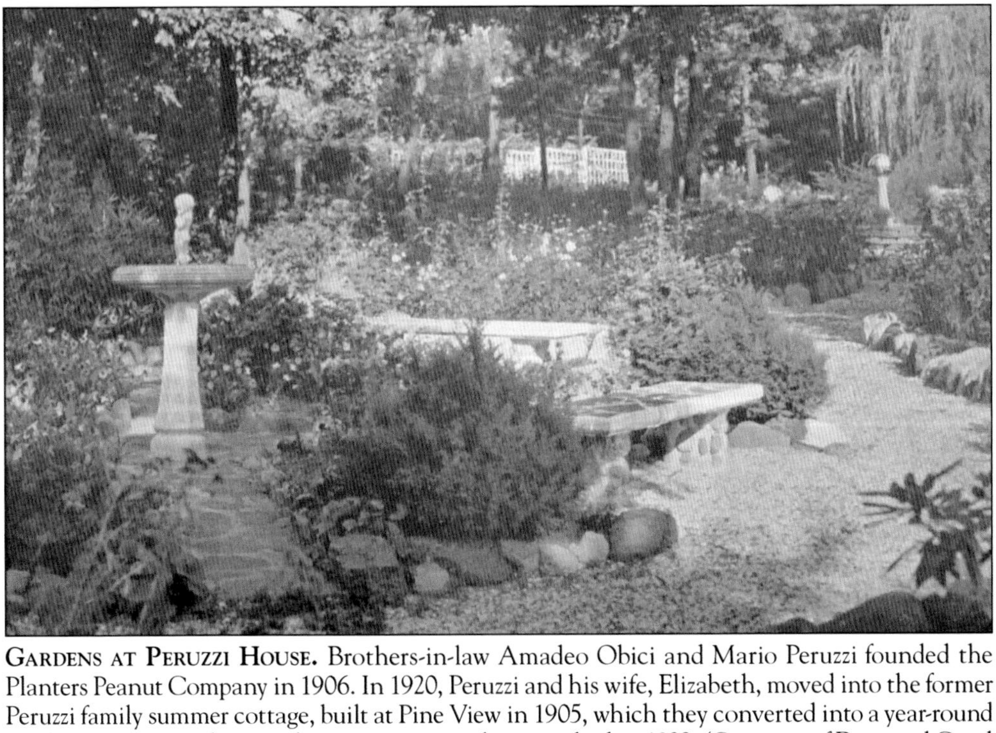

Gardens at Peruzzi House. Brothers-in-law Amadeo Obici and Mario Peruzzi founded the Planters Peanut Company in 1906. In 1920, Peruzzi and his wife, Elizabeth, moved into the former Peruzzi family summer cottage, built at Pine View in 1905, which they converted into a year-round residence. Large gardens on the property were photographed in 1933. (Courtesy of Dave and Carol Lippincott: Atkins, *Picture Tour of Wilkes-Barre and Vicinity.*)

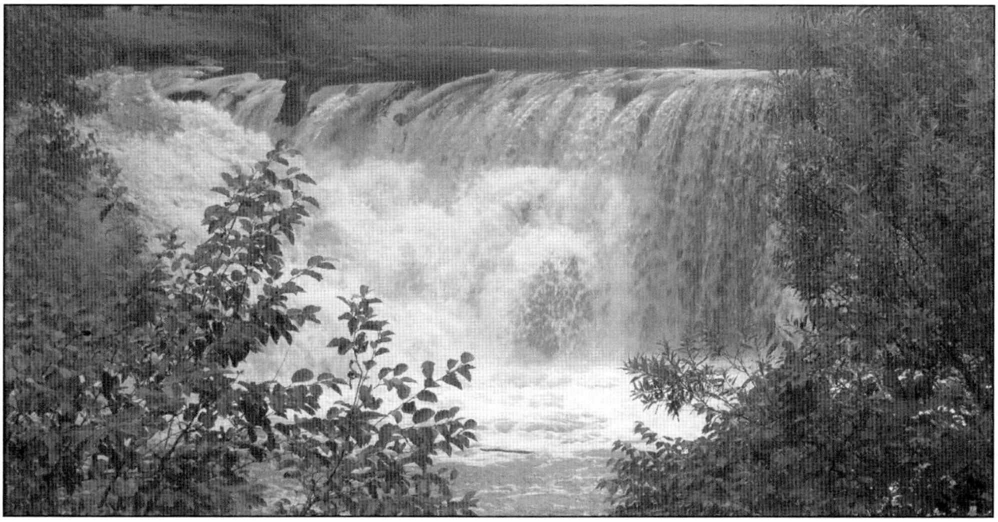

BLYTHEBURN DAM ON THE BIG WAPWALLOPEN CREEK. In 1911, developers Thomas and Wells established the planned community of Blytheburn, meaning "bright or sparkling stream," along the Big Wapwallopen Creek. Amenities included a dam and nearby "Kiddie Pool" for swimming. Blytheburn was served by the Wilkes-Barre & Hazleton Railway, which crossed the Big Wapwallopen Creek above the dam on a steel trestle. (Courtesy Darlene Miller-Lanning.)

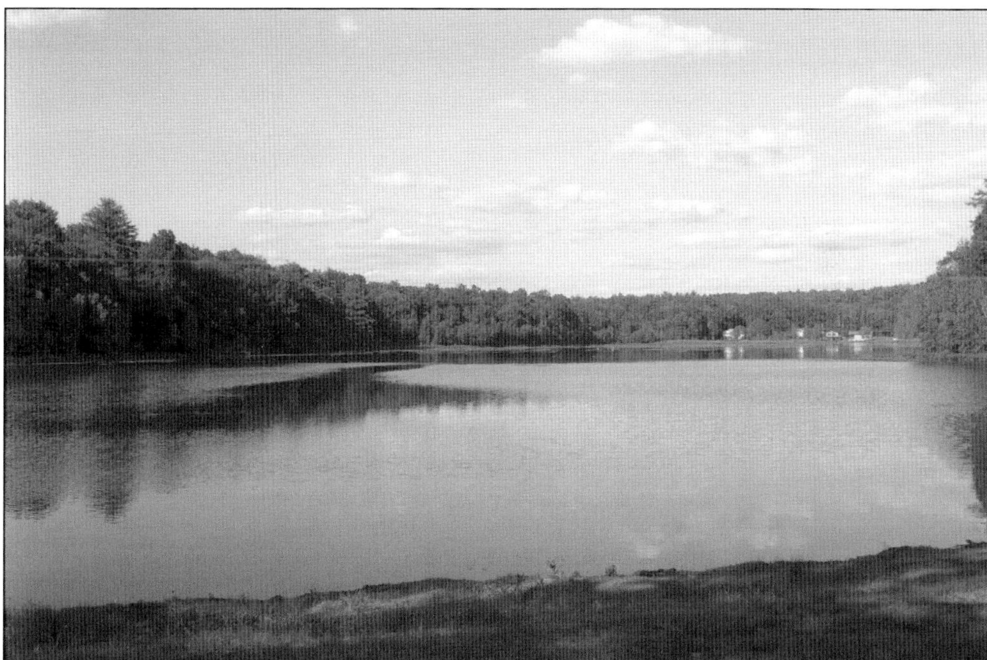

BLYTHEBURN LAKE. Another feature of the Blytheburn settlement was Blytheburn Lake, a popular site for boating, fishing, and skating. Today, it is maintained by the Blytheburn Lake Association. (Courtesy Darlene Miller-Lanning.)

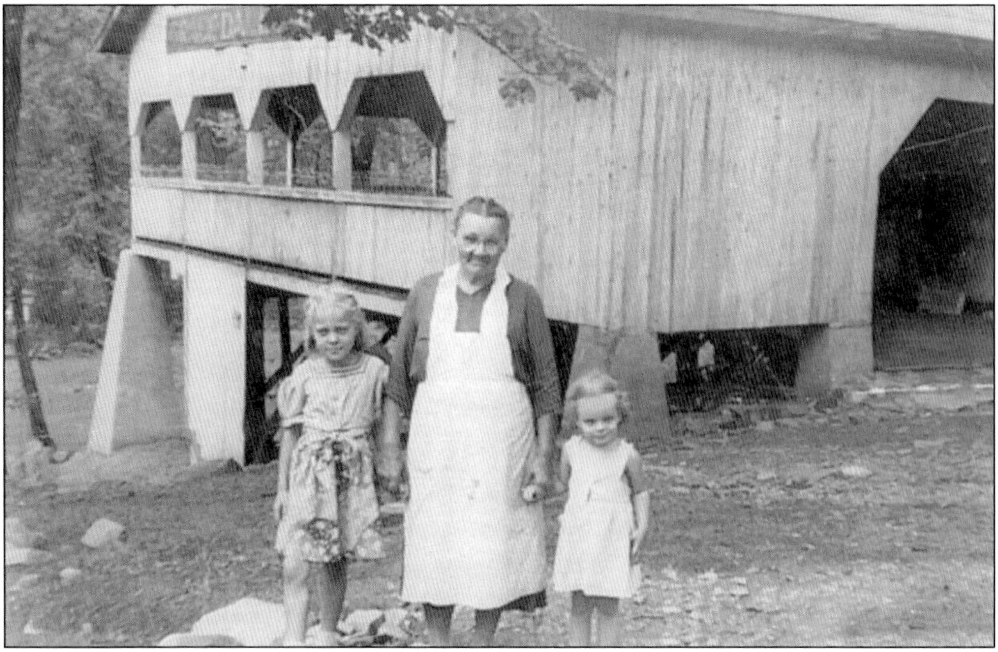

GRACEDALE PARK. Many small parks and groves provided weekend recreation for residents of the Mountain Top area. Gracedale Park, located on Woodlawn Avenue near Penobscot, was purchased by the Sledziewski family in the 1940s and operated through the 1960s. Activities included picnics, clambakes, children's rides, and square and farmer dances held in a pavilion. Loretta, Amelia, and Adeline Sledziewski were photographed there in the 1940s. (Courtesy of Lori Sledziewski.)

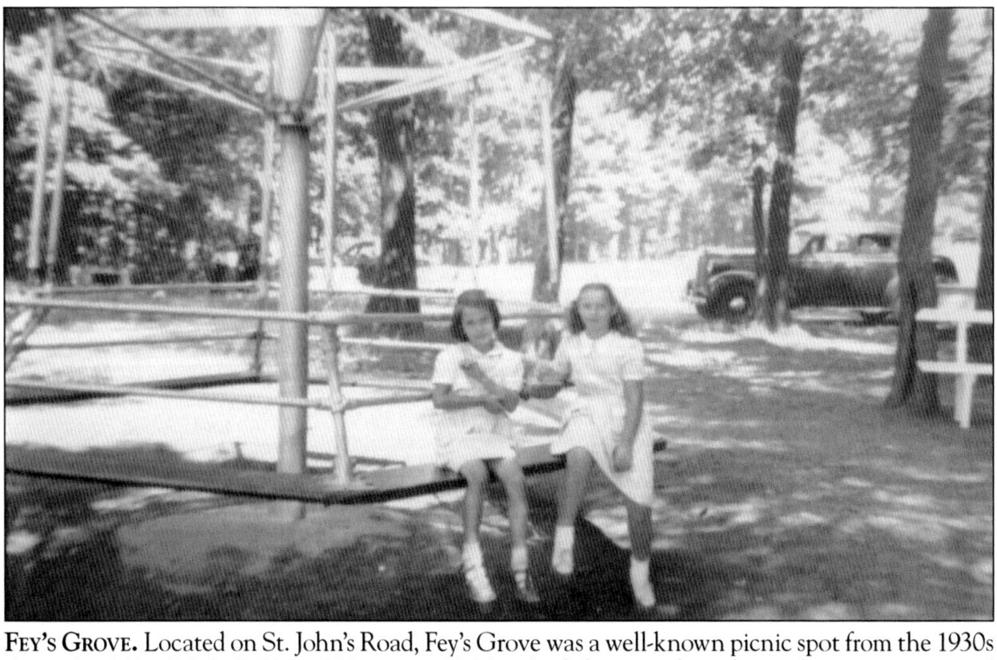

FEY'S GROVE. Located on St. John's Road, Fey's Grove was a well-known picnic spot from the 1930s through 1960s. Edith (left) and Henrietta Kahley (right) enjoyed a ride on the merry-go-round during a family Fourth of July outing in 1949. Other activities at the grove included baseball and horseshoes. (Courtesy of James and Edith Miller.)

Four

HIGHWAYS AND COMMERCE

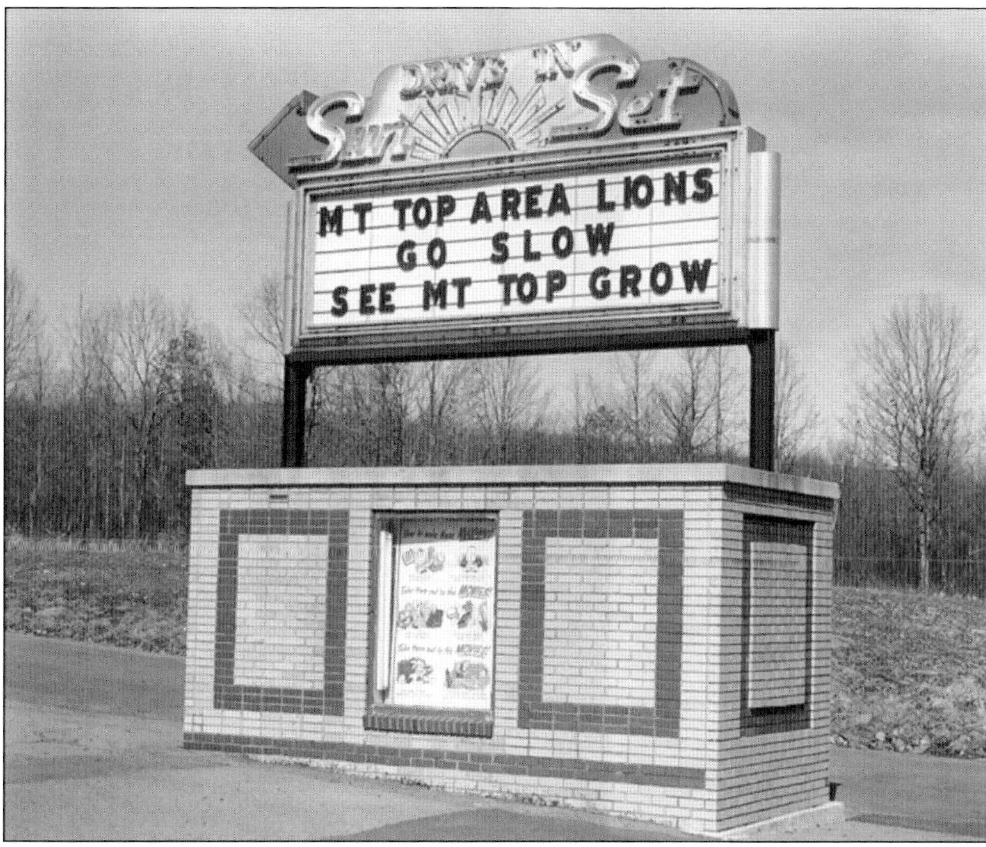

SUNSET DRIVE-IN. During the 1950s, the Sunset Drive-in was Mountain Top's family entertainment spot, hosting a crowd with every new movie feature. Located on Route 309 at what is now the Weis Shopping Center, the facility was owned and operated by the Novitski family of Nanticoke. The drive-in's neon sign displayed movie titles and community messages. In this photograph, the slogan "Go Slow See Mountain Top Grow" was presented by the Mountain Top Lions Club, a civic organization established in 1950. (Courtesy of the Mountain Top Historical Society: *Pieces of the Past.*)

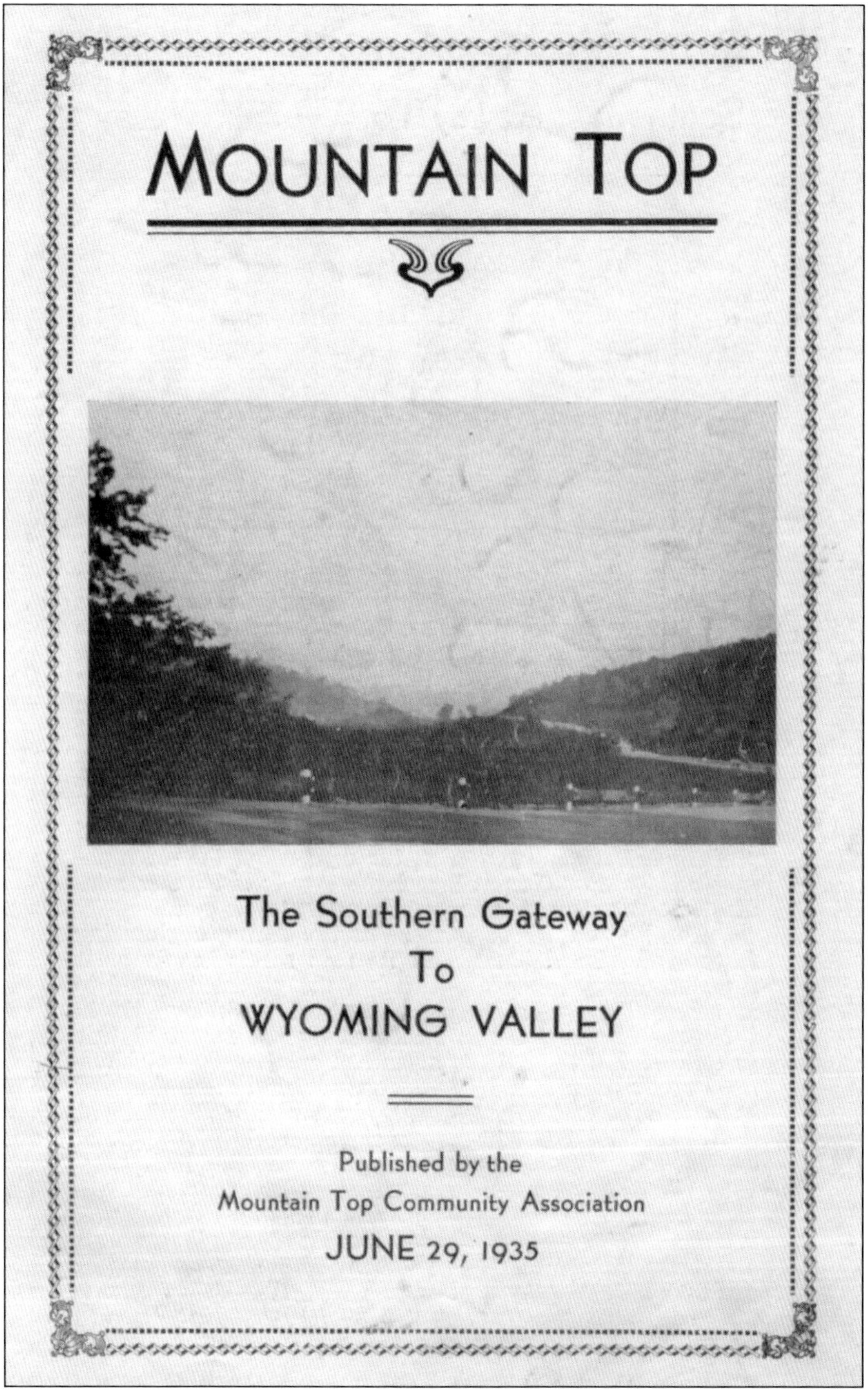
MOUNTAIN TOP

The Southern Gateway
To
WYOMING VALLEY

Published by the
Mountain Top Community Association
JUNE 29, 1935

MOUNTAIN TOP. In 1935, the Mountain Top Community Association published the booklet *Mountain Top: Southern Gateway to the Wyoming Valley*. The publication celebrated the opening of Route 309, which provided easy access to Mountain Top during the 20th century and contributed greatly to the region's growth. (Courtesy of James and Edith Miller.)

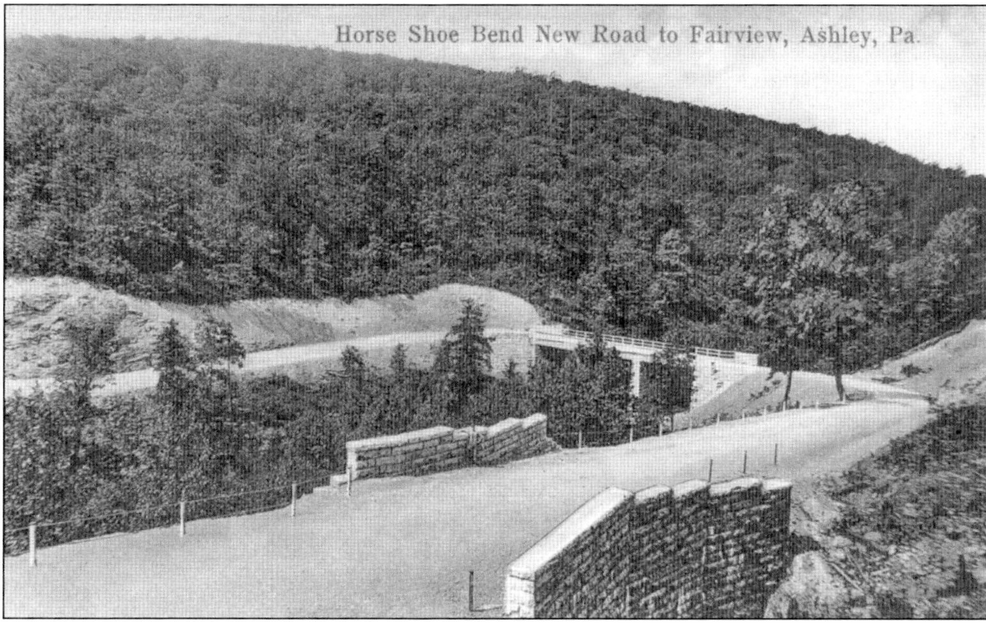

HORSESHOE BEND ON NEW ROAD TO FAIRVIEW. The road over the Penobscot Mountain was first called the Wilkes-Barre and Hazleton Turnpike. Improved in 1908, it became scenic Ashley Boulevard and crossed a curving stone bridge over Pine Run. When Route 309 was constructed, the bridge was replaced by fill. The stones were reused in a retaining wall, still visible along the highway. (Courtesy of Thomas Hollock.)

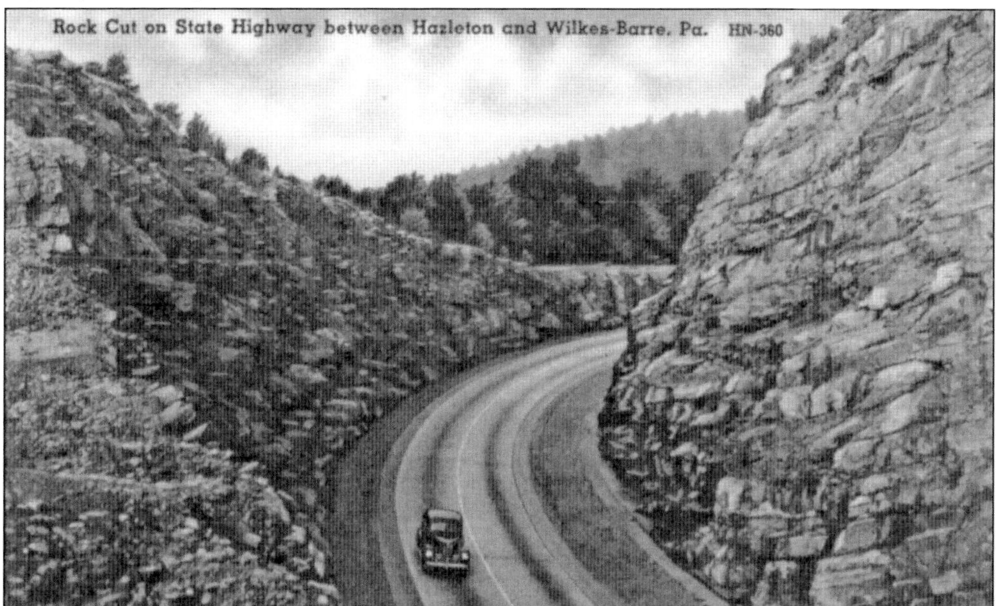

ROCK CUT ON STATE HIGHWAY BETWEEN WILKES-BARRE AND HAZLETON. Route 309 featured two impressive rock cuts. The first, excavated to a depth of 96 feet, measured 800 feet in length. The second, excavated to a depth of 1,200 feet, measured 126 feet in length. Roughly 200 tons of dynamite were needed to clear some 318,000 cubic yards of rock from the cuts. (Courtesy of Thomas Hollock.)

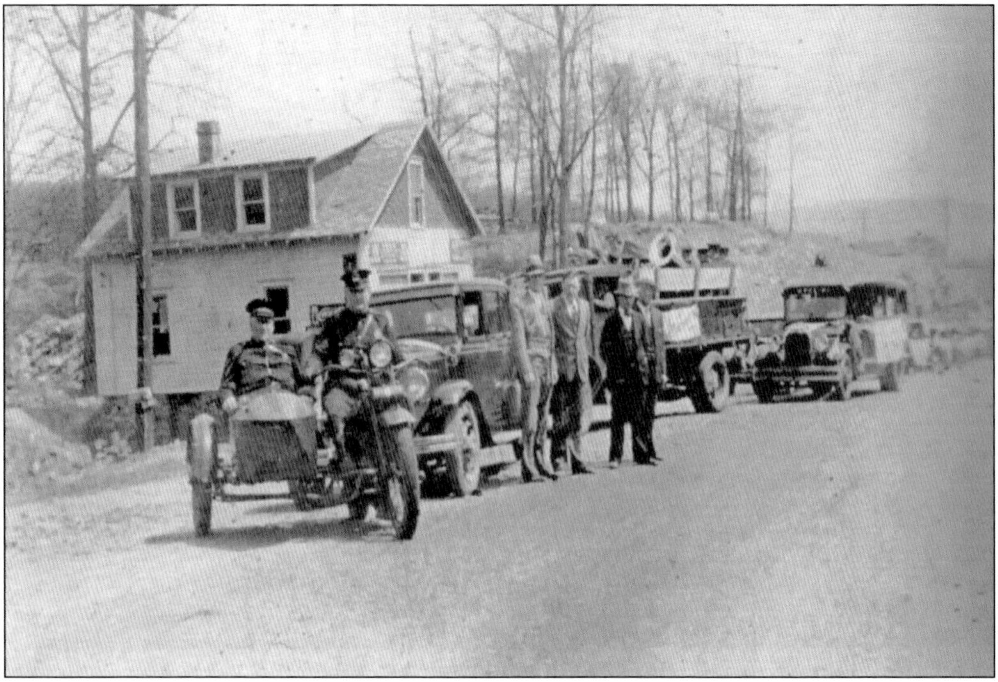

PARADE CELEBRATING THE OPENING OF ROUTE 309. In 1935, residents of Mountain Top celebrated the opening of Route 309 with a parade and dedication ceremony. Many vehicles decorated by community businesses joined in the procession. (Courtesy of Russell Koons.)

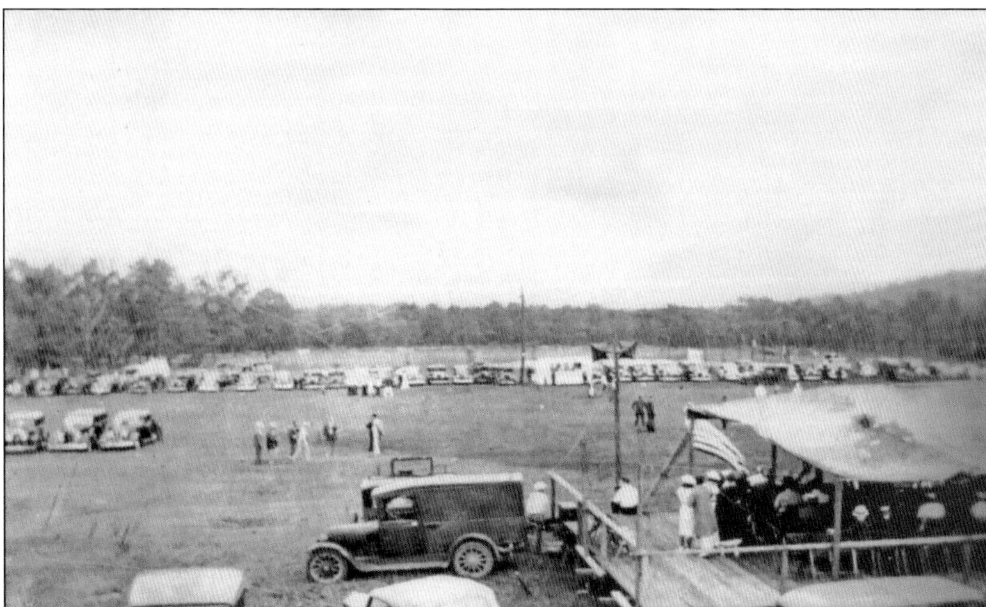

CEREMONY CELEBRATING THE OPENING OF ROUTE 309. In conjunction with the parade, a ceremony took place at the ball field near the new Fairview Heights housing development. The completion of the highway during the Great Depression was no small event; the cost for improvements on three miles of road was near a half-million dollars. (Courtesy of Minnie Koons Peters.)

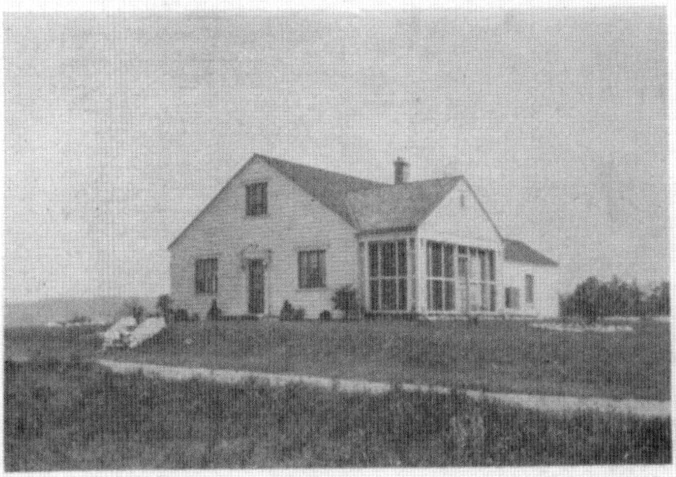

FAIRVIEW HEIGHTS
HOME SITES

BEAUTIFUL SCENERY FINE NEIGHBORHOOD
GOOD SCHOOLS AND CHURCHES

Buy your lot on easy terms and build your home above the noise and dirt and mine caves of the city

FAIRVIEW HEIGHTS HOMESITES. Following construction of Route 309, Bradley Ayers opened Mountain Top's first suburban developments. An advertisement in *Mountain Top: Southern Gateway to the Wyoming Valley* encouraged families to buy lots on easy terms and build homes above "the noise and dirt and mine caves of the city." Included in the ad was a photograph of the Ayers home on Birch Street. (Courtesy of James and Edith Miller.)

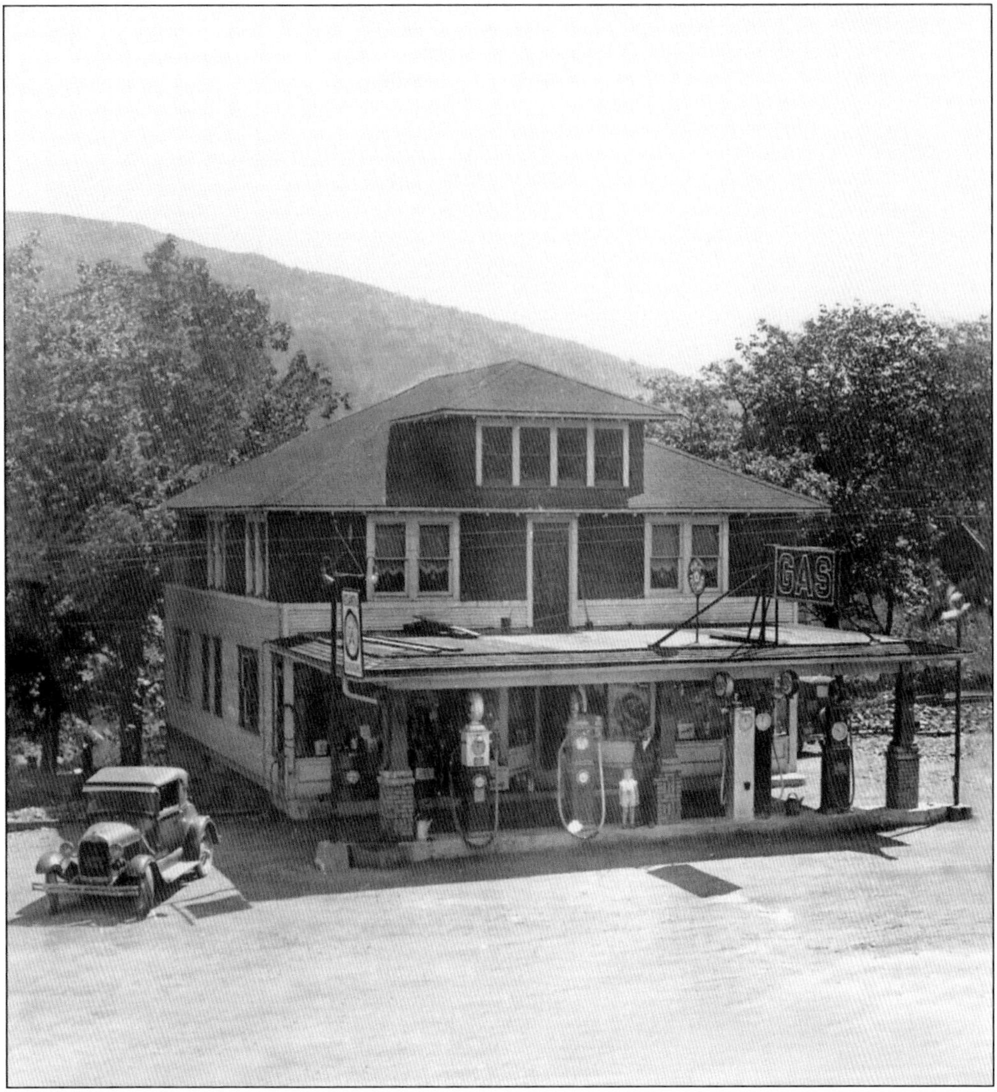

Mountain View Gas Station. The Mountain View Gas Station was built by Arthur Yocum in 1931 and operated by James "Fuzzy" Cornelius. Located at the summit of Penobscot Mountain on the newly improved Route 309, the business had many customers and soon became a well-known landmark. Cornelius and his son Jimmy were photographed next to the station's four gas pumps, with a 1932 Model A Ford nearby. In 1937, with the addition of a bar on the left side of the building, the business expanded to become the Mountain View Tavern. Later, a dance hall was added on the right. The business operates today as the Broadway Tavern. (Courtesy of George and Mary Hollock.)

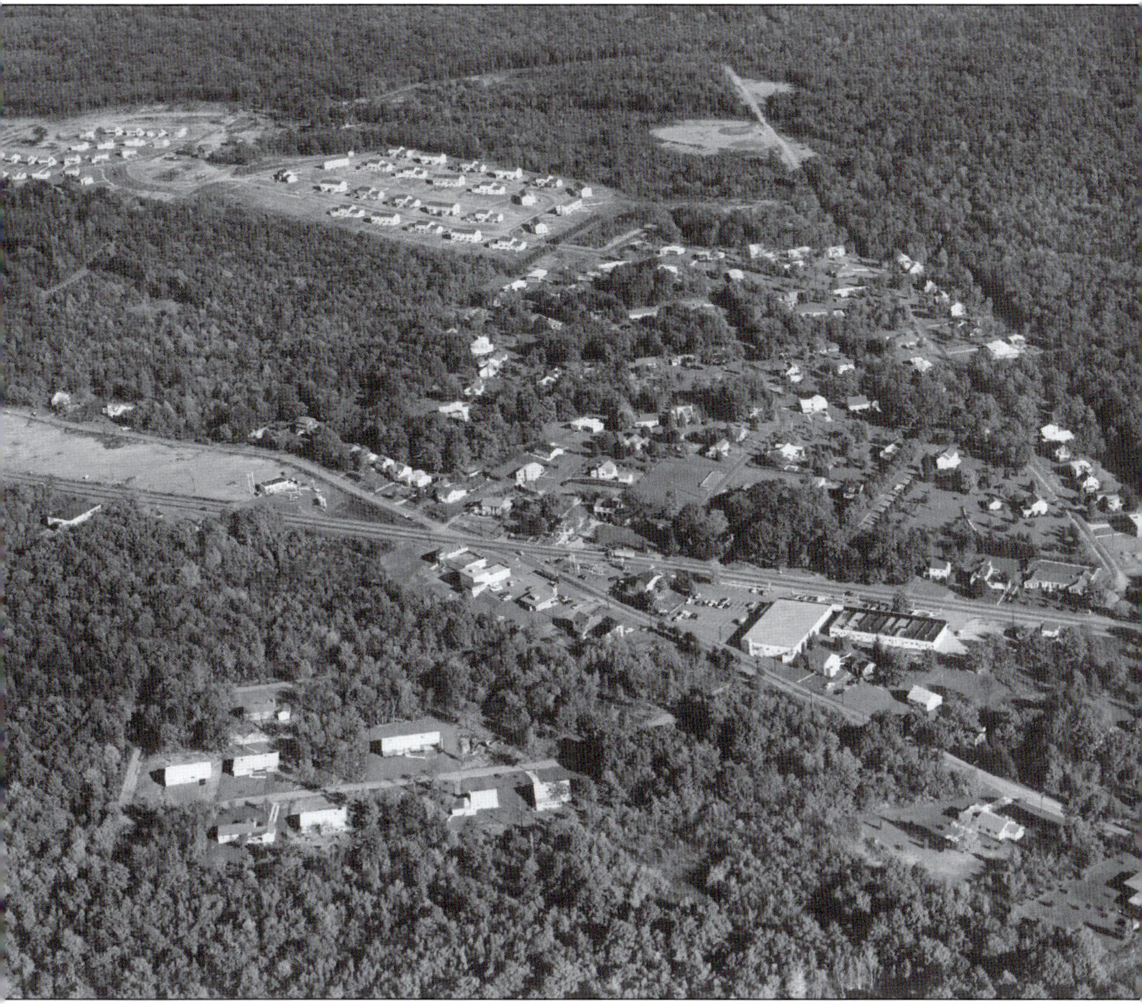

MOUNTAIN TOP AT TRIANGLE INTERSECTION. This aerial photograph of Mountain Top depicts the area in the 1960s. Shown is the Triangle intersection of Main Road and Route 309, including the Gulf gas station, now the site of Subway; Mountain Top Hardware, now the site of the *Mountaintop Eagle* newspaper office; Triangle Pharmacy; Miners Bank, now the Lewith and Freeman Real Estate office; Triangle Restaurant, now the site of the Petroleum Service Company gas station; and Acme Market, now the site of Carone's Market. Also shown are houses in Fairview Heights and town houses in Fairview Park. (Courtesy of the Luzerne County Historical Society.)

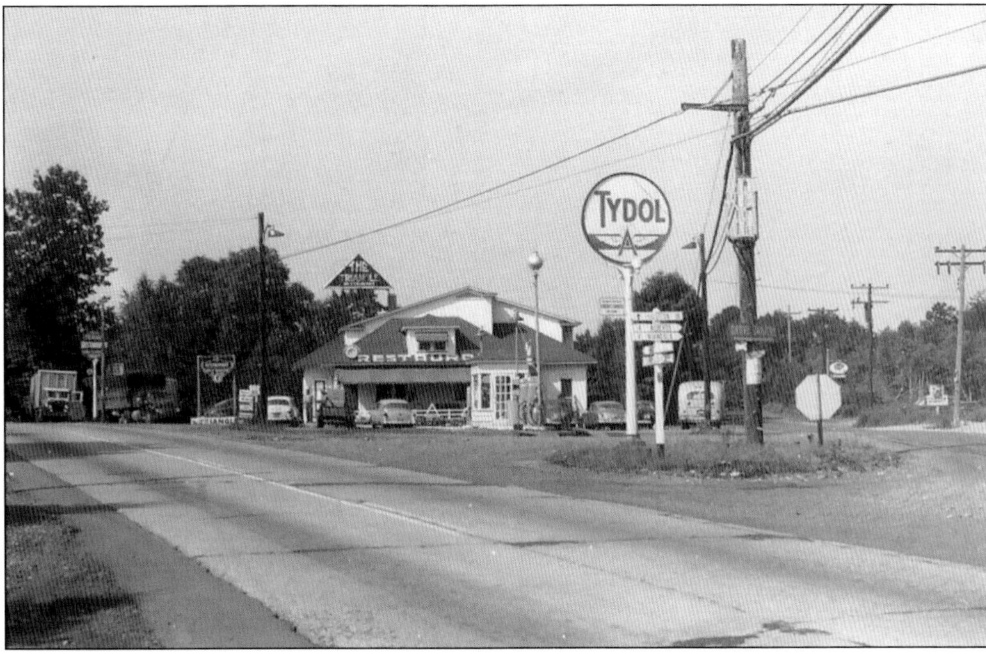

TRIANGLE INTERSECTION ON ROUTE 309. The Triangle Restaurant and Tydol gas station were built by Lymon Milory after Route 309 was constructed. The restaurant, later owned and operated by Charles and Anne Locke, became a popular gathering place as well as a Trailways bus stop. It is now the site of the Petroleum Service Company gas station. (Courtesy of Charles and Anne Locke.)

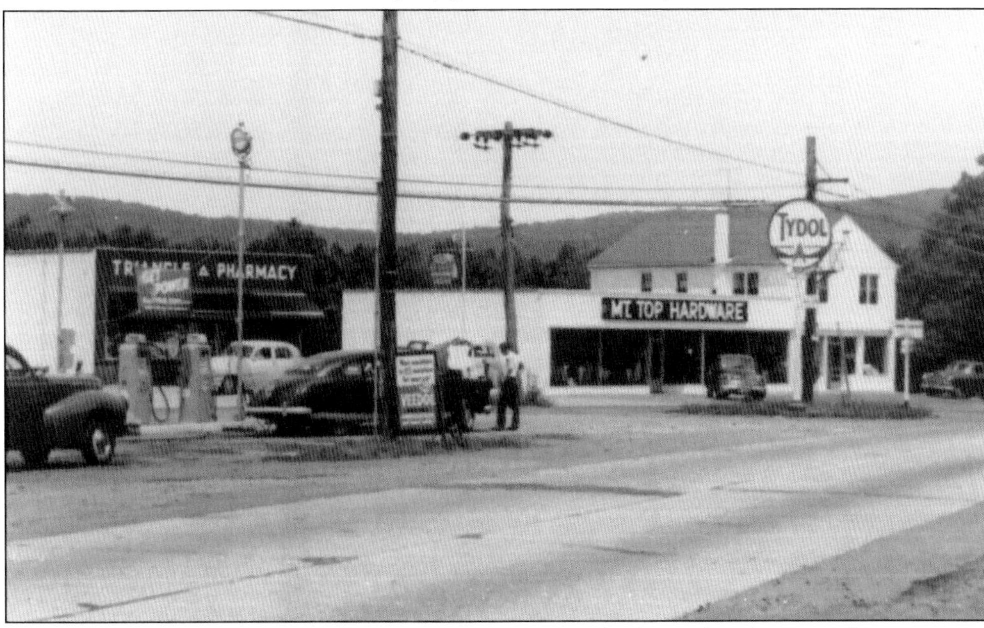

TRIANGLE PHARMACY AND MOUNTAIN TOP HARDWARE. Also located at the Triangle intersection in Fairview Township were the Triangle Pharmacy and Mountain Top Hardware store. Built by the Yuscavages, the pharmacy continues today as a family business. The building of Mountain Top Hardware is now the site of the *Mountaintop Eagle* newspaper and other businesses. (Courtesy of Charles and Anne Locke.)

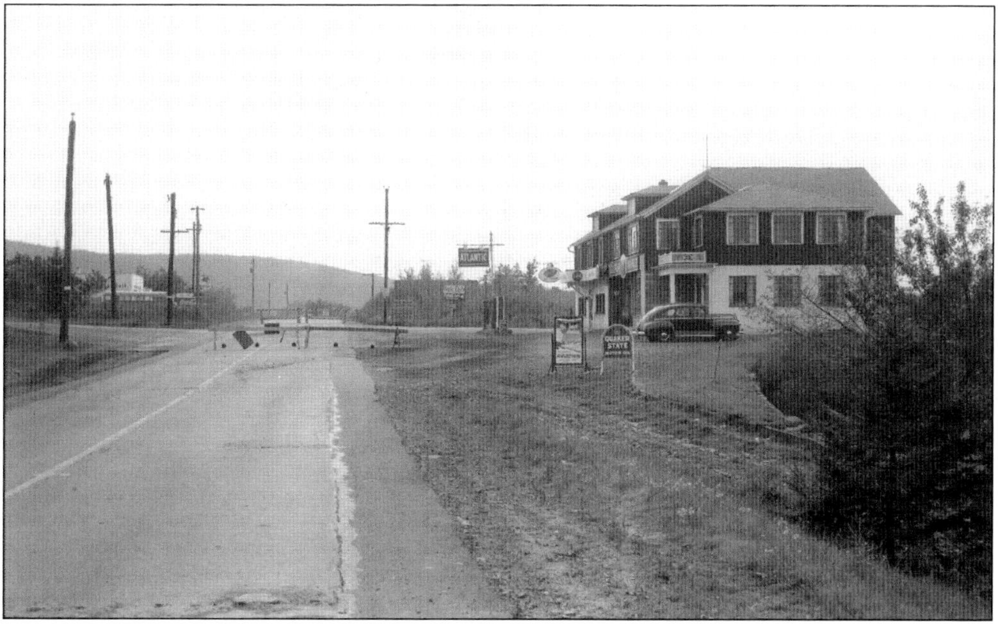

Konn's Corners on Route 309. With the completion of Route 309 in Wright Township, Tony and Mary Konn built a grocery store and gas station at the intersection of the highway and Church Road. The location was later known as Konn's Corners. After the closing of Konn's grocery, the building became home to a variety of businesses in subsequent years. (Courtesy of Genevieve Petroski.)

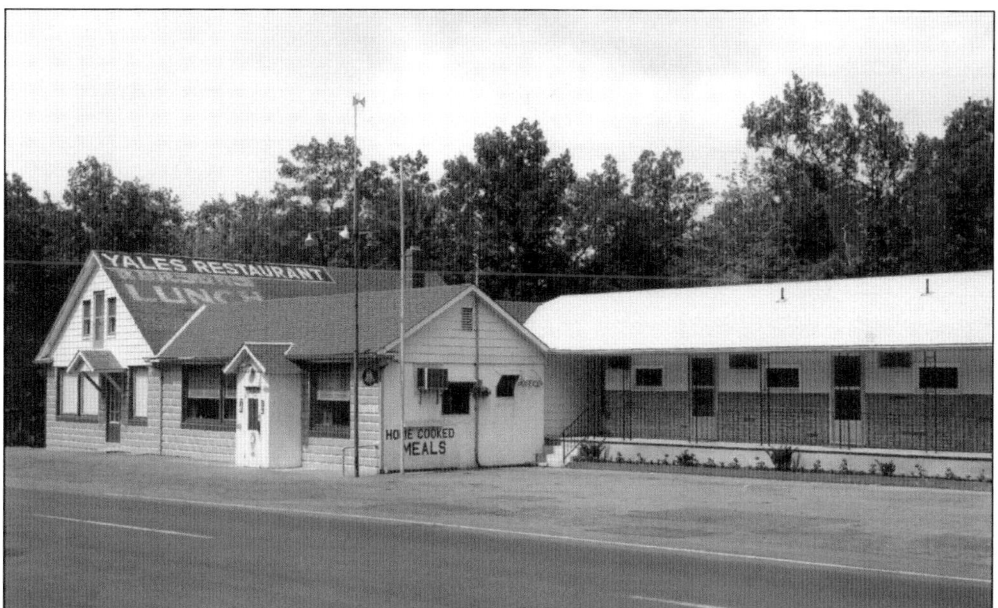

Yale's Restaurant. Known for its fine home cooking, Yale's Restaurant was built in 1943 by Frank Kreuzer for Worthy and Francis Yale, who expanded it to become a motel. While campaigning in 1959, Pres. John F. Kennedy stopped there to address a group of people who had gathered to watch his motorcade on Route 309. The restaurant is now the Shalimar Lounge. (Courtesy of Joe Yale.)

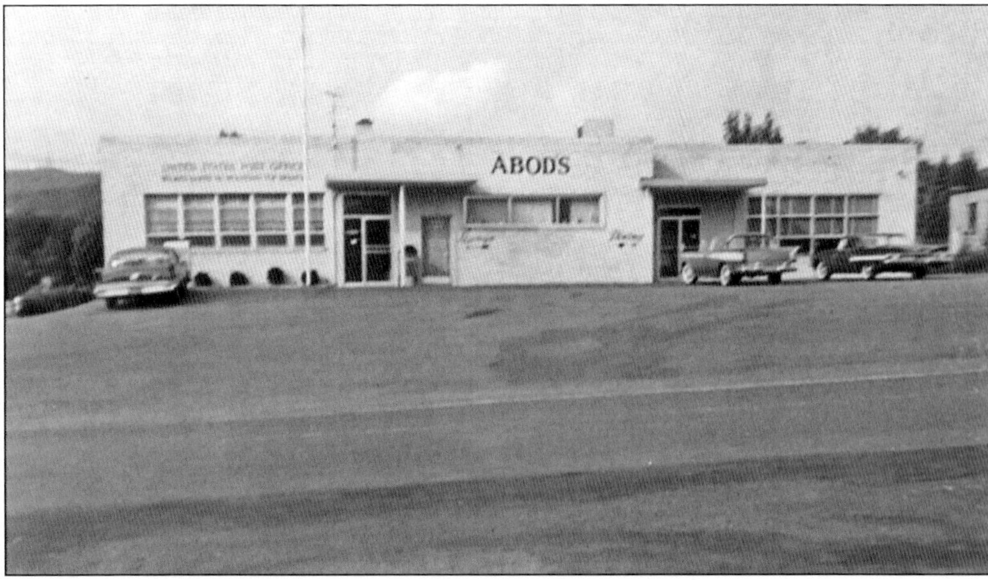

Mountain Top Post Office and Abod's Lounge. The Mountain Top Post Office moved from its location on North Main Street in 1957, opening in a facility at the corner of Kirby Avenue and Route 309 next to Abod's Lounge. This is now the site of the Rite-Aid pharmacy. (Courtesy of James and Edith Miller.)

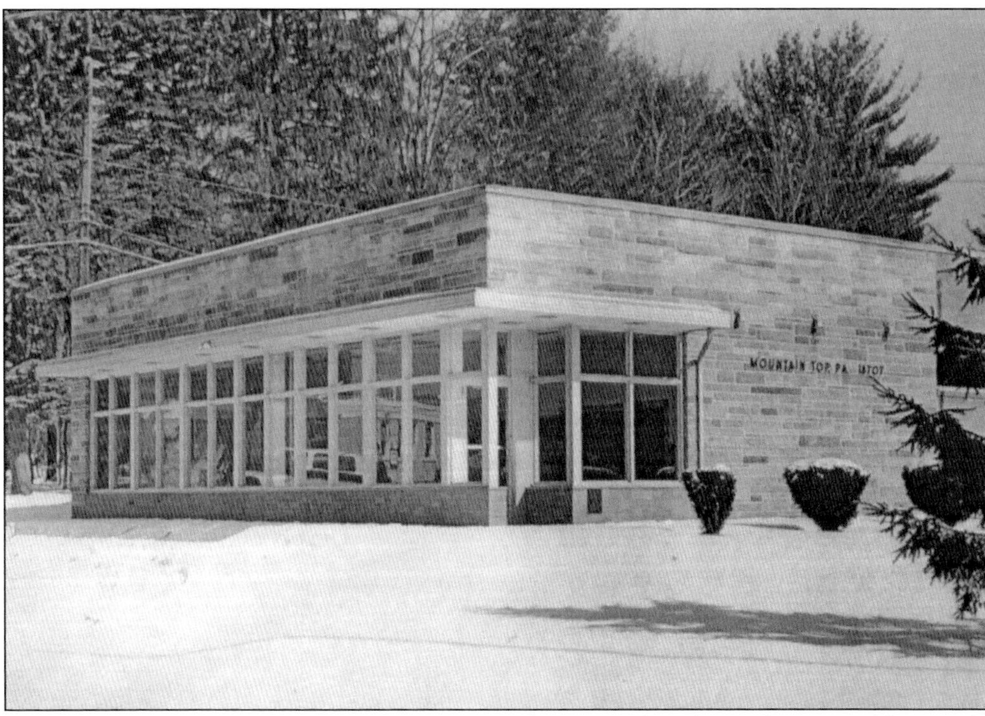

Mountain Top Post Office. In 1970, the post office moved to the Wideman Building at the corner of North Main Street and Kirby Avenue. Today, this structure is home to the Geisinger Health Center. The post office is currently located in the Simoncavage Building on Route 309. (Courtesy of the Luzerne County Historical Society.)

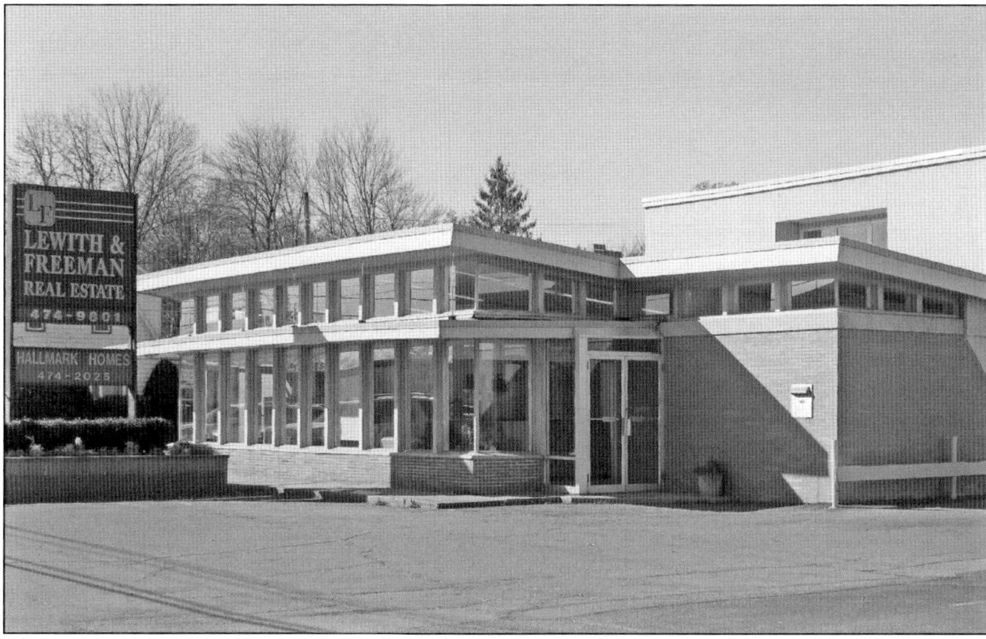

Lewith and Freeman Real Estate Office. During the 1950s, the Miners National Bank became the first to open in Mountain Top. The building, located on South Main Road near the Triangle intersection, is now used as the Lewith and Freeman Real Estate office. (Courtesy of Darlene Miller-Lanning.)

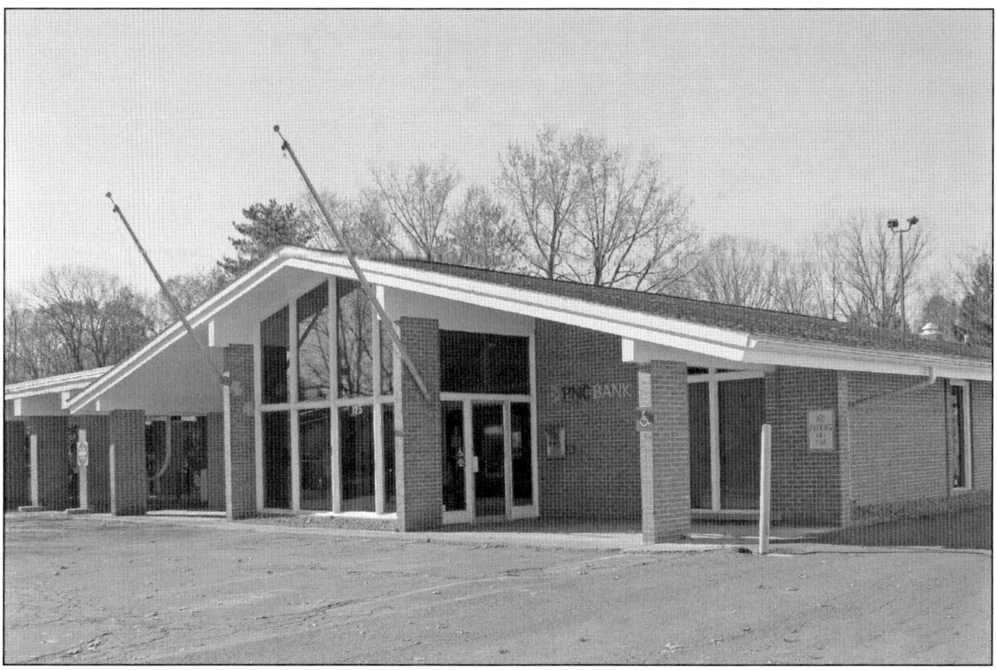

PNC Bank. Shortly after the opening of the Miners National Bank, the First National Bank constructed a facility in Mountain Top near the shopping center of Acme Market between Route 309 and South Main Road. It operates today as PNC Bank. (Courtesy of Darlene Miller-Lanning.)

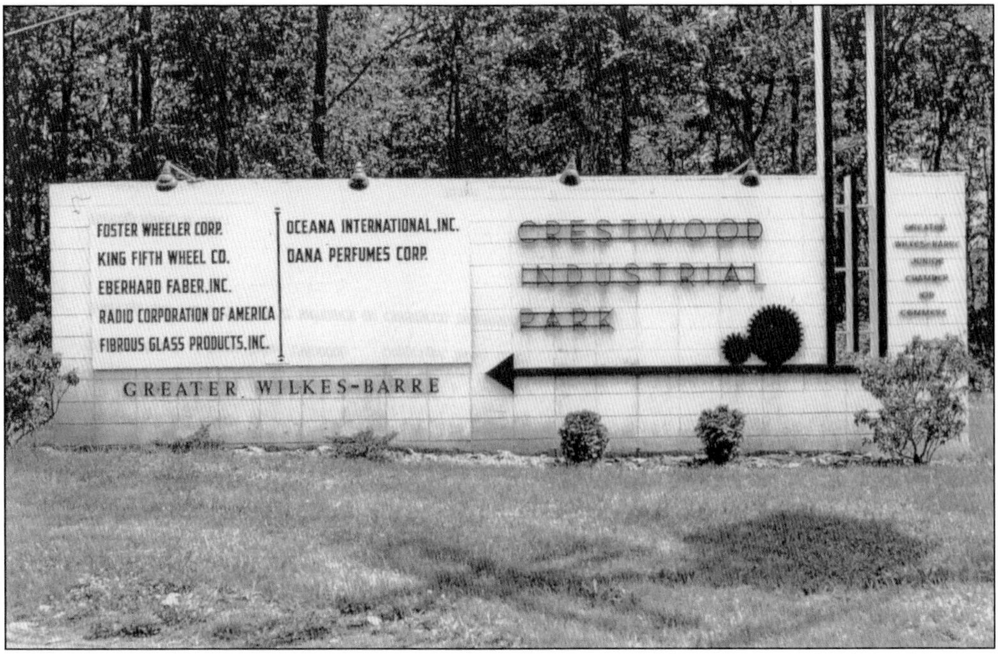

ENTRANCE TO CRESTWOOD INDUSTRIAL PARK IN THE 1960s. Established in 1952 by the Committee of 100, a predecessor of the Greater Wilkes-Barre Chamber of Business and Industry, the Crestwood Industrial Park was the first industrial park in Luzerne County. By the late 1960s, seven companies had located there. (Courtesy of the Luzerne County Historical Society.)

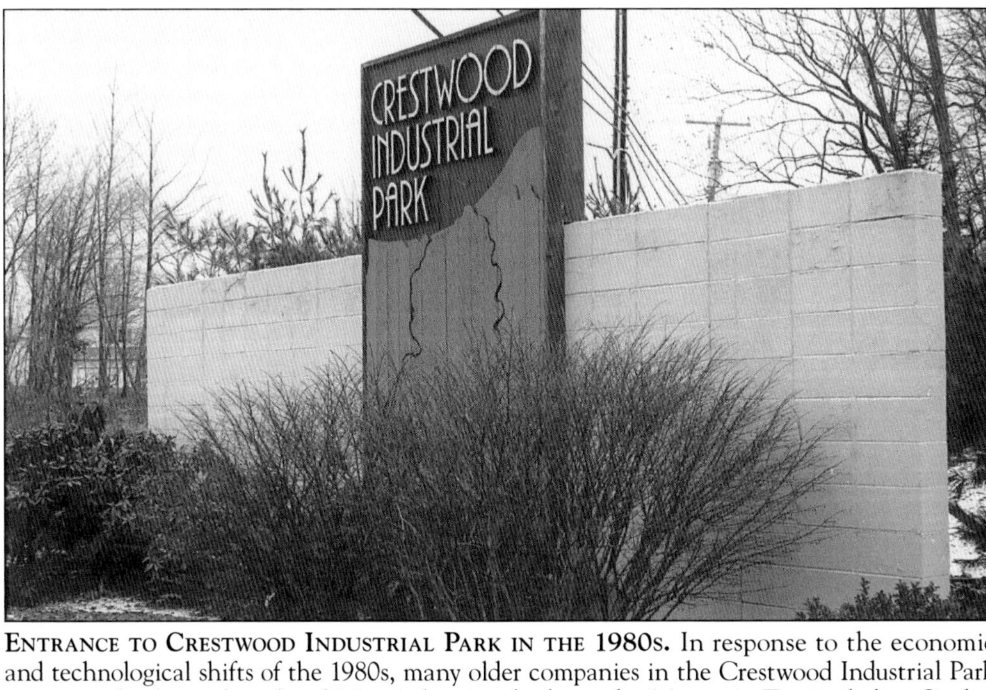

ENTRANCE TO CRESTWOOD INDUSTRIAL PARK IN THE 1980s. In response to the economic and technological shifts of the 1980s, many older companies in the Crestwood Industrial Park reorganized, relocated, or closed. New industries also located at Mountain Top, including Quaker Oats, Mission Foods, and Mideast Aluminum, among others. (Courtesy of Mountain Top Historical Society: *Pieces of the Past*.)

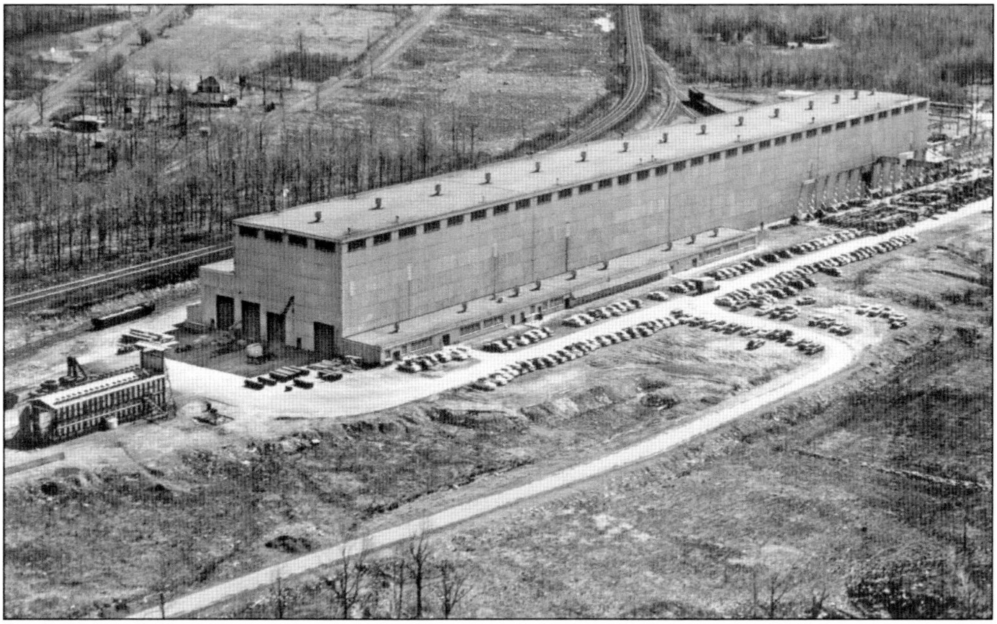

FOSTER WHEELER CORPORATION. The Foster Wheeler Corporation opened in 1953 as the first factory in the Crestwood Industrial Park. The company built heat exchangers and pressure vessels there until it closed in 1984. The complex was purchased by Morrison-Knudson Company Inc., which repaired railcars there for several years before closing. The building was torn down in 2005. (Courtesy of the Luzerne County Historical Society.)

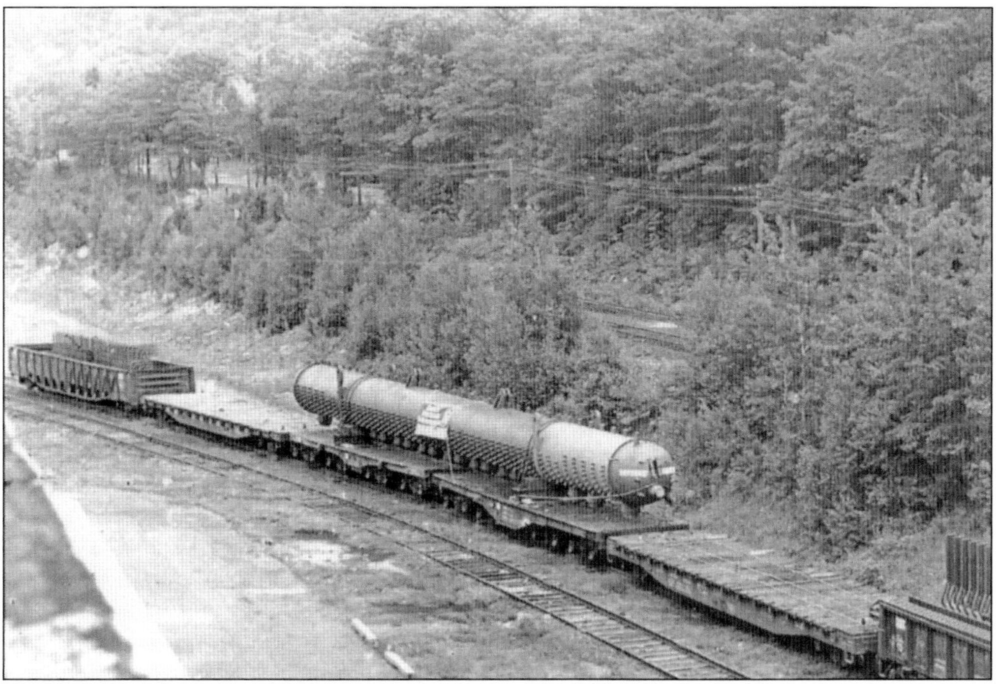

FOSTER WHEELER HEAT EXCHANGER. The large vessels fabricated by the Foster Wheeler Corporation were often shipped by rail. The heat exchanger shown here spanned two flatbed railcars. (Courtesy of Florence Lenahan.)

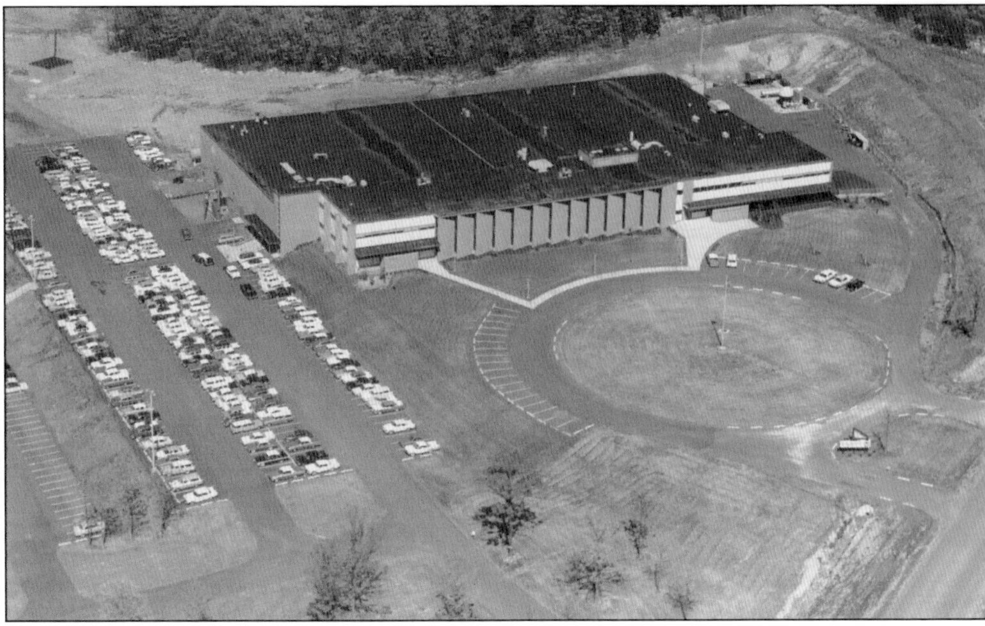

RADIO CORPORATION OF AMERICA. The Radio Corporation of America built a factory in the Crestwood Industrial Park in 1968. The company was a leading manufacturer of transistors before electronics were produced overseas. The facility was later home to General Electric Solid State, Harris Semiconductor, Intersil, and currently, Fairchild Semiconductor. (Courtesy of the Luzerne County Historical Society.)

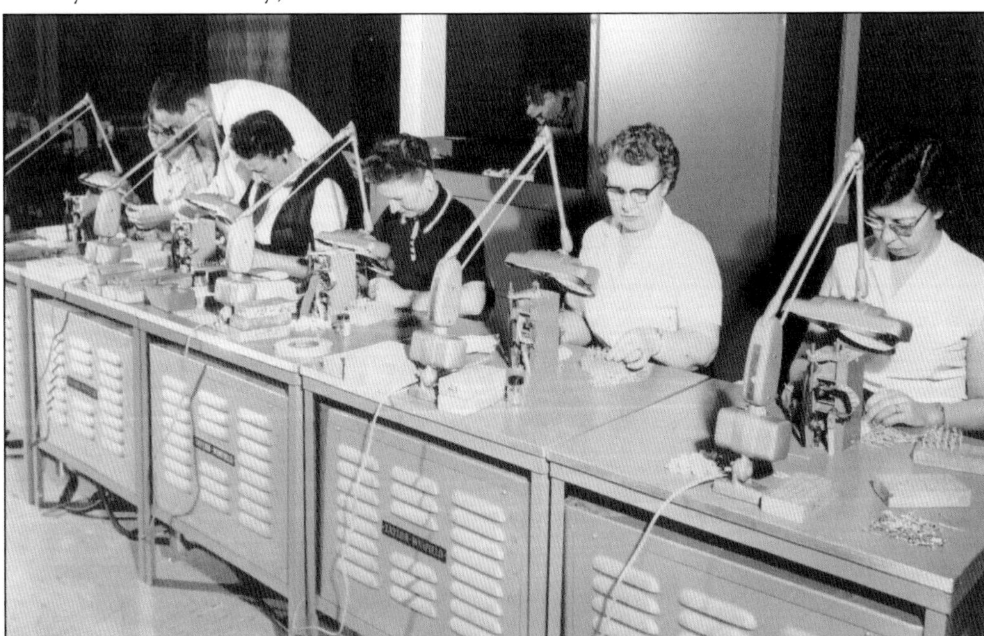

WORKERS AT RADIO CORPORATION OF AMERICA. Workers at the Radio Corporation of America plant looked through magnifying lenses as they assembled small and delicate components. The labor force included a large number of female employees. (Courtesy of the Luzerne County Historical Society.)

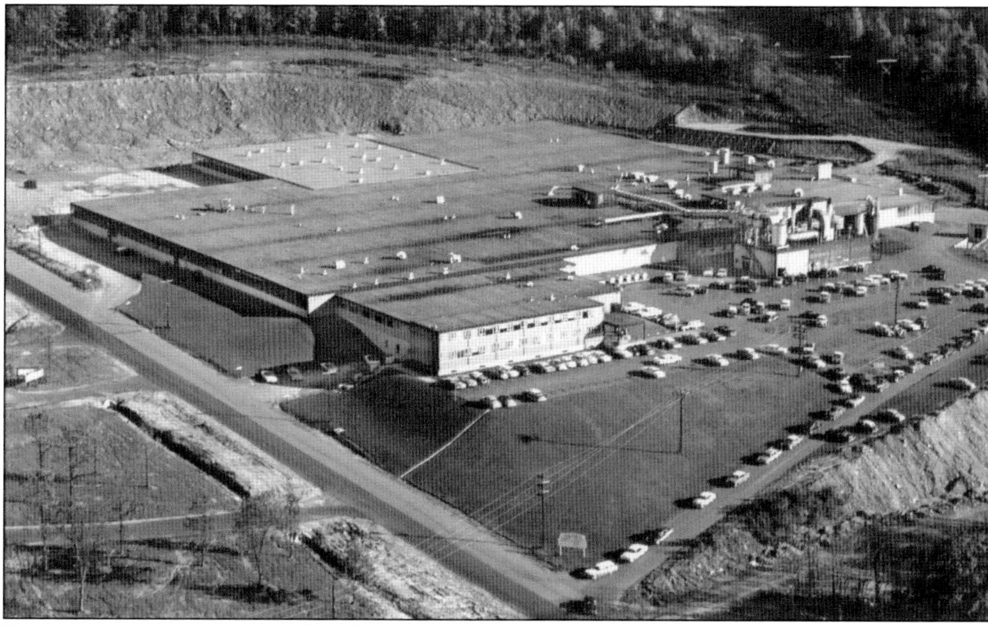

EBERHARD FABER INC. Eberhard Faber Inc. relocated from Brooklyn, New York, to its new Mountain Top facility in 1956. In 1986, some departments moved to Nogales, Mexico. Operations at the Crestwood Industrial Park closed in 1988 after the company was sold to the Faber-Castell Corporation in Lewisburg, Tennessee. The building, owned by Poseidon Pools until 1998, was demolished in 2010. (Courtesy of the Luzerne County Historical Society.)

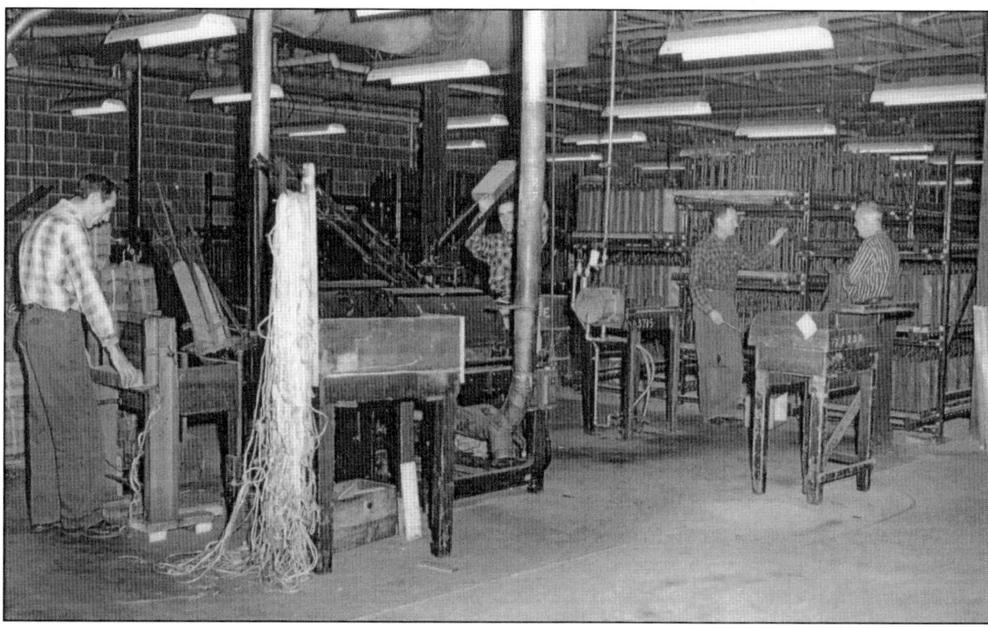

EBERHARD FABER WOOD ROOM. Eberhard Faber Inc. was a widely known manufacturer of pencils, erasers, pens, and markers. In the Wood Room, wooden slats were cut and grooved to hold graphite cores as a first step in making pencils. "Sandwiches" of slats and cores were then glued, shaped, and cut to form individual pencils, which were painted and fitted with eraser tips. (Courtesy of the Luzerne County Historical Society.)

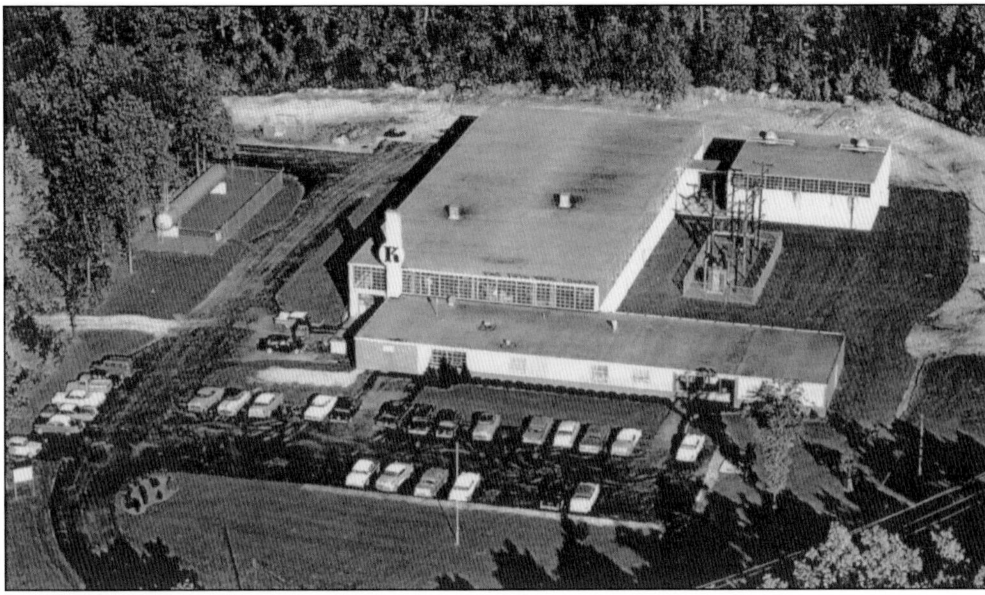

King Fifth Wheel Company. The King Fifth Wheel Company, originally a manufacturer of "fifth-wheel" connections for horse-drawn carriages, opened a modern Mountain Top facility producing engine ring components in 1954. The company's logo, featuring a "K" inside a circle, was prominently displayed on the new building. In later years, the company became Unison Engine Components. The facility is now owned by Wyman Gordon. (Courtesy of the Luzerne County Historical Society.)

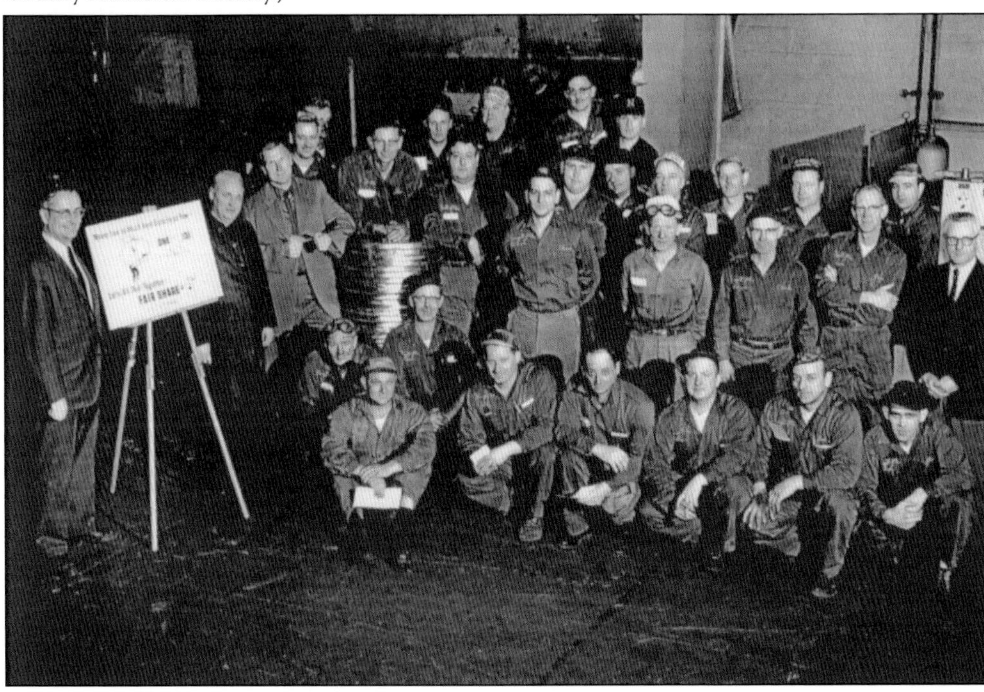

King Fifth Wheel Employees. Workers at the King Fifth Wheel Company posed for a publicity photograph in the 1960s. Metalworking and welding skills were necessary in the plant's heavy-industrial environment. (Courtesy of the Luzerne County Historical Society.)

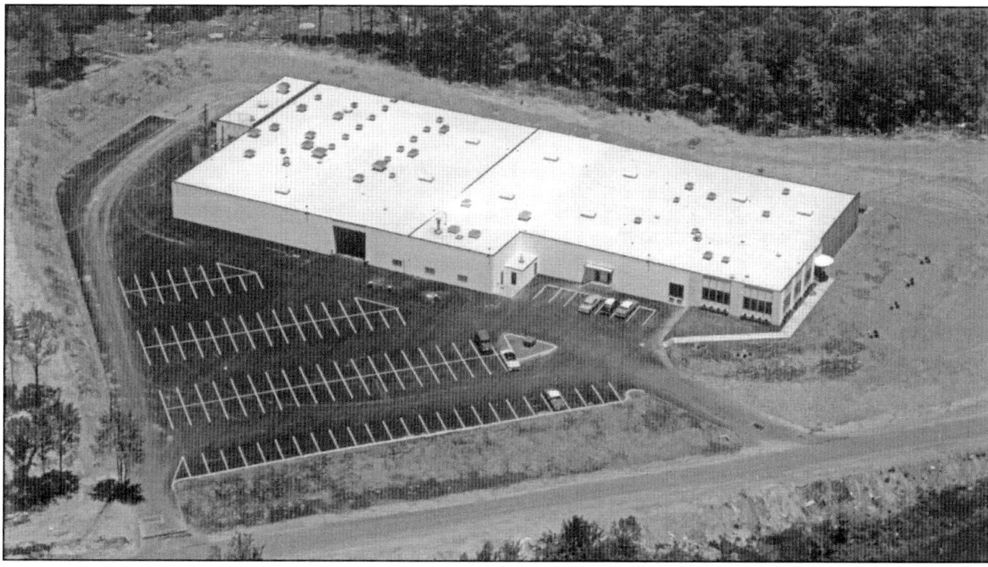

Oceana International Inc. The button manufacturer Oceana International Inc. came to the Crestwood Industrial Park in 1962. The seashell-shaped awning over its main entrance was a distinctive feature of the "Button Factory," as it was locally known. After the business closed, the building was sold to the Bergen Machine and Tool Company. (Courtesy of the Luzerne County Historical Society.)

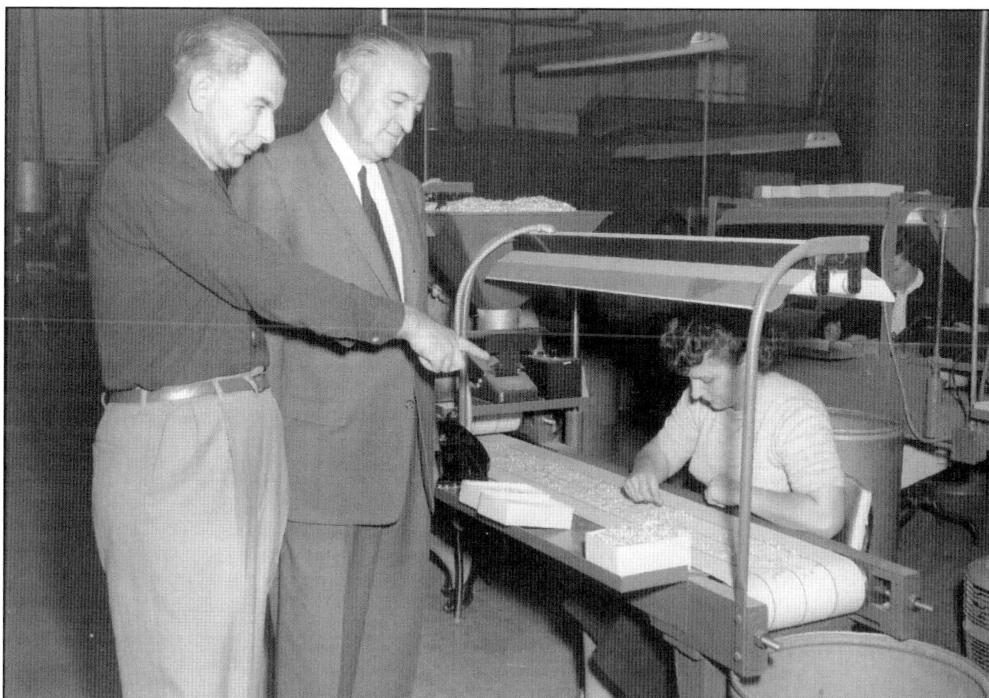

Workers at Oceana International Inc. After being formed, buttons were passed through hoppers onto brightly lit conveyor tables where quality control workers sorted them by hand. Buttons with imperfections were collected and discarded. (Courtesy of the Luzerne County Historical Society.)

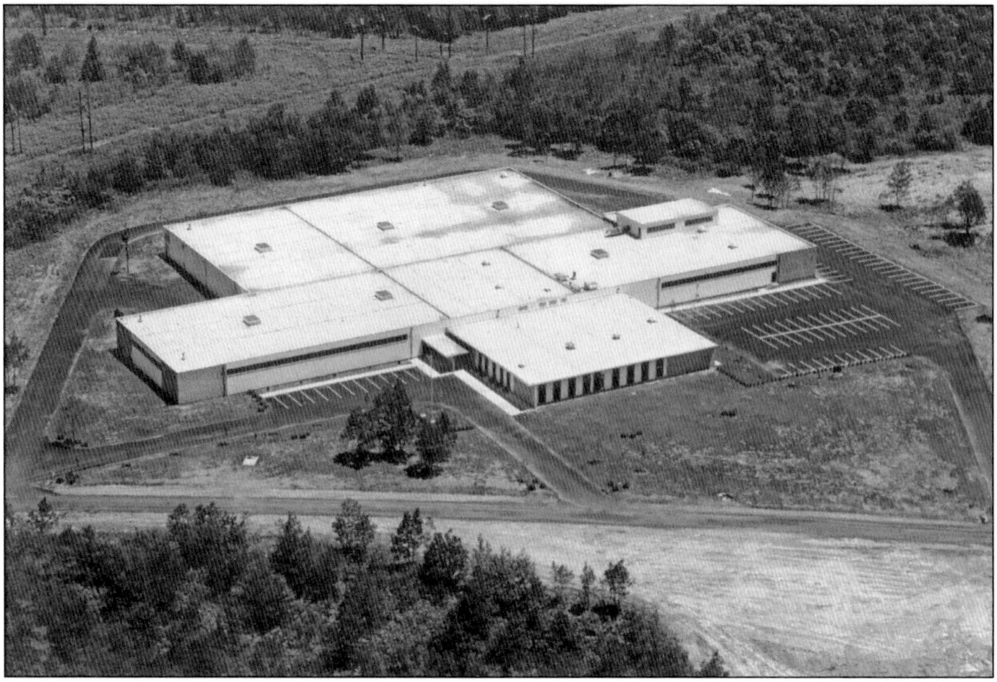

Dana Perfume Corporation. The Dana Perfume Corporation opened its Mountain Top facility in 1963. Popular fragrances produced there included Tabu and Canoe. (Courtesy of the Luzerne County Historical Society.)

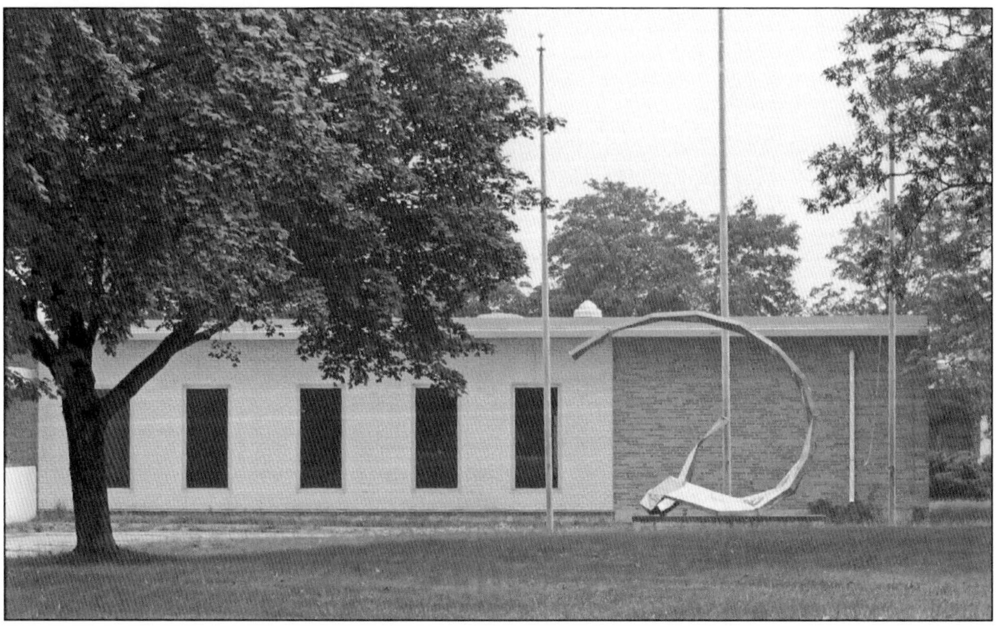

New Dana Perfume Corporation. After a period of restructuring, the Dana Perfume Corporation began operating as the New Dana Perfume Corporation in 1999. A sculpture in the form of the company's trademark "D" was installed outside of its facility at the Crestwood Industrial Park. Despite efforts to revitalize business, the company closed its Mountain Top facility in 2005. (Courtesy of Darlene Miller-Lanning.)

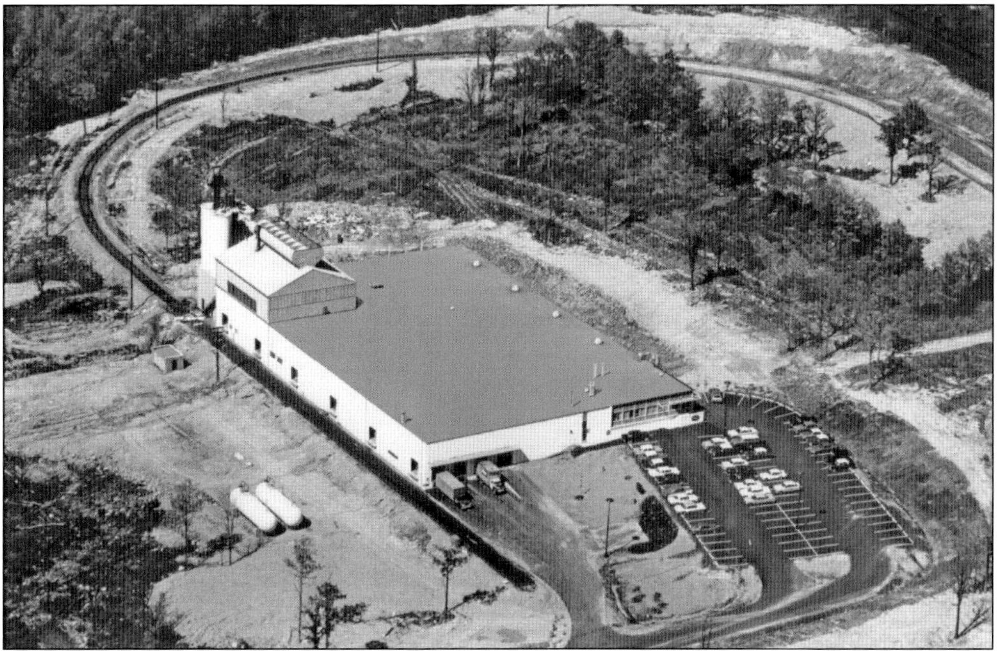

Fibrous Glass Products Inc. In 1961, Fibrous Glass Products Inc. opened a manufacturing complex in the Crestwood Industrial Park. The company, which produced fiberglass insulation, became the CertainTeed Corporation in 1964. In subsequent years, it doubled the size of its facilities, adding product lines and a large warehouse. (Courtesy of the Luzerne County Historical Society.)

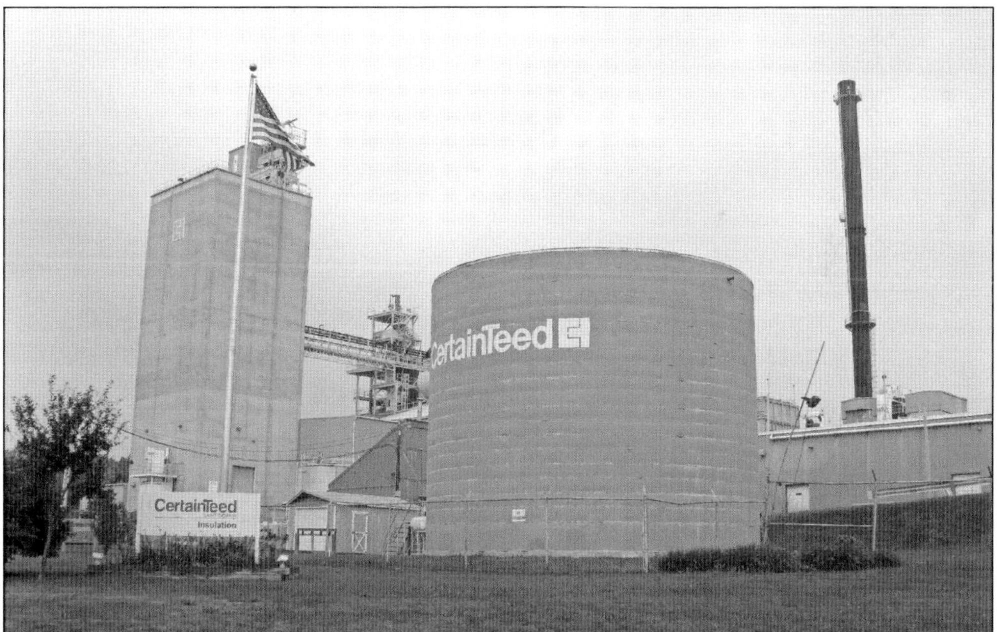

CertainTeed Corporation. As a result of economic crises in the early 21st century, particularly in relation to the housing industry, CertainTeed Corporation closed its plant at the Crestwood Industrial Park in 2010. Many employees had worked there for decades. (Courtesy of Darlene Miller-Lanning.)

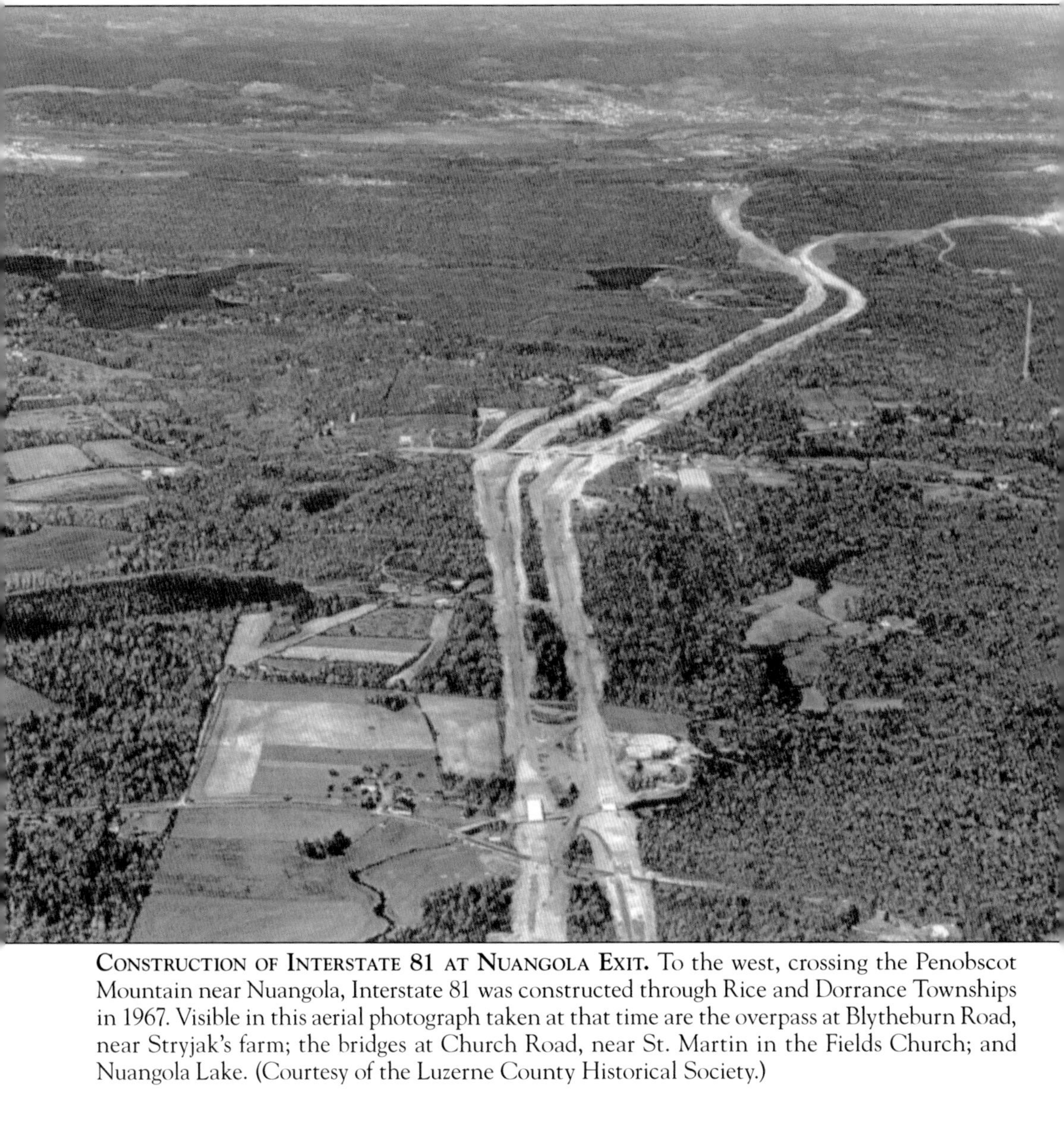

Construction of Interstate 81 at Nuangola Exit. To the west, crossing the Penobscot Mountain near Nuangola, Interstate 81 was constructed through Rice and Dorrance Townships in 1967. Visible in this aerial photograph taken at that time are the overpass at Blytheburn Road, near Stryjak's farm; the bridges at Church Road, near St. Martin in the Fields Church; and Nuangola Lake. (Courtesy of the Luzerne County Historical Society.)

Five

SCHOOLS AND CHURCHES

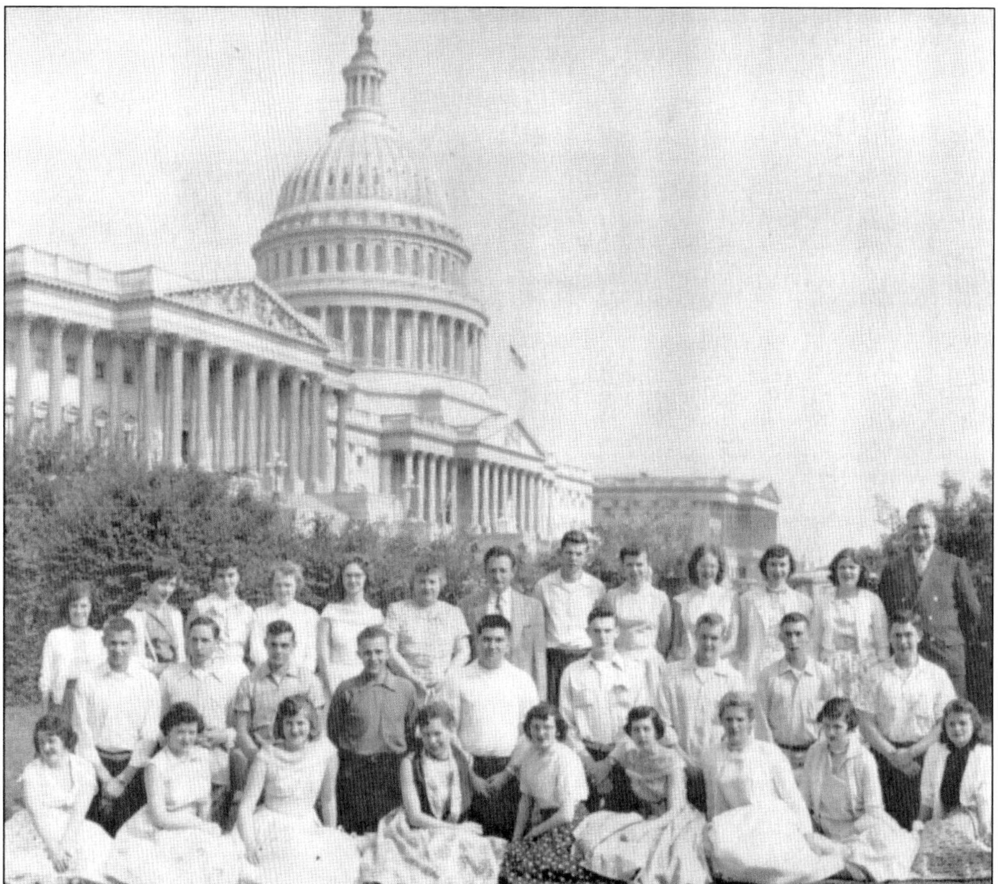

FAIRVIEW HIGH SCHOOL SENIOR CLASS TRIP TO WASHINGTON, DC. During the 1950s, Fairview High School conducted annual senior class trips to Washington, DC. Members of the class of 1956 were photographed in front of the US Capitol. (Courtesy of James and Edith Miller.)

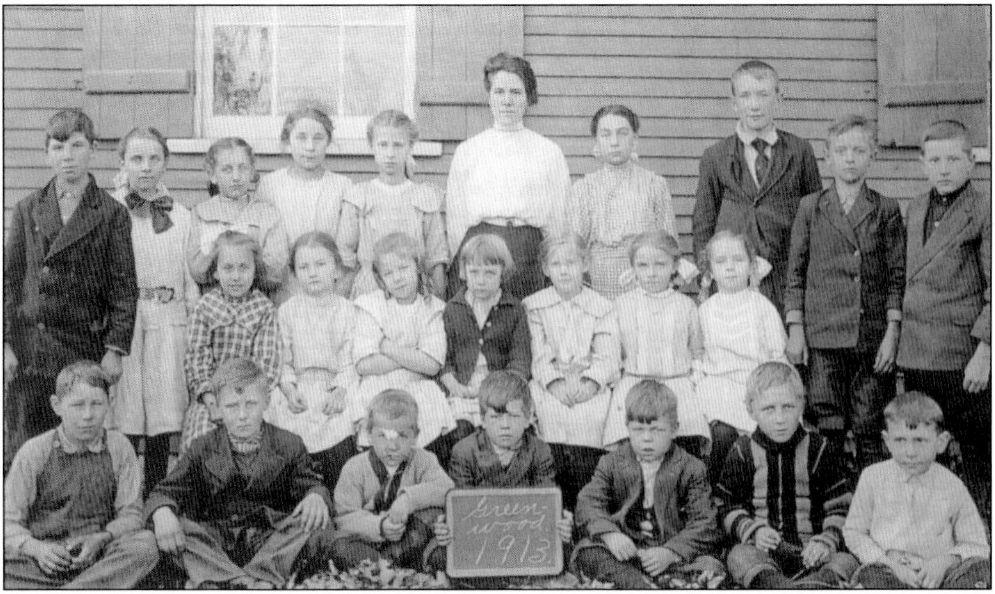

GREENWOOD SCHOOL. In the early 20th century, most neighborhoods in the Mountain Top area were served by one-room schools. Among these were the Slocum, Badman, and Lily Lake Road Schools in Slocum Township as well as the Greenwood and Wenner Schools in Dorrance Township. Students at the Greenwood School were photographed in 1913. (Courtesy of the Mountain Top Historical Society: *Pieces of the Past.*)

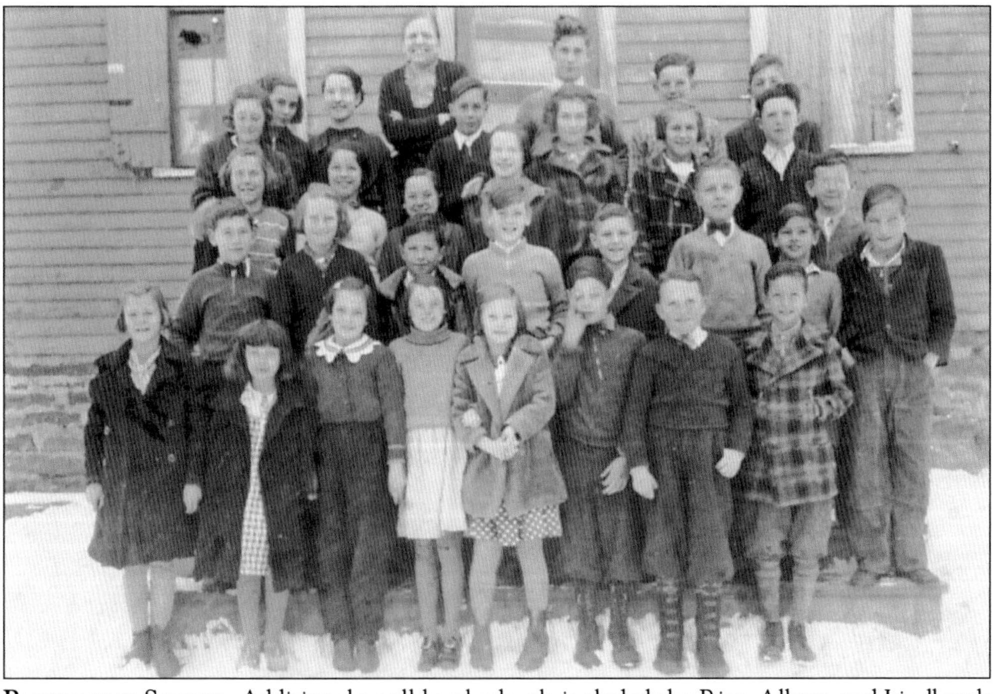

BLYTHEBURN SCHOOL. Additional small local schools included the Rita, Albert, and Lindbergh Schools in Wright Township and the Stivers, Jones, and Blytheburn Schools in what is now Rice Township. Students at the Blytheburn School were photographed around 1927. (Courtesy of the Mountain Top Historical Society: *Pieces of the Past.*)

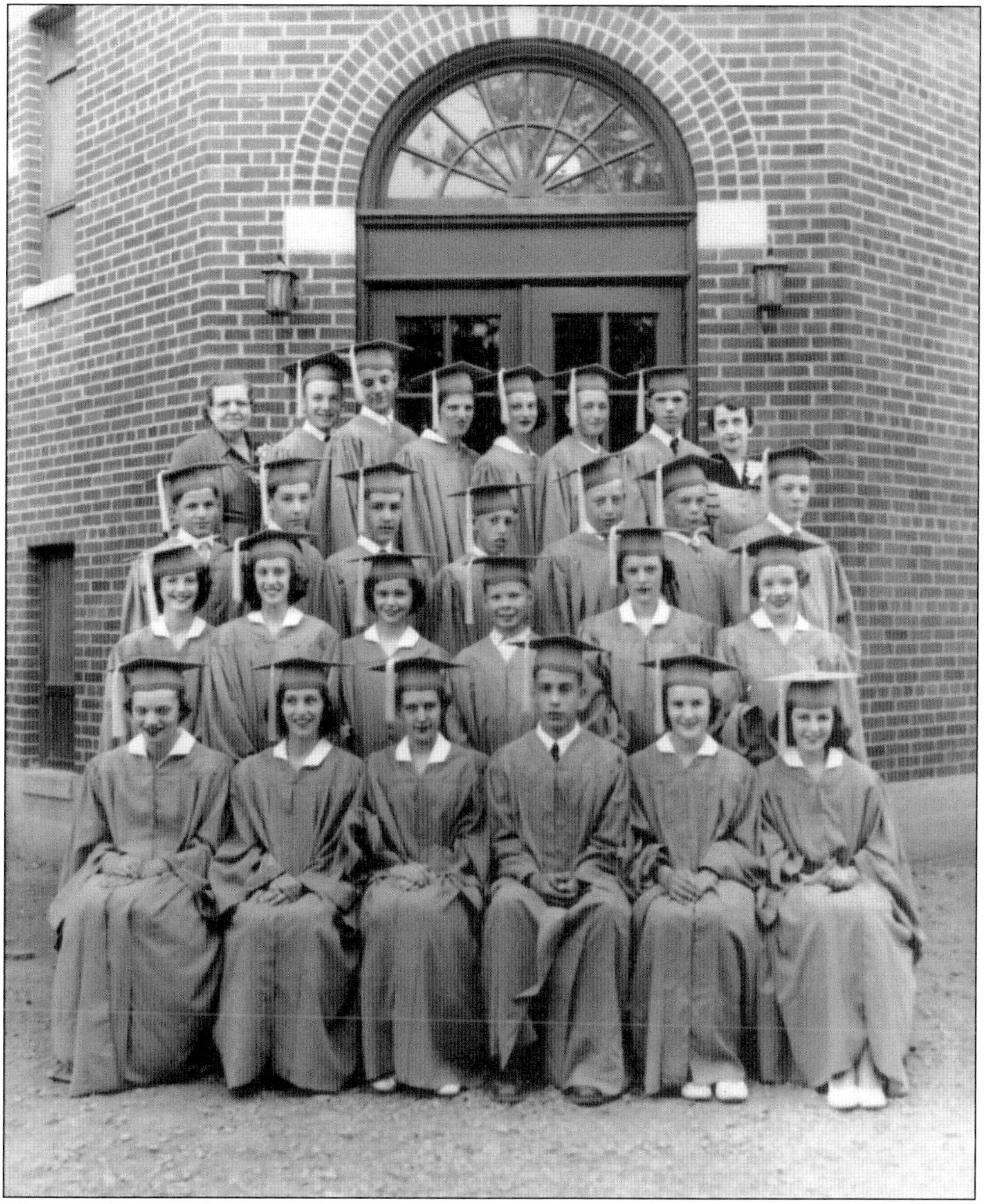

Wright Township School Eighth-Grade Graduation. In 1937, the Wright Township School was constructed on South Main Road to accommodate students in first through eighth grades. The new building included a library, cafeteria, gymnasium, and stage. The eighth-grade class of 1954 was photographed outside of Wright Township School during its graduation ceremony. Students then attended the ninth through twelfth grades at Fairview High School. (Courtesy of James and Edith Miller.)

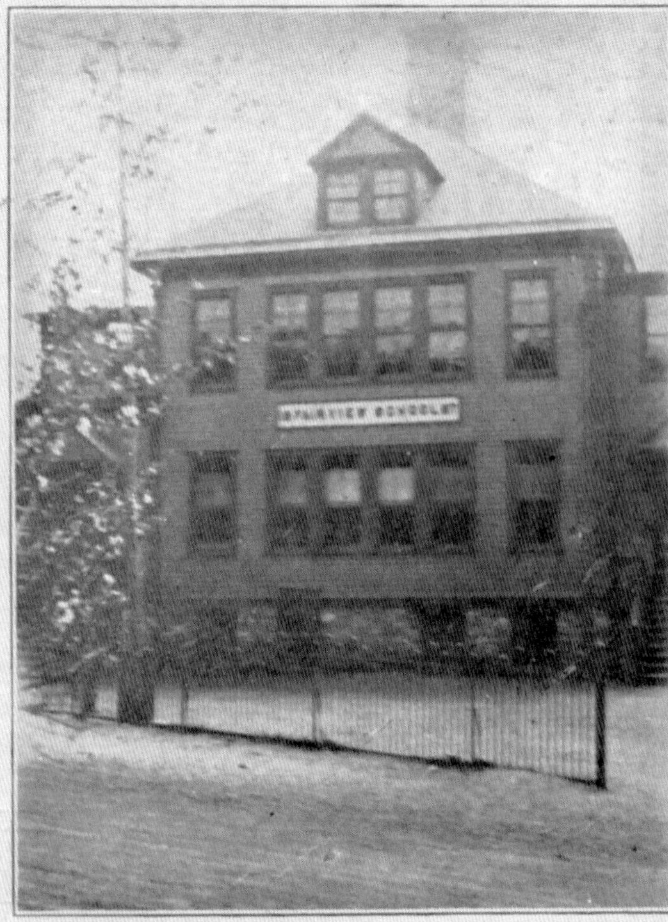

SWEET REMEMBRANCES

Let Fate do her worst; there are relics of joy,
Bright dreams of the past, which she cannot destroy;
And which come in the night-time of sorrow and care,
And bring back the features that joy used to wear;
Long, long be my heart with such memories filled;
Like the vase in which roses have once been distilled,
You may break, you may shatter the vase, if you will,
But the scent of the roses will hang around it still.

Fairview School. Several small schools initially served Fairview Township. In 1897, a new school, constructed on Woodlawn Avenue, was the first in the Mountain Top area to offer both elementary and four-year high school curriculums. John Berilla, Myers Delp, Earl Johnson, and Asher Snyder were the first to graduate from Fairview School as the class of 1901. (Courtesy of James and Edith Miller.)

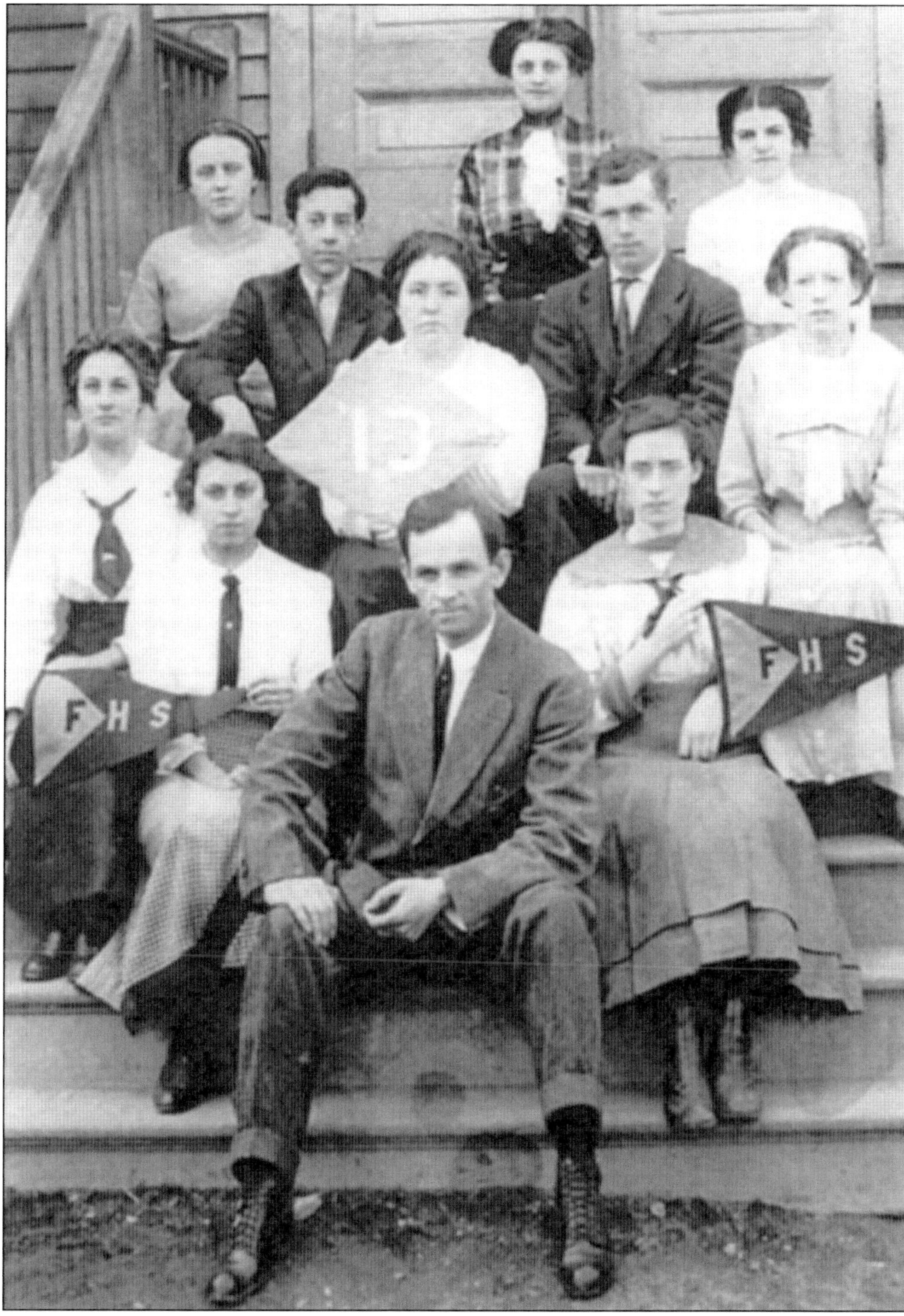

Fairview High School Class of 1913. Students in the Fairview High School class of 1913 included Charles Berilla, Jennie Hayes, Gertrude Meade, Gladys McKay, Emily Morrison, Mamie Murphy, Leona Schentz, and John Swandick. (Courtesy of the Mountain Top Historical Society, *Fairview High School Alumni: 1901–1962.*)

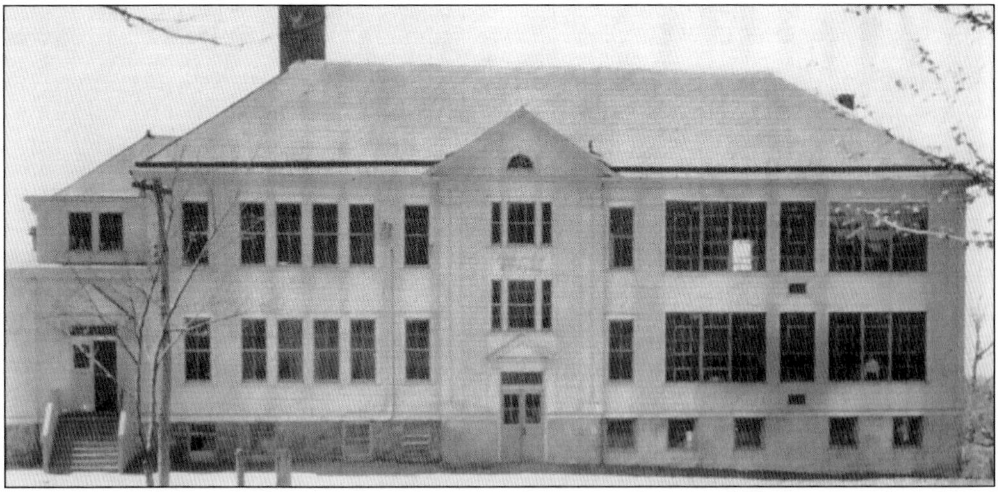

FAIRVIEW SCHOOL WITH FIRST ADDITION. Considered a model school at the time of its initial construction, Fairview School soon proved to be too small to accommodate growing numbers of students. During the 1930s, a series of additions increased classroom space in the building. The renovated structure was photographed for the school's annual in 1934. (Courtesy of James and Edith Miller.)

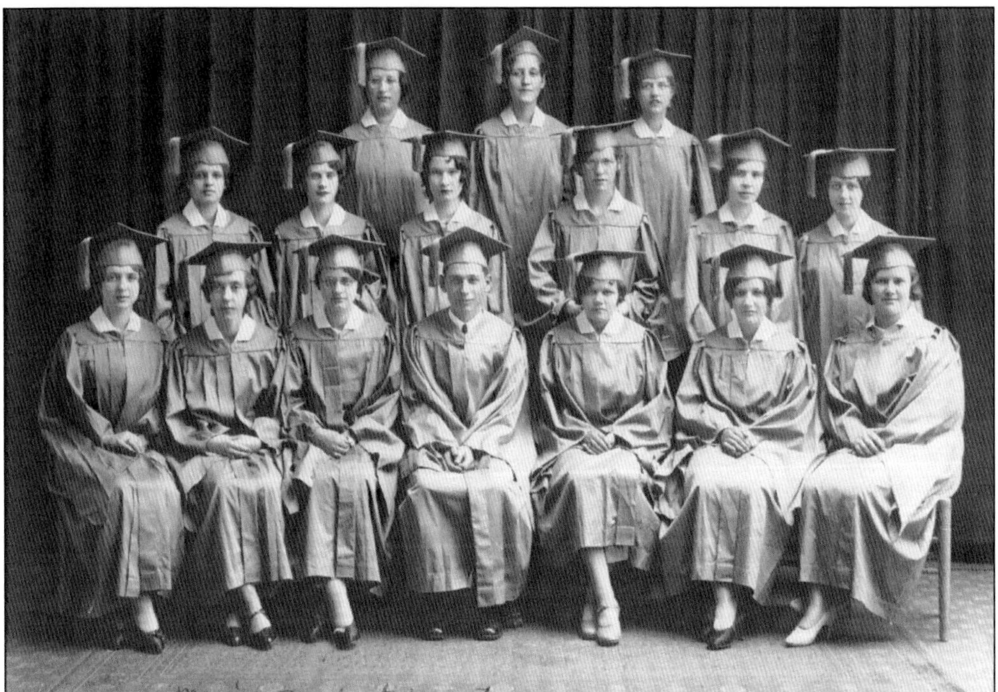

FAIRVIEW HIGH SCHOOL CLASS OF 1932. The Fairview High School class of 1932 included Charlotte Arbogast, Dorothy Devitt, Marvin Drendall, Ethel Houser, Ella Kneal, Lottine Knoll, Mildred McKay, John McGovern, Helen Moyer, Edna Reed, Dorothy Schultz, Sara Searfoss, and Florence Zerfoss. Members of the class of 1931, including Helen Dickinson, Helen Shea, Anna Swartwood, and Johanna Devitt, returned for a group photograph. Drendall was not pictured. (Courtesy of James and Edith Miller.)

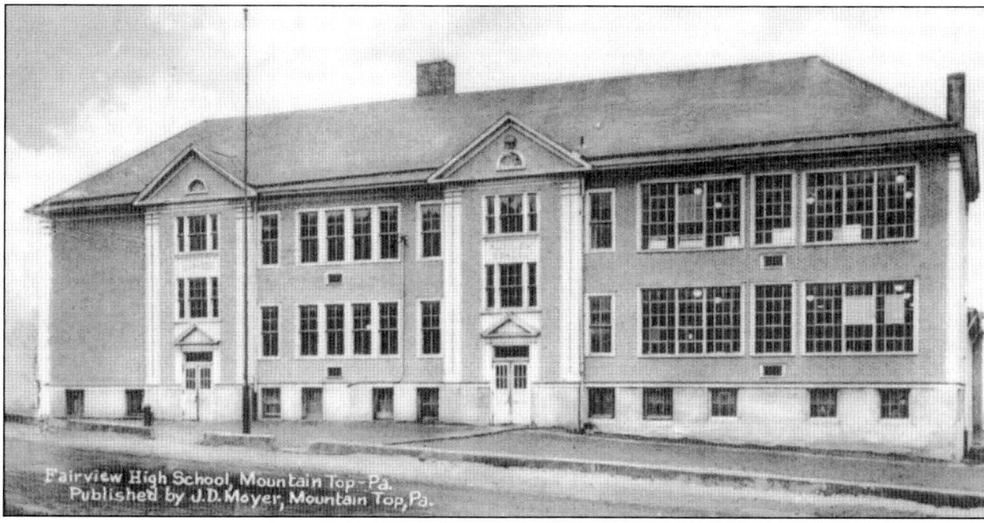

FAIRVIEW SCHOOL WITH SECOND ADDITION. Fairview School was further renovated by 1938. The building contained high school classes until construction of Crestwood High School in 1963 and elementary classes until construction of Fairview Elementary School in 1973. This postcard, published by Jerry Moyer, shows the school as it appeared during the late 20th century. The building burned in 1977, and the lot was cleared. (Courtesy of James and Edith Miller.)

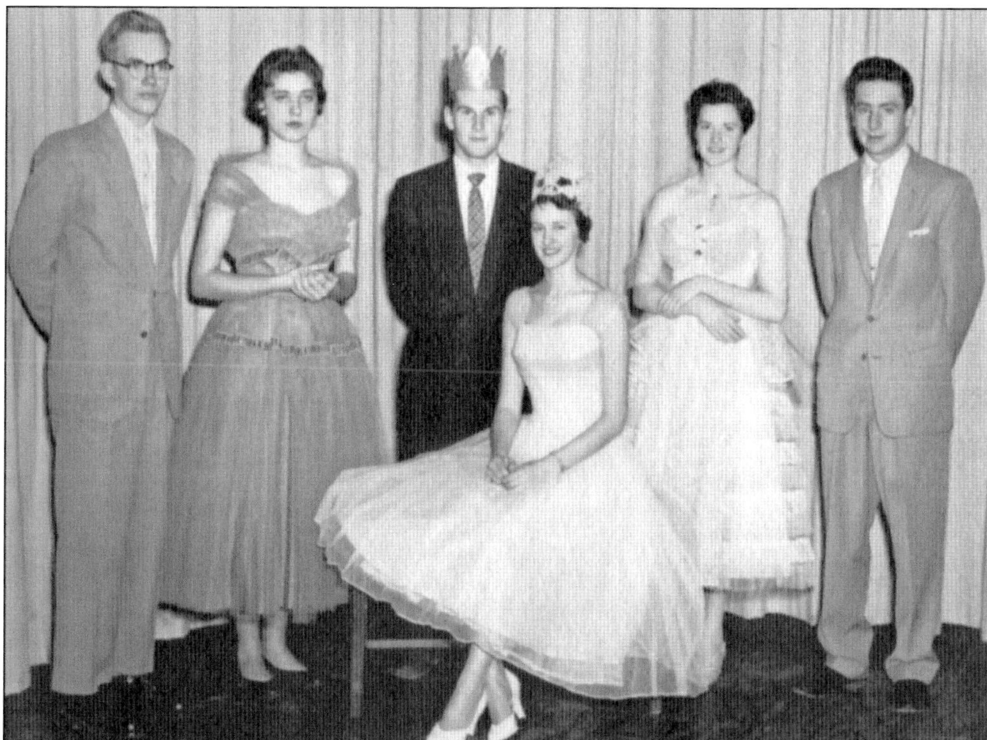

FAIRVIEW HIGH SCHOOL JUNIOR-SENIOR PROM. In 1956, the Royal Court of the Fairview High School junior-senior prom posed for a group photograph. Prom royalty included queen Marion Brush and king John Frankenfield, with attendants David Lear and Catherine Halloway (left) and Sharon Rehn and James Henry (right). (Courtesy of the Mountain Top Historical Society: *Pieces of the Past*.)

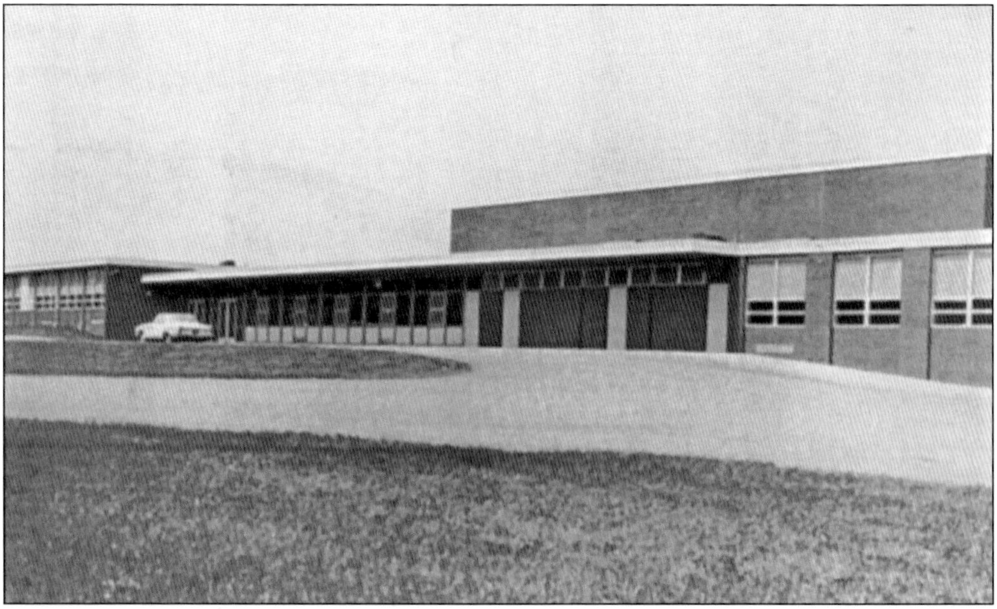

Central Luzerne County High School. Located on Route 309, the Central Luzerne County High School was built by Boyd H. Kline General Contractors in 1962. The school was dedicated in 1963, and Kenneth Hawk was the first supervising principal. It was renamed Crestwood High School in 1969. (Courtesy of the Mountain Top Historical Society: *Pieces of the Past.*)

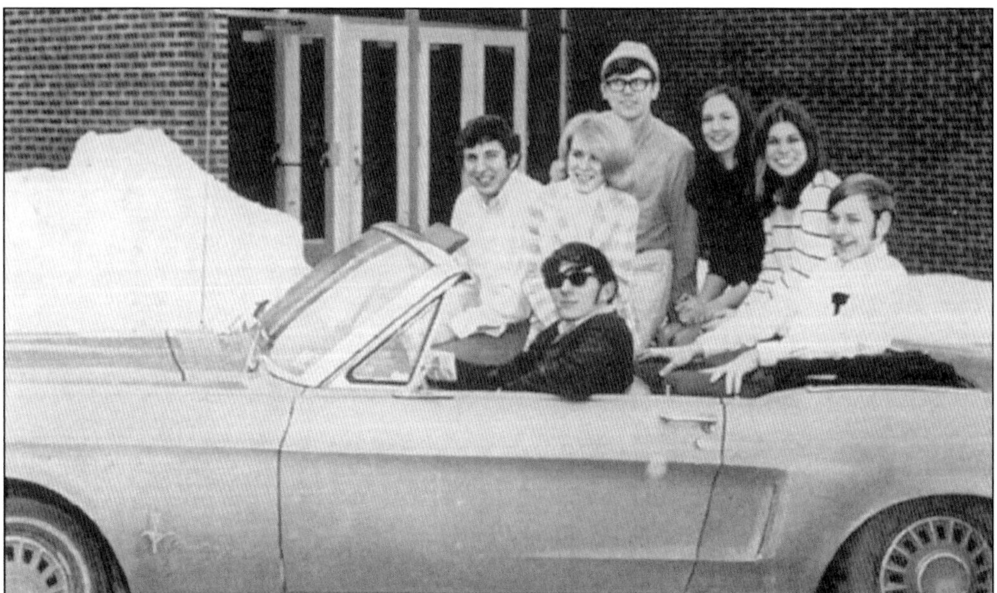

Crestwood High School Yearbook Staff. In 1970, members of the Crestwood High School yearbook staff posed for a photograph in a Ford Mustang convertible outside the school. (Courtesy of the Mountain Top Historical Society: *Pieces of the Past.*)

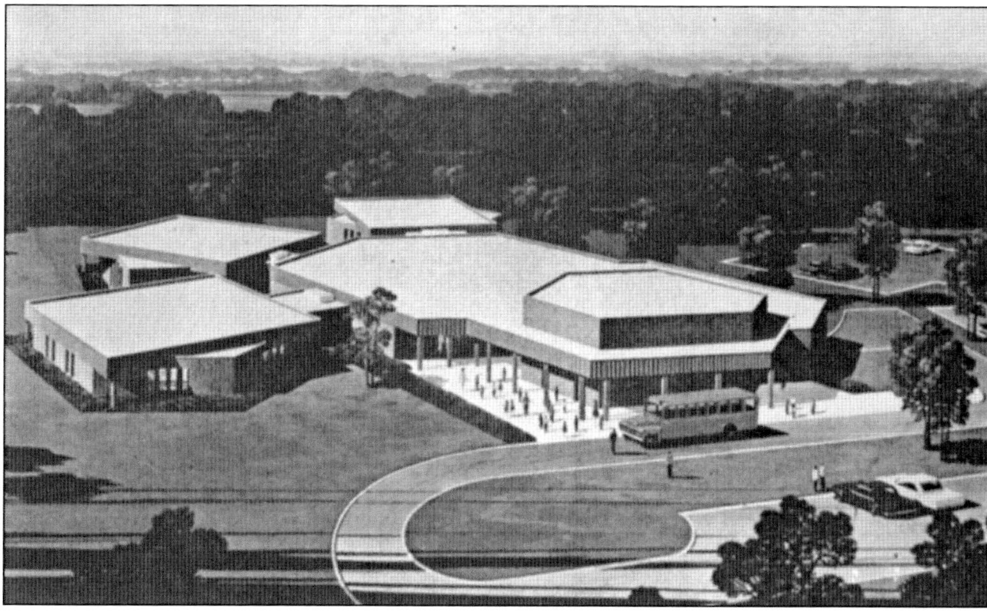

Rice Elementary School. Constructed in 1970 at the corner of Church and St. Mary's Roads, Rice Elementary School featured a contemporary "pod" design. Asymmetrical classrooms were fitted with wall-to-wall carpeting and floor-to-ceiling "blackboards" of colored slate. In keeping with the school's open floor plan, classrooms were clustered around central gathering spaces and had no doors. (Courtesy of James and Edith Miller.)

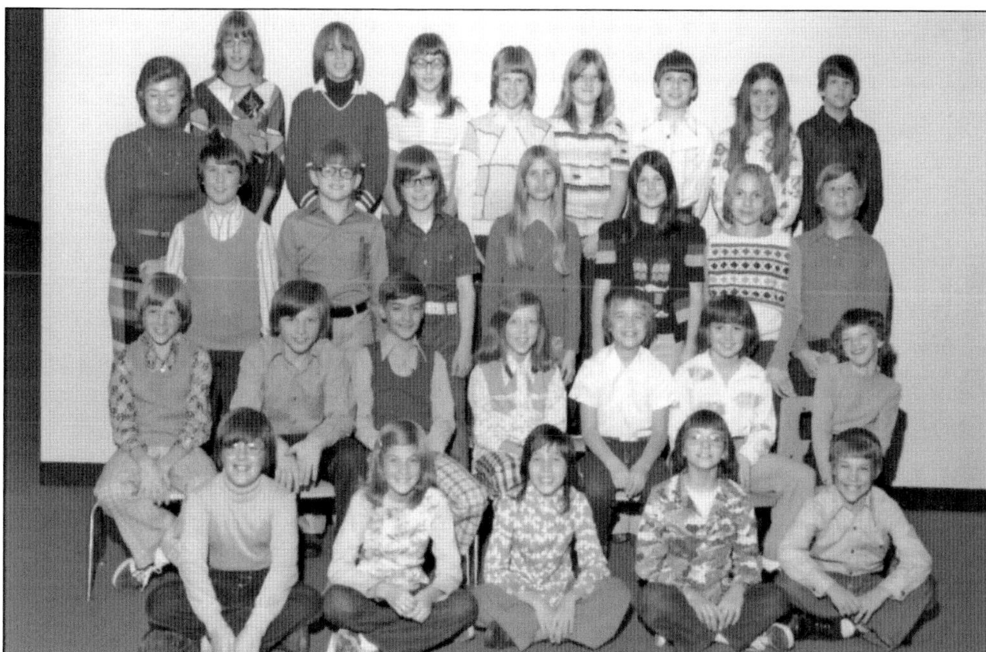

Rice Elementary School Sixth-Grade Class. Mrs. Noss and her homeroom students, members of the sixth-grade class of 1976, posed for a group picture at Rice Elementary School. That year, sixth-grade students took a special field trip to Philadelphia in honor of the US bicentennial. (Courtesy of James and Edith Miller.)

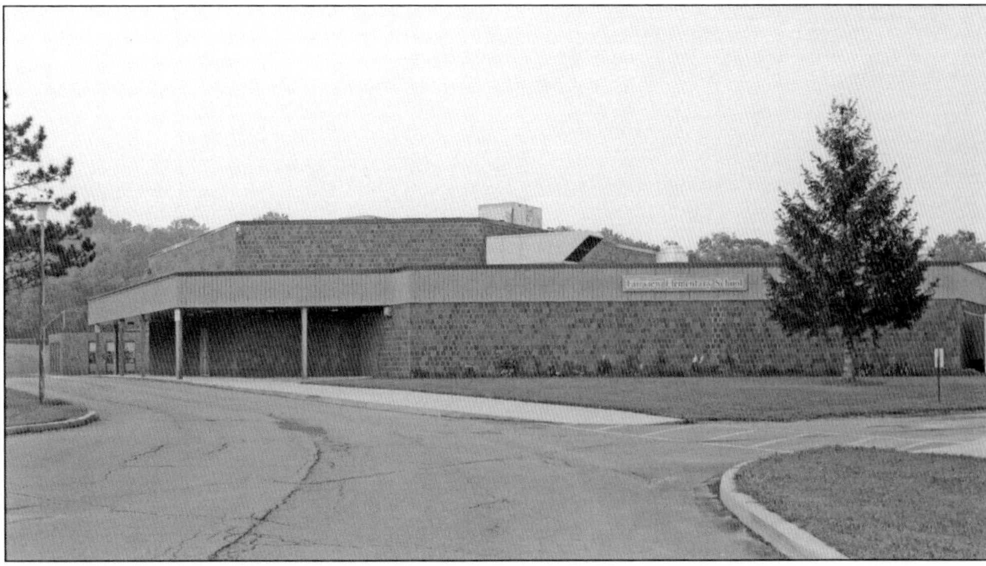

Fairview Elementary School. Built in 1973, Fairview Elementary School, located on Spruce Street, was the architectural twin of Rice Elementary School. During the course of its construction, students from both Rice and Fairview attended half-day sessions at Rice Elementary School. Both schools now provide instruction for students enrolled in kindergarten through sixth grade. (Courtesy of Darlene Miller-Lanning.)

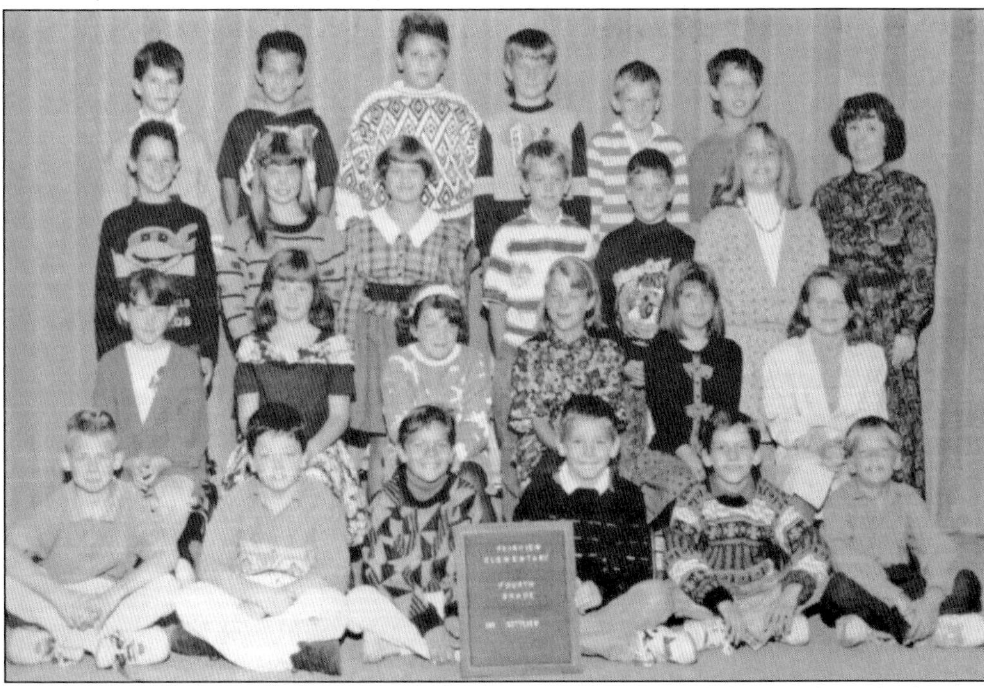

Fairview Elementary School Fourth-Grade Class. Miss Gottlieb's fourth-grade class was photographed at Fairview Elementary School. During the 1991–1992 academic year, they participated in the "Book-It" reading program, the "Sergeant Seymour" vision presentation, the "Toys for Tots" holiday campaign, and the "Create a Molecule" science contest. (Courtesy of Amanda Davenport Detrick.)

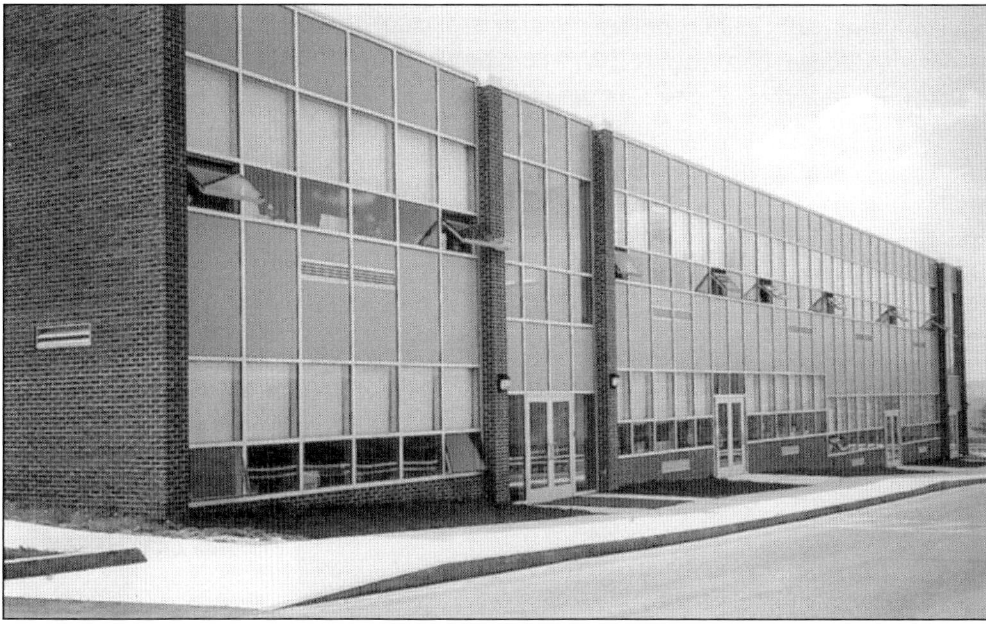

CRESTWOOD MIDDLE SCHOOL. Built as an extension of the Crestwood High School, the Crestwood Middle School opened in 2000. Seventh- and eighth-grade students attend classes there. (Courtesy of the Mountain Top Historical Society: *Pieces of the Past.*)

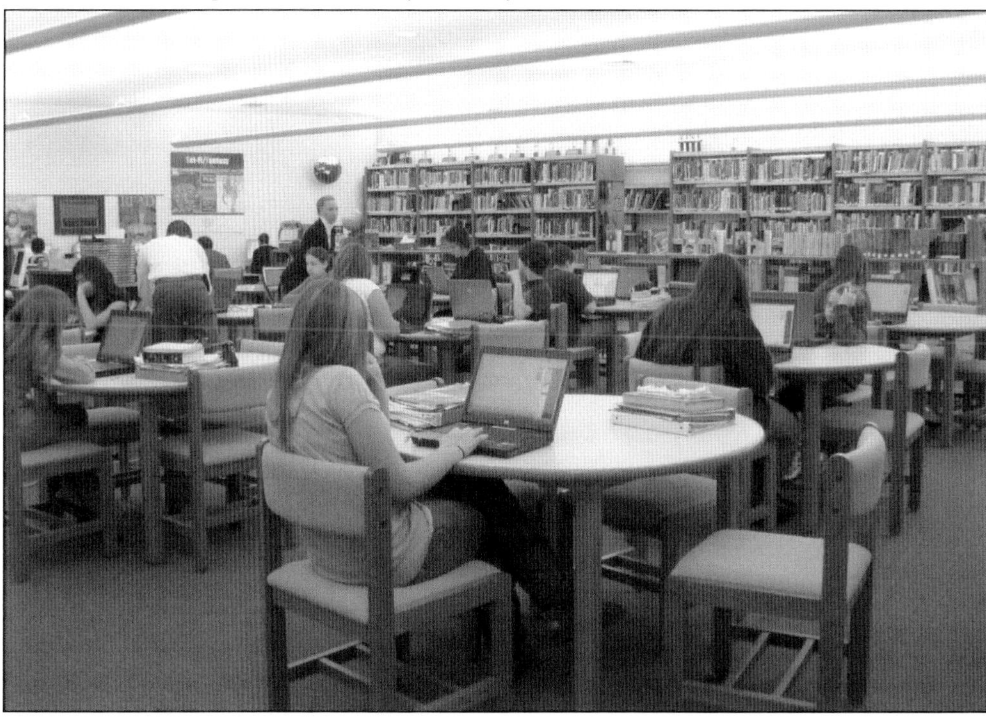

CRESTWOOD MIDDLE SCHOOL LIBRARY. Students log on in the Crestwood Middle School Library to take advantage of 21st-century learning resources, including Quest Atlantis. Other instructional technologies recently incorporated throughout the Crestwood School District include Promethean boards, class wiki-spaces, and online testing. (Courtesy of the Crestwood Middle School.)

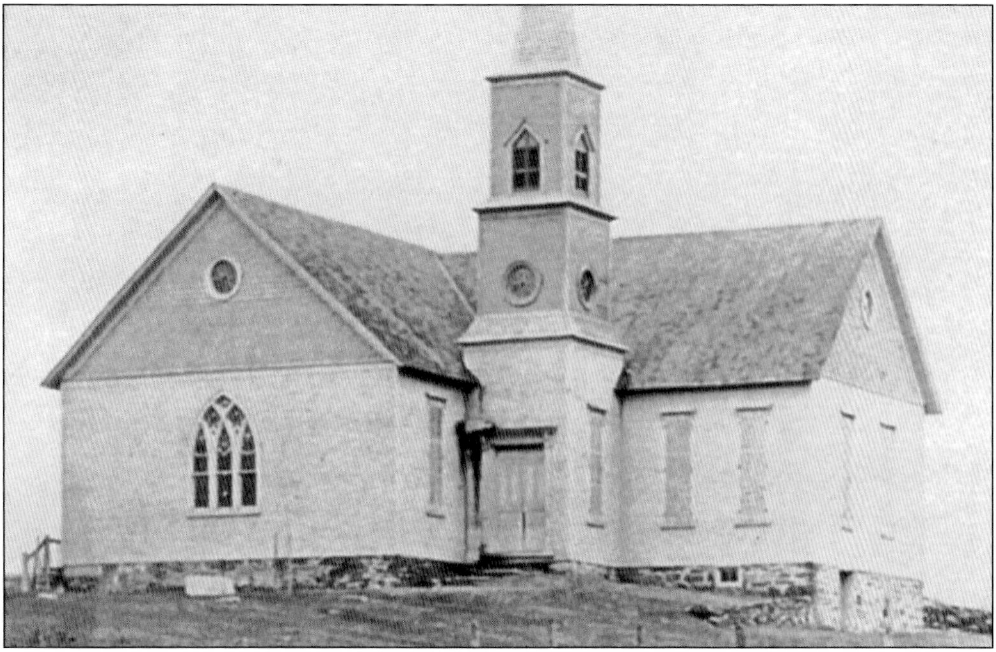

LUTHERAN REFORMED CHURCH. Reformed Lutheran ministers conducted services in a school near the present-day intersection of Alberdeen Road and Blue Ridge Trail around 1849. The Union Evangelical Reformed and Evangelical Lutheran Congregation was organized in 1859. A church was constructed in 1869 and enlarged in 1895. In 1968, the Emmanuel United Church of Christ purchased the building. (Courtesy of the Mountain Top Historical Society: *Pieces of the Past*.)

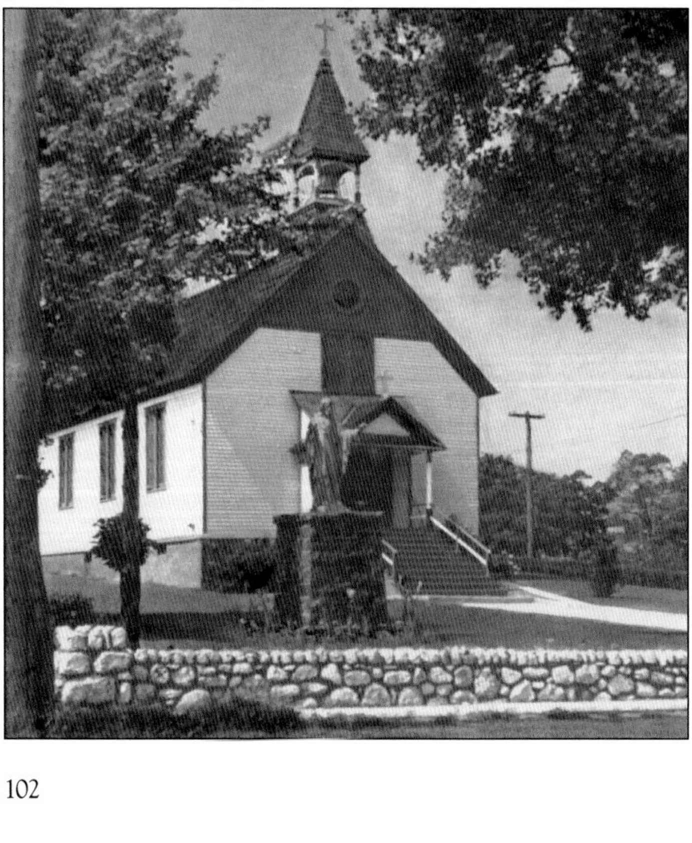

ST. CATHERINE'S CHURCH. Catholics in Solomon's Gap celebrated Mass in private homes as early as the 1850s. As attendance grew, St. Catherine's Mission Church was built at the corner of Lehigh and Mary Streets in 1886. The church closed in 2000 after serving Mountain Top parishioners for 114 years. (Courtesy of Hubert McGovern.)

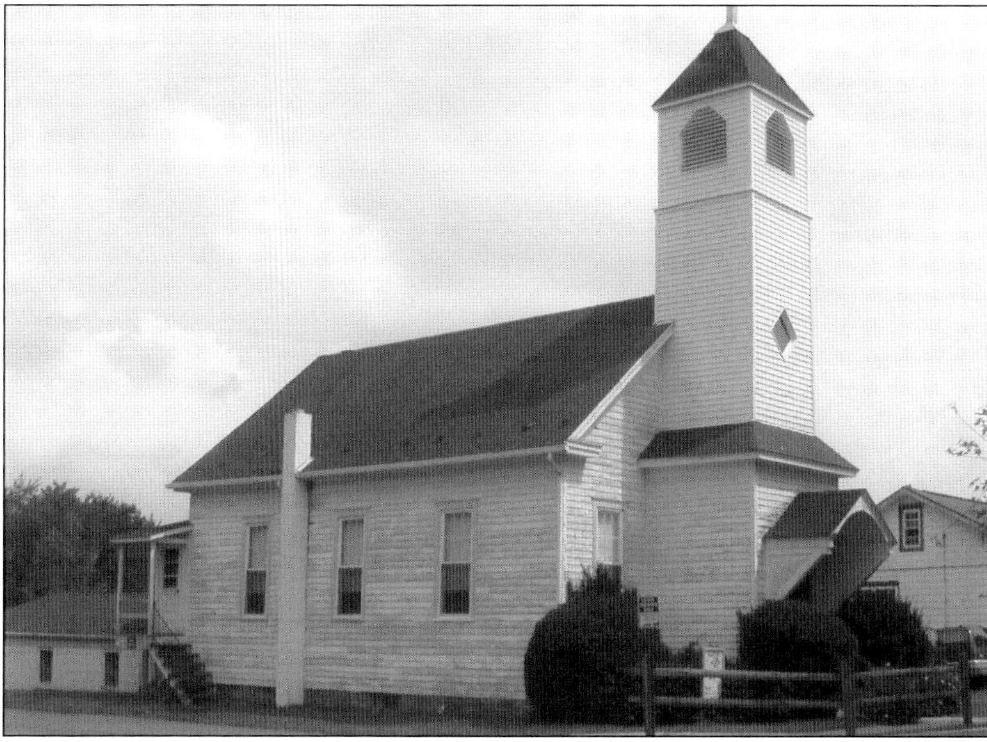

SLOCUM UNITED METHODIST CHURCH. In 1860, a Union church was built for use by the Reformed, Methodist, and Evangelical congregations of Slocum at the intersection of Schmid and Slocum Roads. In 1890, the Evangelicals constructed a new church. The Union church was purchased by the Methodists, dismantled, and moved to a new site on Blue Ridge Trail in 1908. (Courtesy of Mountain Top Photo.)

FAITH UNITED METHODIST CHURCH. The Slocum Evangelical congregation worshipped at the Union Church until 1890, when it constructed its own building nearby. Following denominational mergers with the Evangelical United Brethren in 1946 and the United Methodist Church in 1968, it became the Slocum Evangelical United Brethren and, later, the Faith United Methodist Church. (Courtesy of Mountain Top Photo.)

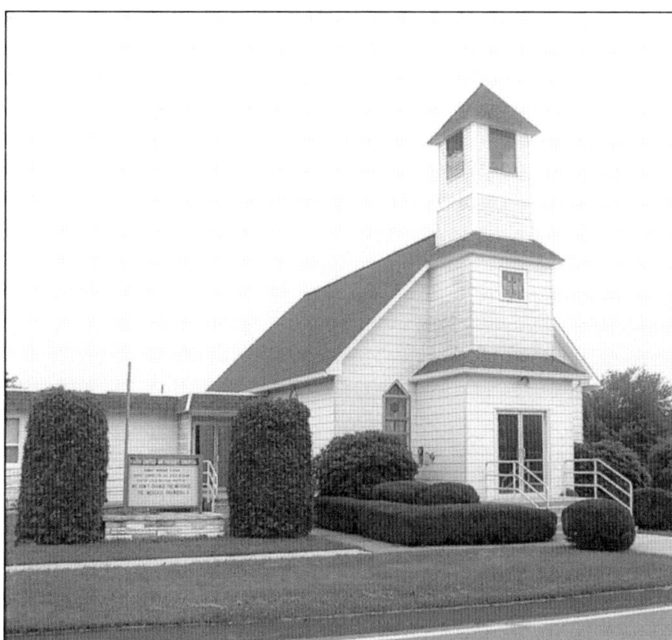

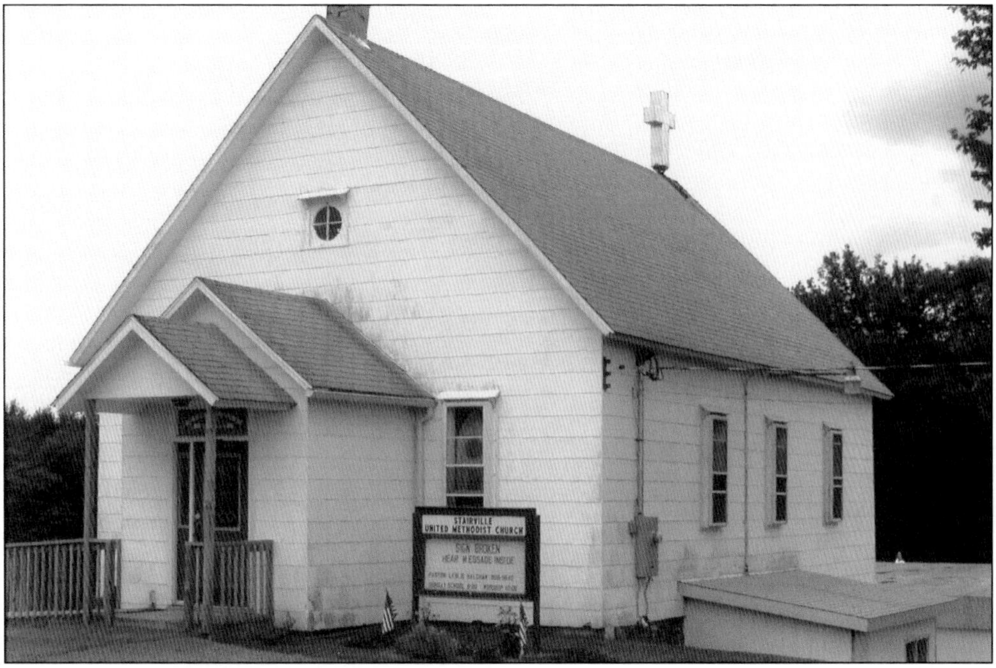

STAIRVILLE UNITED METHODIST CHURCH. During the early 19th century, the Methodist congregation of Dorrance was served by itinerant ministers assigned to the Wyoming Valley and its surrounding regions. Services were held in log homes, barns, groves, and eventually, a school constructed on Stairville Road. In 1873, the Stairville Methodist Episcopal Church, later named the Stairville United Methodist Church, was built on a site nearby. (Courtesy of Mountain Top Photo.)

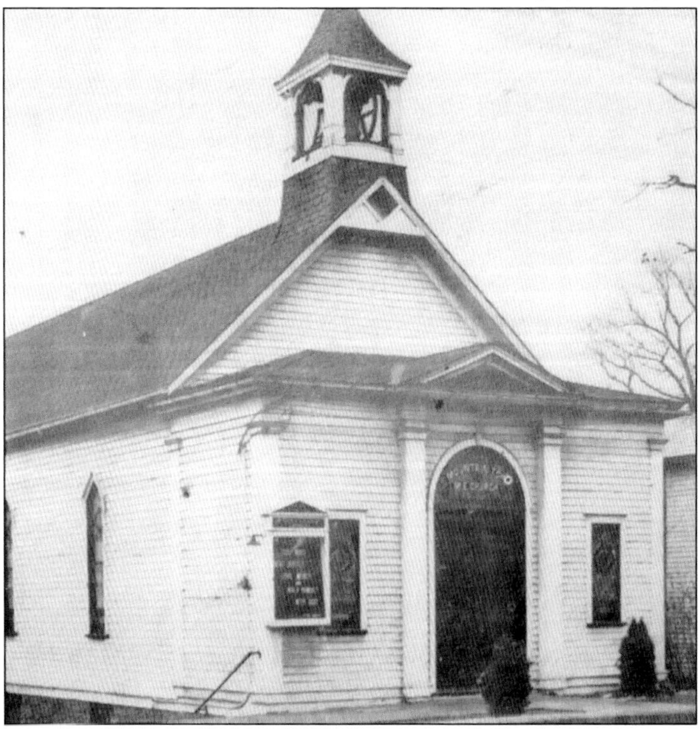

MOUNTAIN TOP METHODIST EPISCOPAL CHURCH. Itinerant preachers were also the first to serve Methodists in Wright Township. In 1880, members in Fairview formed the Mountain Top Methodist Episcopal Society, building a church on Woodlawn Avenue in 1881. This congregation merged with that of the Albert Methodist Church in 1955. (Courtesy of the Mountain Top Historical Society: *Pieces of the Past*.)

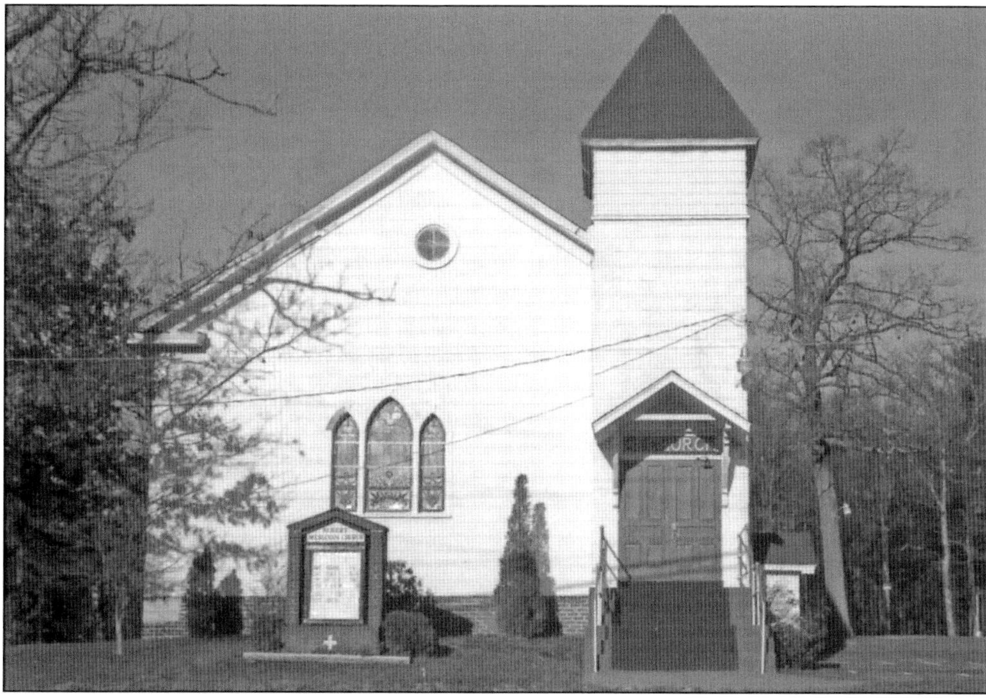

Albert Wesleyan Church. Methodists at Albert's Corners and Rippletown originally met in a one-room school. In 1926, they purchased a church at Powder Glen, near Wapwallopen, dismantling and rebuilding it near the current intersection of Church Road and Lines Lane. After the Mountain Top and Albert Methodist congregations merged, the building was purchased by the Pilgrim Holiness Church, Albert Wesleyan Church, and Mountain Top Baptist Church. (Courtesy of Mountain Top Photo.)

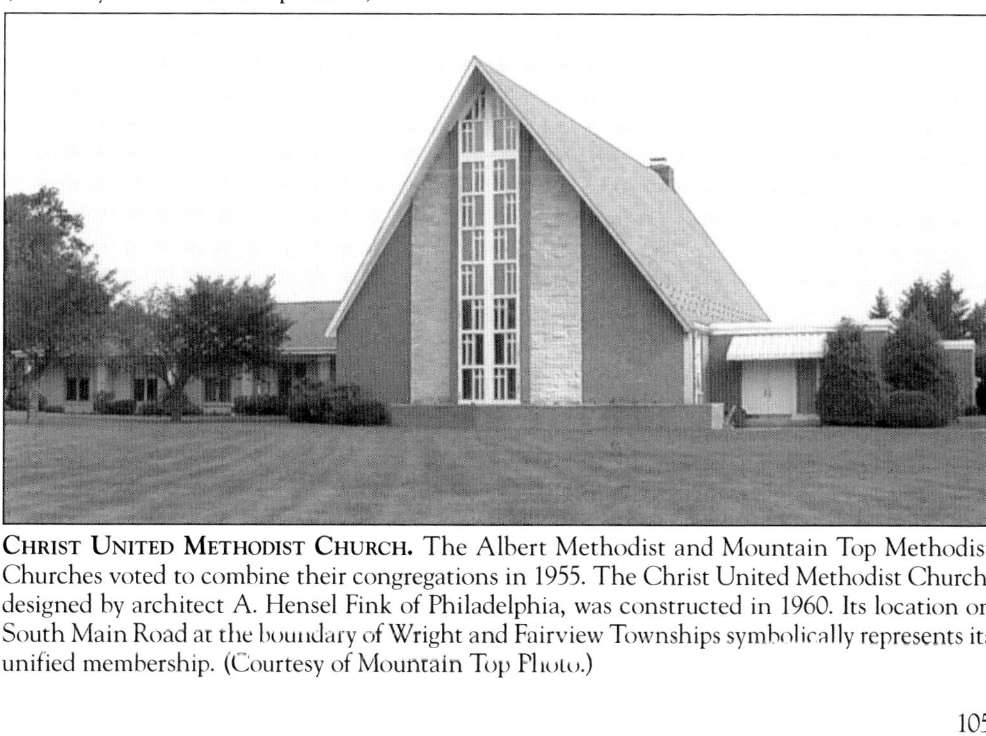

Christ United Methodist Church. The Albert Methodist and Mountain Top Methodist Churches voted to combine their congregations in 1955. The Christ United Methodist Church, designed by architect A. Hensel Fink of Philadelphia, was constructed in 1960. Its location on South Main Road at the boundary of Wright and Fairview Townships symbolically represents its unified membership. (Courtesy of Mountain Top Photo.)

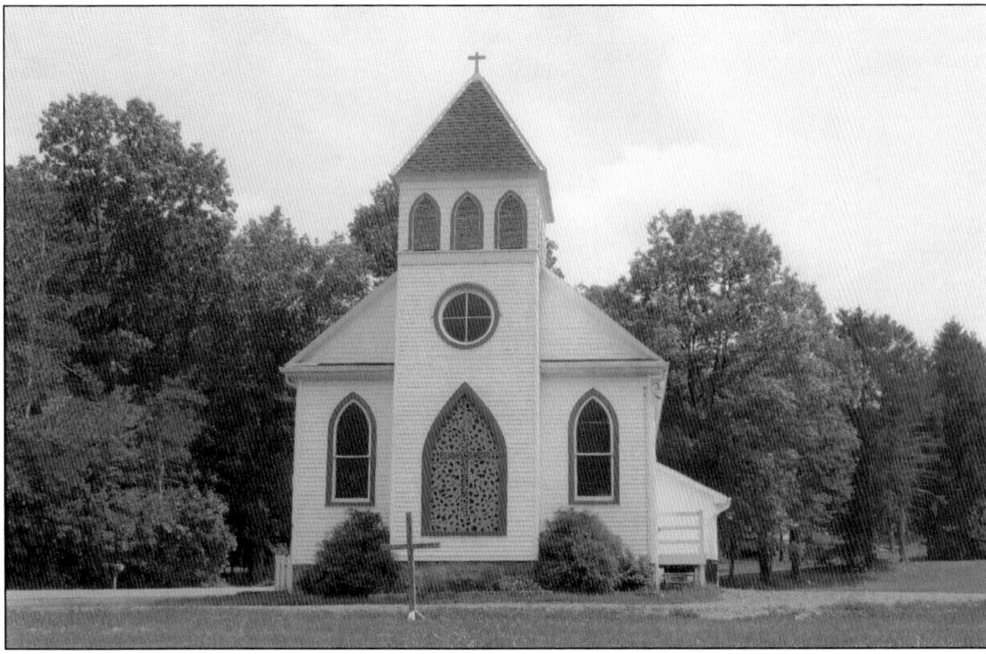

New Life Community Church. Lutheran families in Wright Township first attended services at the Evangelical Lutheran Church in Dorrance and, later, the old Wright Township School. In 1912, they constructed St. Paul's Lutheran Church at Yeager and South Main Roads. After 1968, when a modern church was built on Route 309, the original building was sold. It is now home to the New Life Community Church. (Courtesy of Darlene Miller-Lanning.)

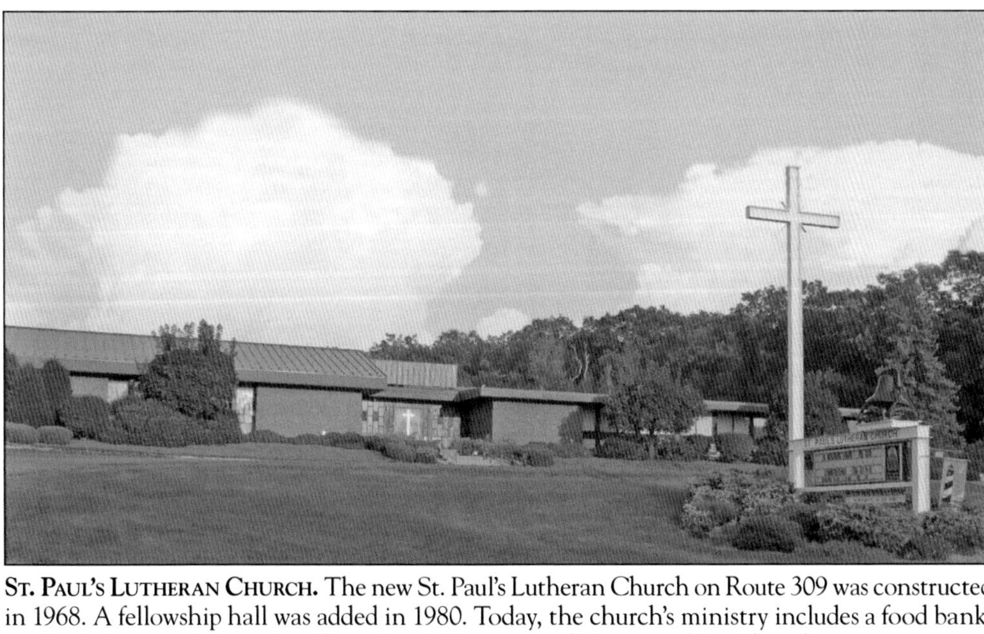

St. Paul's Lutheran Church. The new St. Paul's Lutheran Church on Route 309 was constructed in 1968. A fellowship hall was added in 1980. Today, the church's ministry includes a food bank, medical clinic, and play school/preschool. (Courtesy of Mountain Top Photo.)

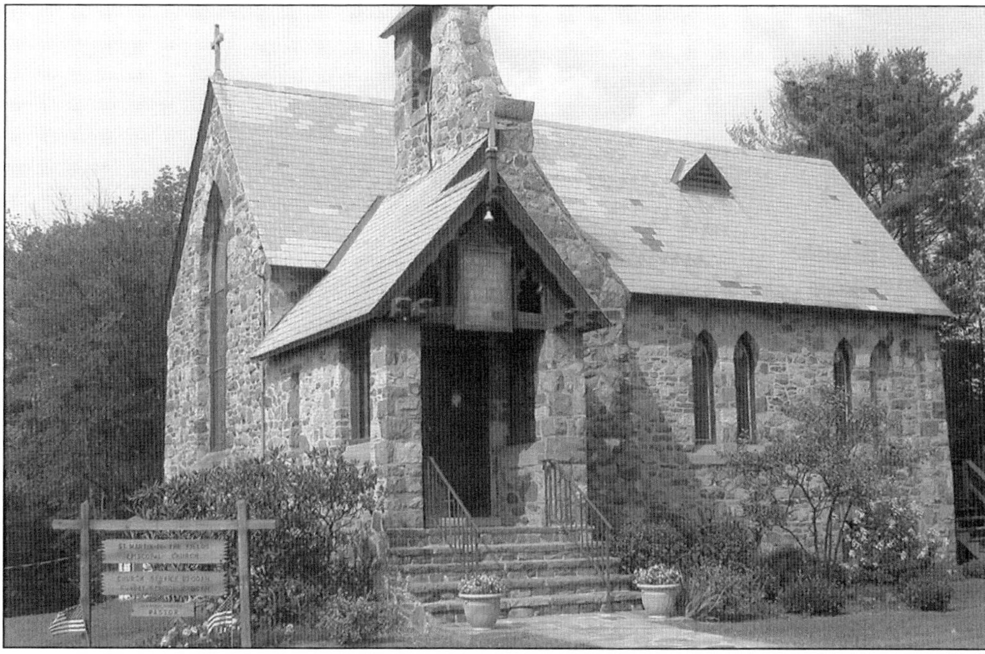

St. Martin in the Fields Episcopal Church. Founding members of the St. Martin in the Fields Episcopal Church first met as a Bible study group in the Fred Pettit home at Nuangola Station. A stone church, designed by architect T. Comers Newman in the Old English Gothic style, was completed in 1926. A notable feature of the church is its stained-glass "West Apostles' Window." (Courtesy of Mountain Top Photo.)

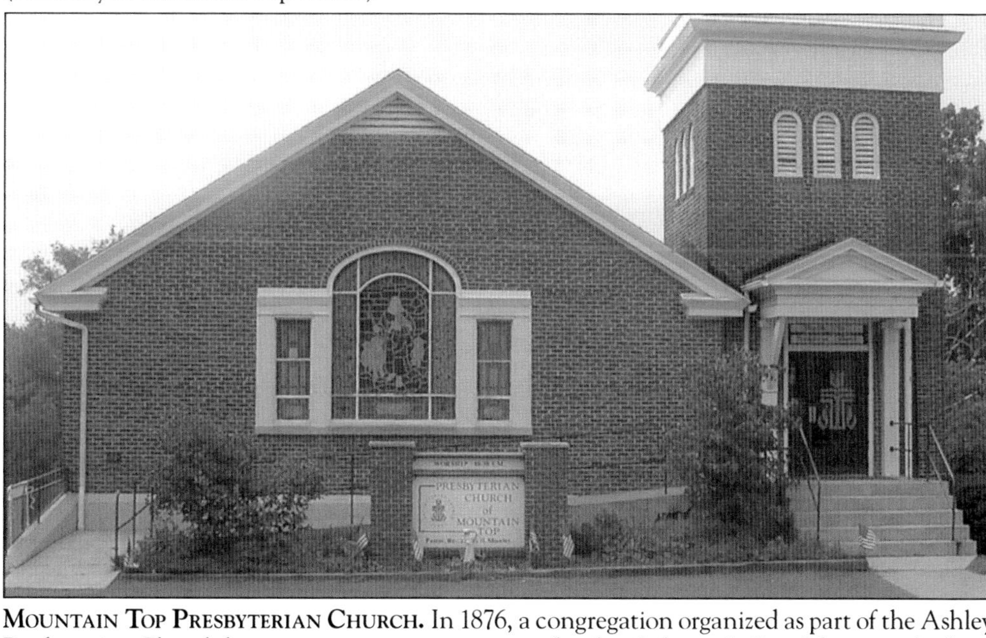

Mountain Top Presbyterian Church. In 1876, a congregation organized as part of the Ashley Presbyterian Church began meeting in a one-room school at Solomon's Gap. The group built its first church at Penobscot in 1880, organizing as the Mountain Top Presbyterian Church in 1887. A new building, constructed on Chestnut Street in 1928, still serves as a house of worship for members today. (Courtesy of Mountain Top Photo.)

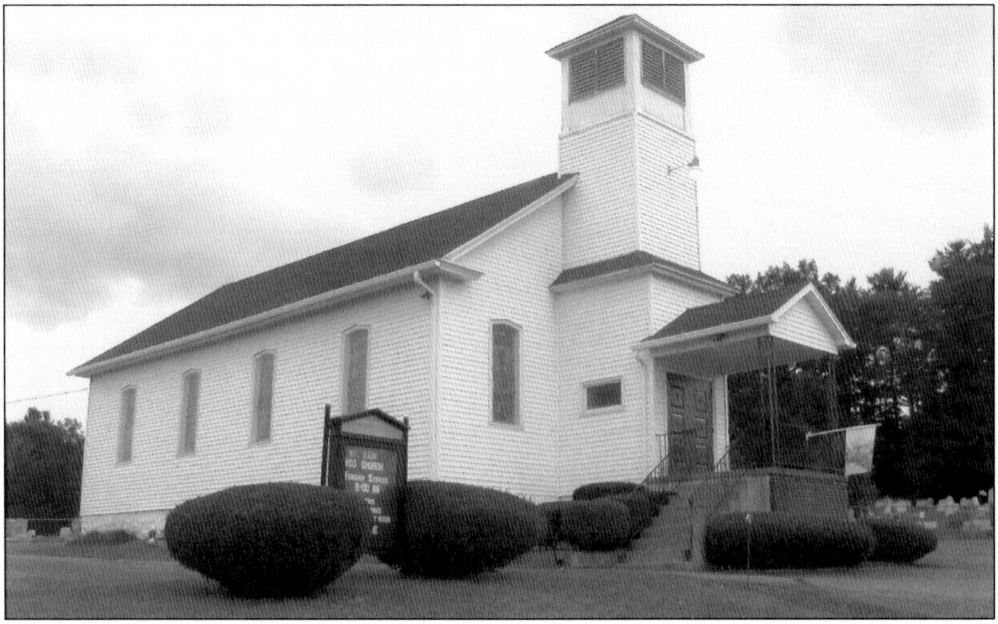

Mount Zion United Church of Christ. Lutherans residing in Slocum Township originally attended services at the Evangelical Lutheran Church in Dorrance. In 1891, they organized as a separate congregation and constructed the Mount Zion Church on Lily Lake Road. In 1997, the congregation reorganized as an independent United Church of Christ. (Courtesy of Mountain Top Photo.)

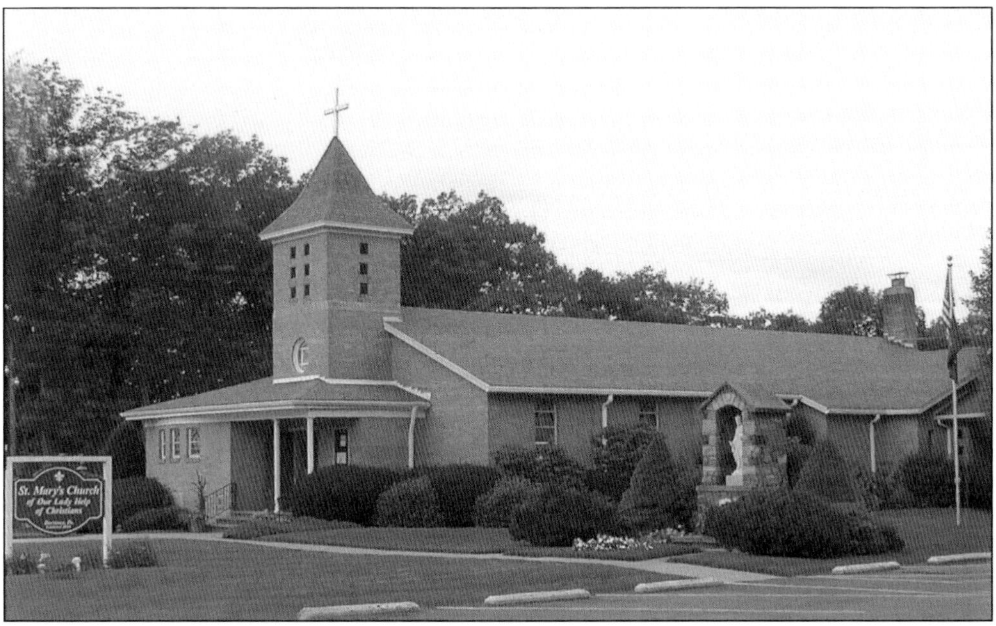

St. Mary's Church of Our Lady Help of Christians. Early Catholics in Slocum and Dorrance worshipped in Wilkes-Barre and Hazleton. In 1923, St. Mary's Church of Our Lady Help of Christians was founded as a mission church of the Church of the Maternity of the Blessed Virgin Mary in Wilkes-Barre. A building was constructed on St. Mary's Road. Following a fire, the church was rebuilt in 1955. (Courtesy of Mountain Top Photo.)

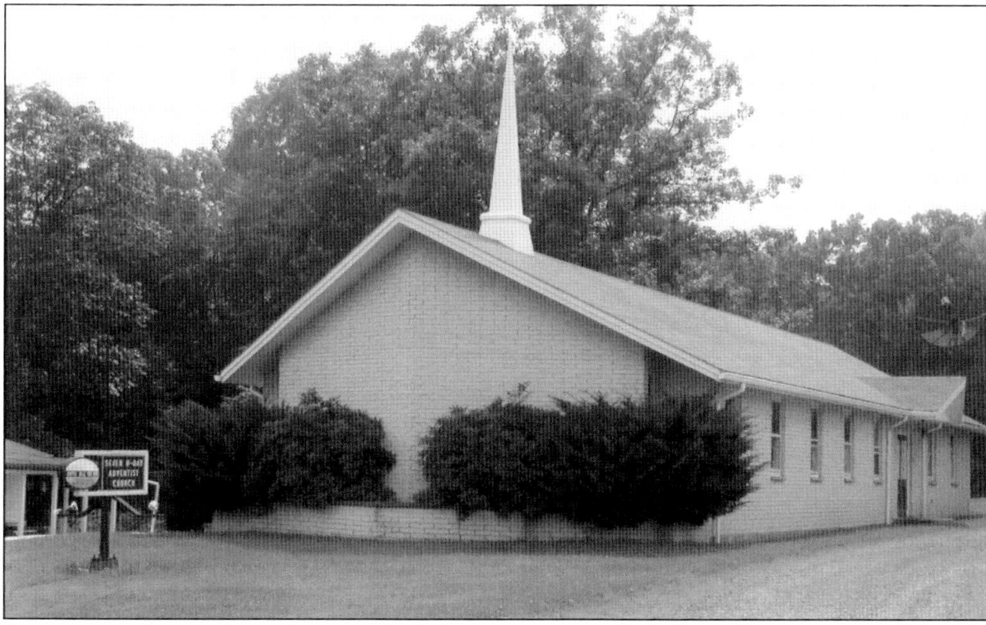

SLOCUM SEVENTH-DAY ADVENTIST CHURCH. The Stairville Polish Seventh-day Adventist Church was organized in 1933. Members first met in family homes and the Slocum Junior Mechanics Hall. In 1942, a church was built on Blue Ridge Trail. In 1964, it was renamed the Slocum Seventh-day Adventist Church. The church was dismantled, and a new structure was built in 1967. (Courtesy of Mountain Top Photo.)

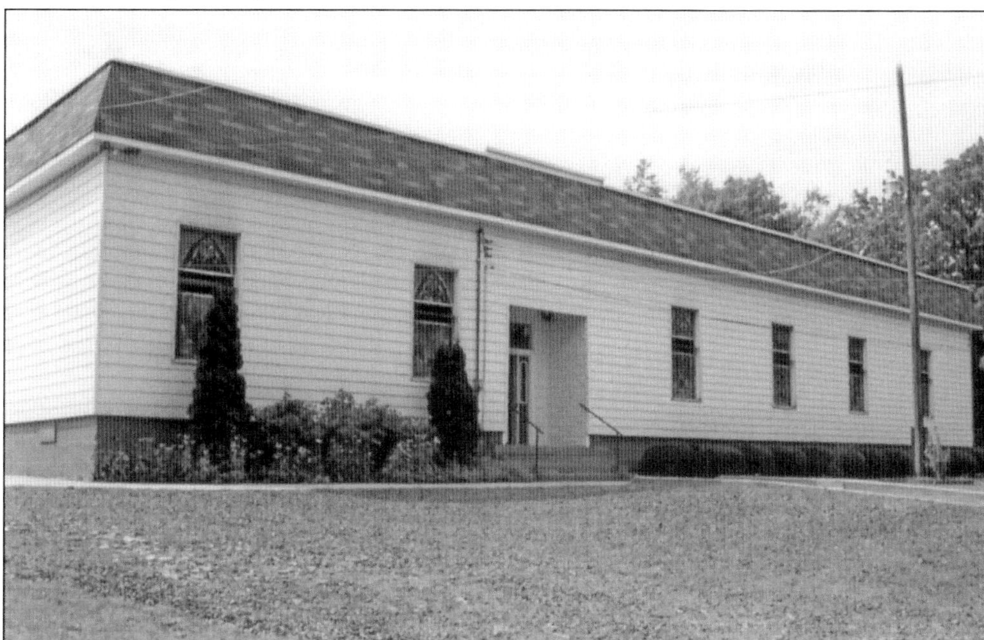

GRACE INDEPENDENT BAPTIST CHURCH. The Grace Independent Baptist Church was founded in 1973 by a small group of families who gathered together for Bible study and fellowship. The congregation is housed on Blue Ridge Trail in the former Slocum Township School, which was built in 1925. (Courtesy of Mountain Top Photo.)

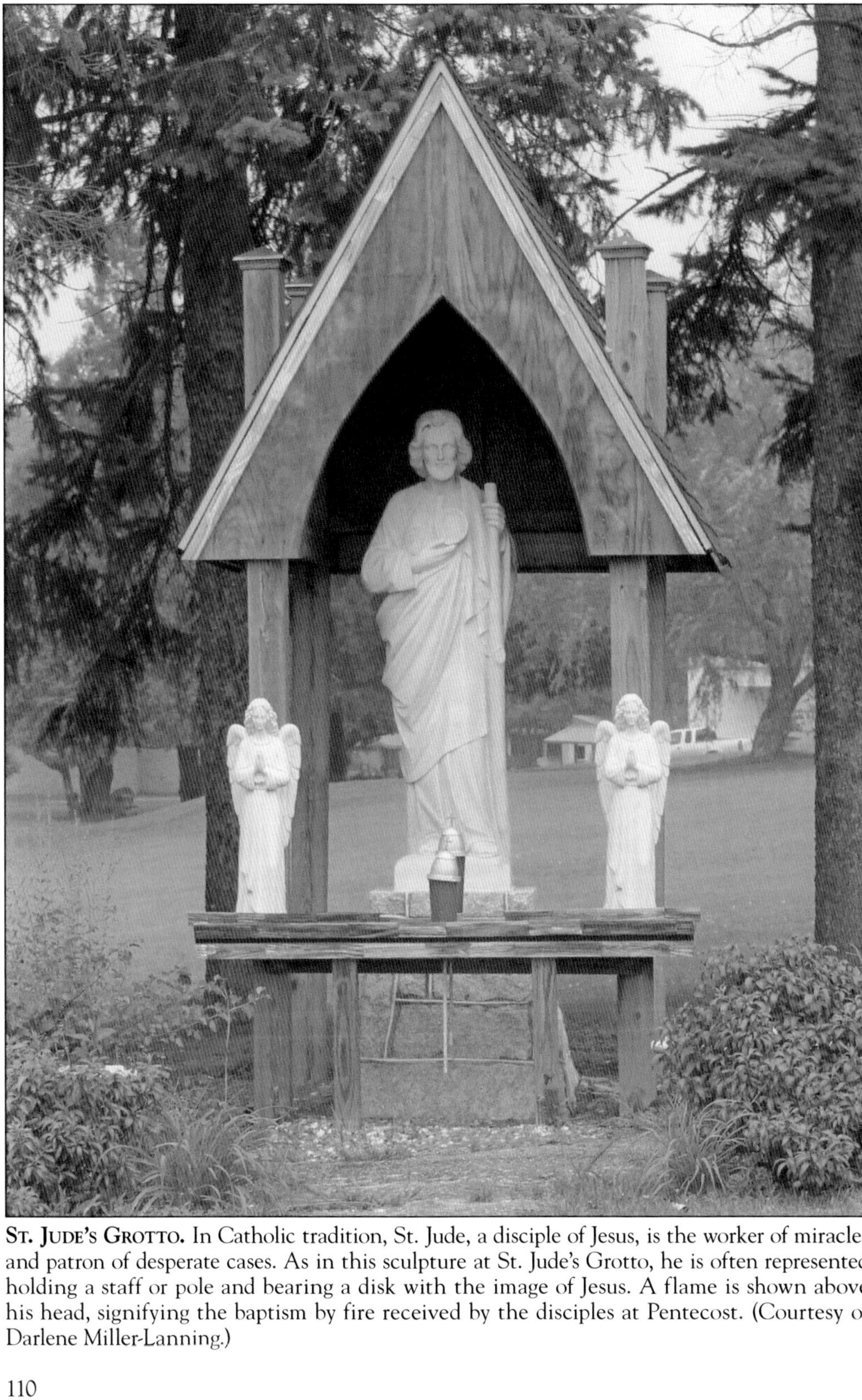

St. Jude's Grotto. In Catholic tradition, St. Jude, a disciple of Jesus, is the worker of miracles and patron of desperate cases. As in this sculpture at St. Jude's Grotto, he is often represented holding a staff or pole and bearing a disk with the image of Jesus. A flame is shown above his head, signifying the baptism by fire received by the disciples at Pentecost. (Courtesy of Darlene Miller-Lanning.)

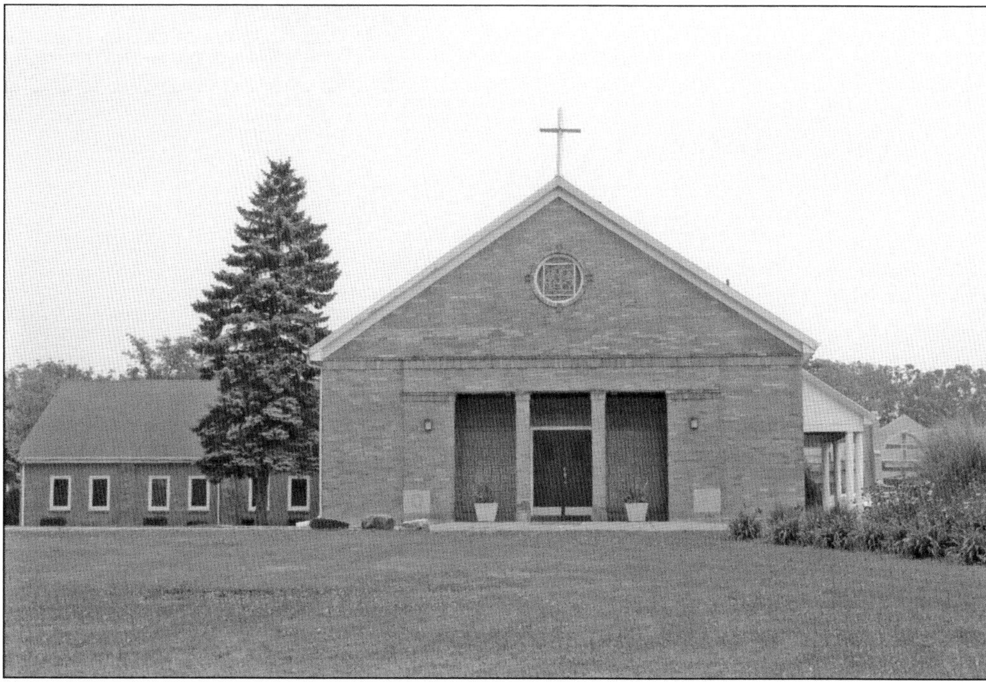

St. Jude's Church. As the population of Mountain Top grew, St. Jude's Catholic Church was constructed in 1954 at the intersection of Route 309 and Church Road. Expansion of facilities continued, and church grounds soon included a rectory, convent, church hall, picnic grounds, and an elementary school. (Courtesy of Darlene Miller-Lanning.)

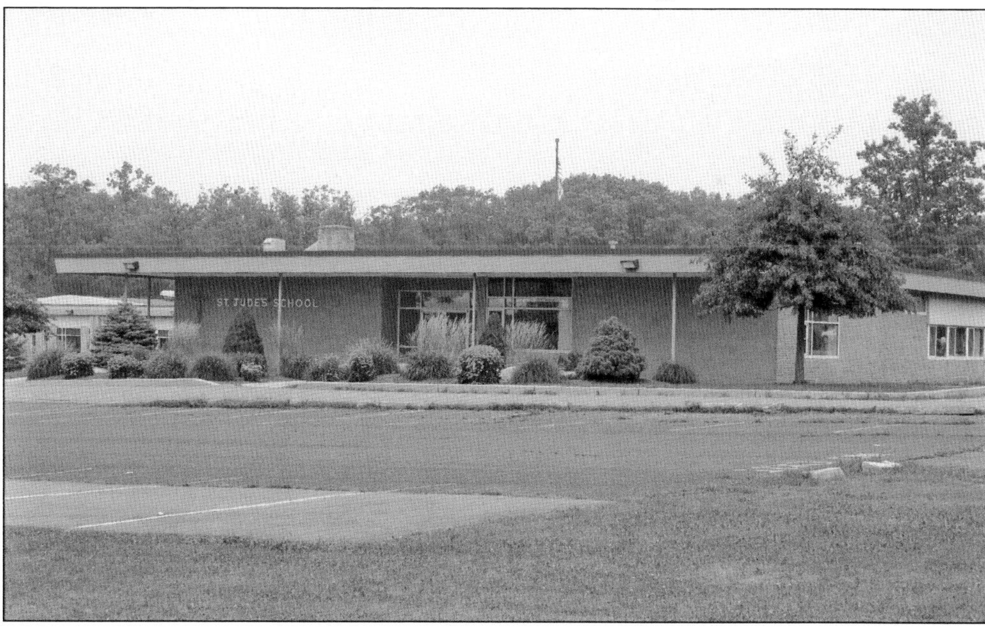

St. Jude's School. In 1958, St. Jude's Church opened a parochial elementary school under the direction of the Sisters of Christian Charity from Mendham, New Jersey. Today, the facility, which includes a cafeteria, library, and gym/auditorium complex, offers instruction for students from preschool through the eighth grade. (Courtesy of Darlene Miller-Lanning.)

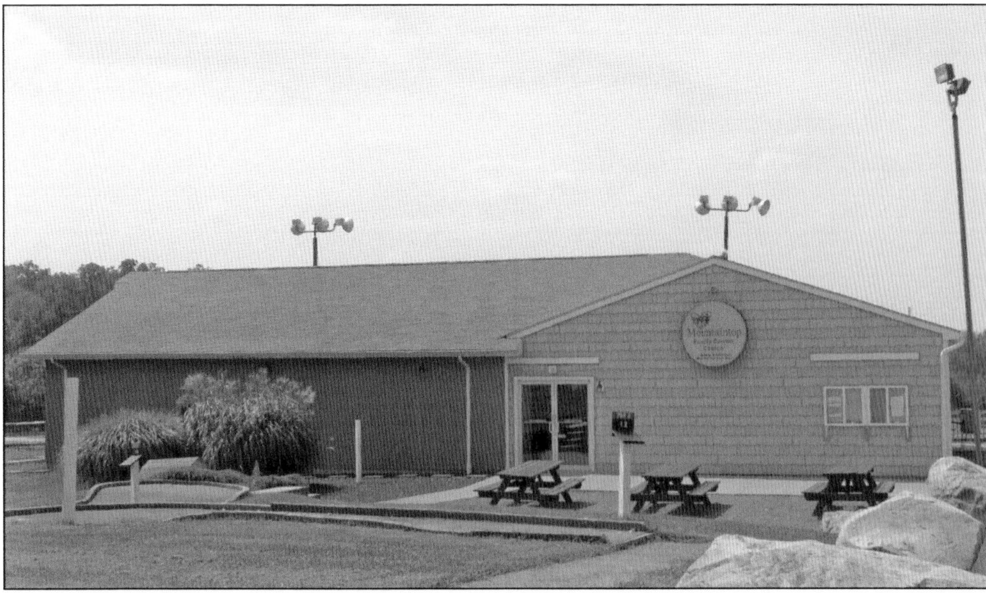

MOUNTAIN TOP FAMILY CENTER CHURCH. Members of the Mountain Top Family Center Church began meeting in family homes in 2002. They then met in the cafeteria of the Crestwood High School before moving into the Grouse Hill Complex on Route 309 in 2005. (Courtesy of Mountain Top Photo.)

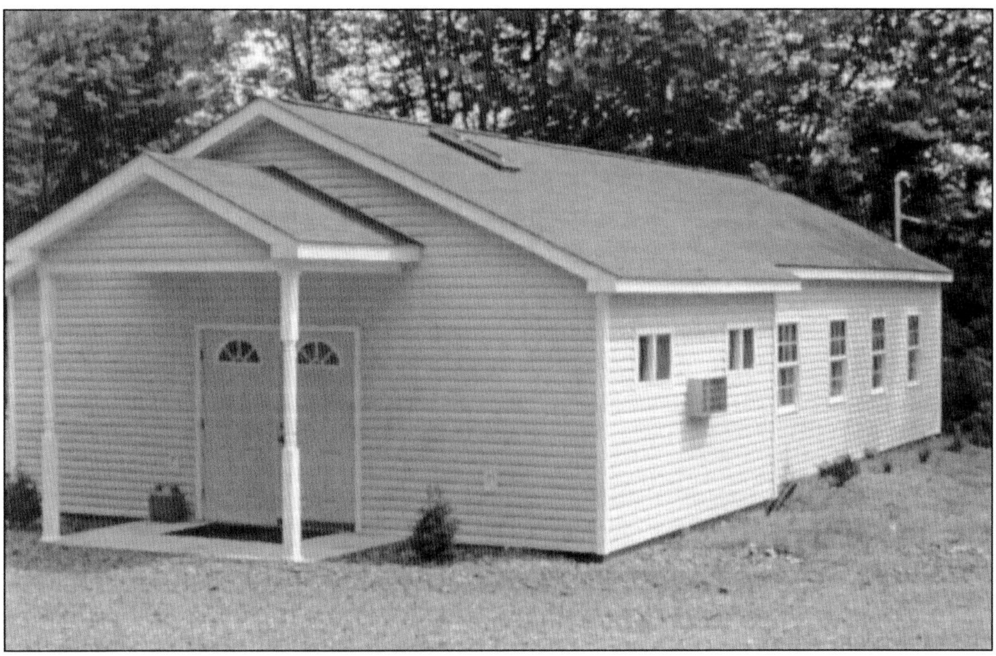

CORNERSTONE CHRISTIAN FELLOWSHIP. The Cornerstone Christian Fellowship is located on Church Road near the intersection of Stairville Road. The Fellowship recognizes its relationship to the Lancaster Conference of the Mennonite Church through the Weaverland District. (Courtesy of Mountain Top Photo.)

Six

COMMUNITY AND CONTINUITY

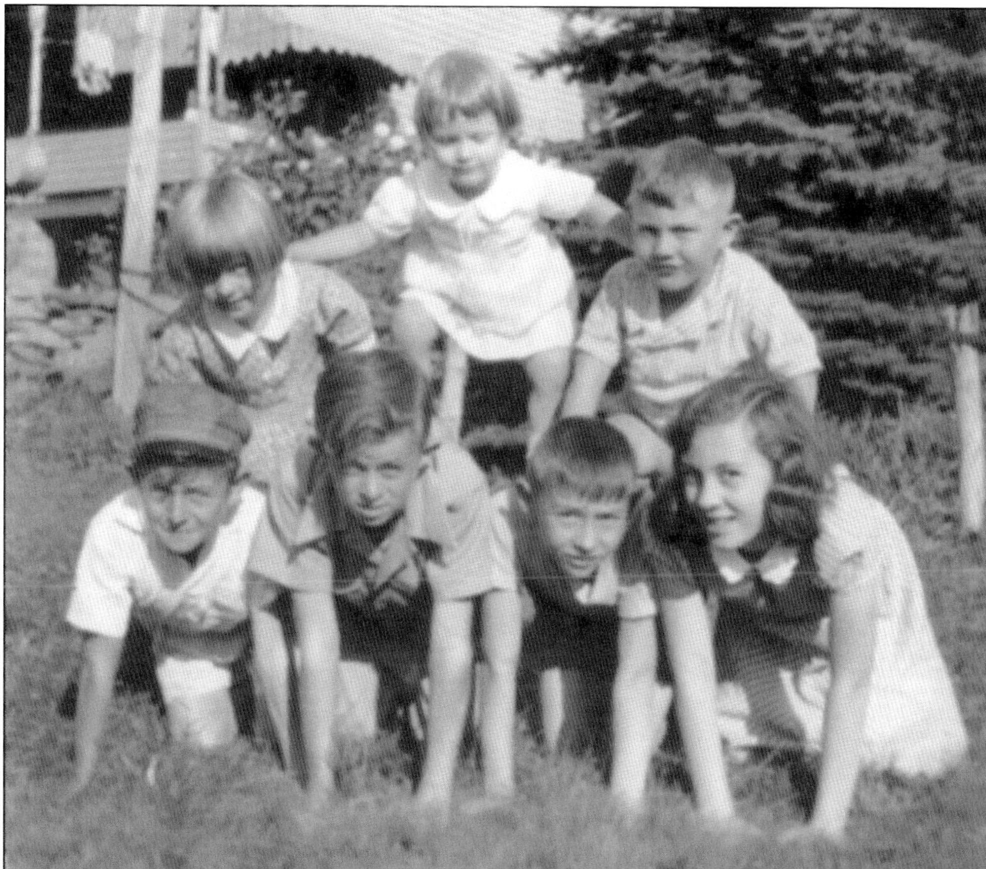

CHILDREN PLAYING "KING OF THE MOUNTAIN." Mountain Top residents consistently state that the community is a great place to raise a family. Generations of children have grown up in the area, enjoying the benefits of open spaces and close-knit neighborhoods. In 1943, from left to right, (top) Edith Kahley, Henrietta Kahley, and Bobby Zerfoss; (bottom) George Fillman, Paul Fillman, Clinton Zerfoss, and Patsy Zerfoss posed for a photograph while playing "king of the mountain" in the Kahley family's backyard. (Courtesy James and Edith Miller.)

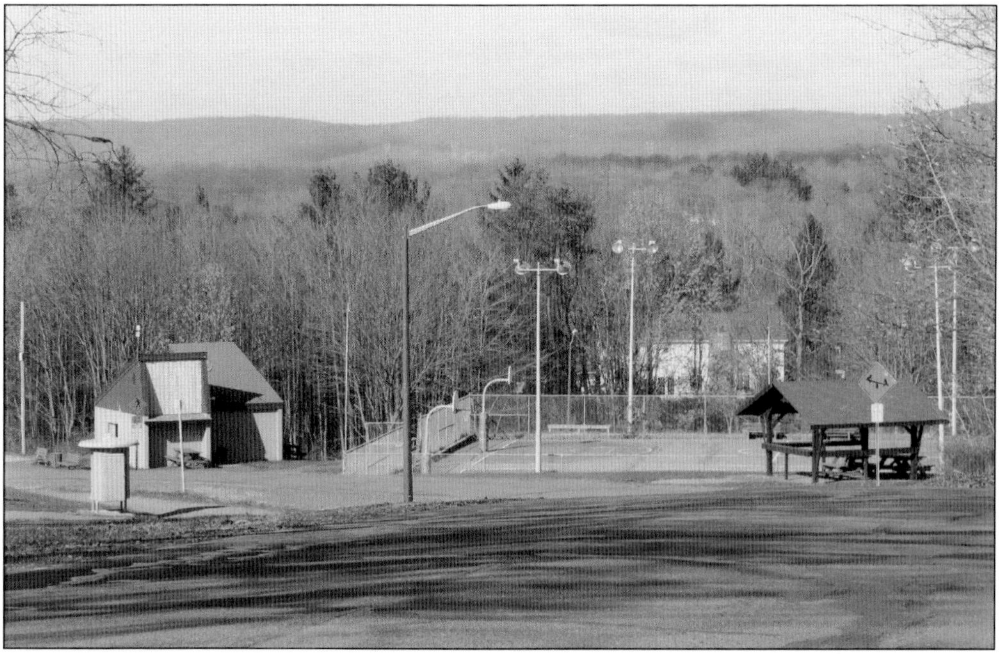

WRIGHT TOWNSHIP MUNICIPAL PARK. The Wright Township Municipal Park, built in 1976, includes a baseball diamond, basketball court, tennis courts, waterpark, playground, picnic grove, and ice-skating rink. It is the site of summer camp programs, fireworks, concerts, and outdoor movies. (Courtesy of Darlene Miller-Lanning.)

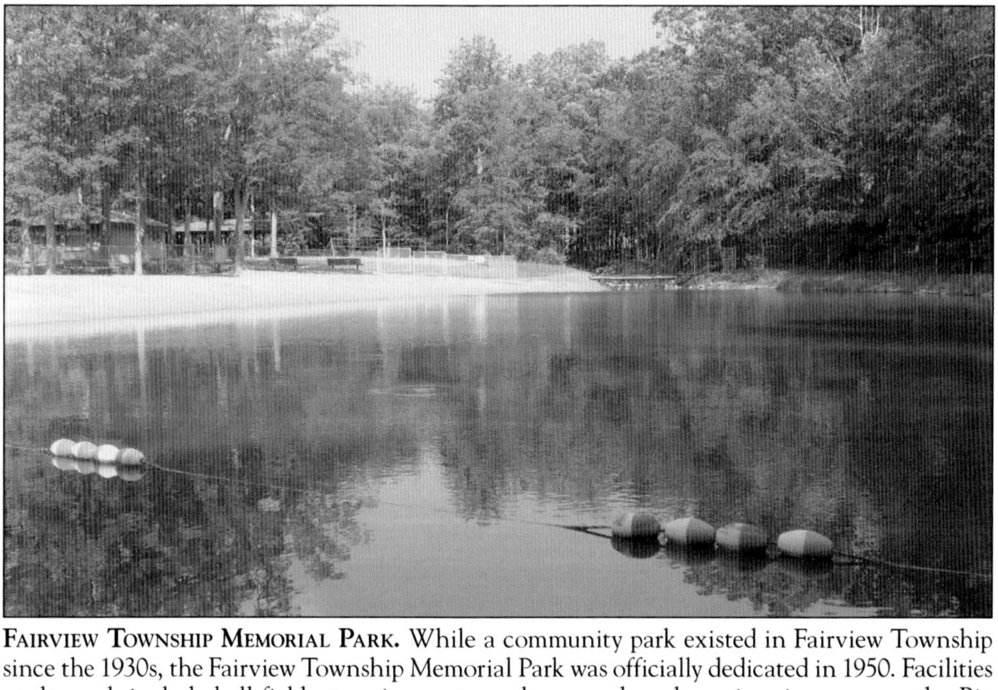

FAIRVIEW TOWNSHIP MEMORIAL PARK. While a community park existed in Fairview Township since the 1930s, the Fairview Township Memorial Park was officially dedicated in 1950. Facilities at the park include ball fields, tennis courts, a playground, and a swimming area on the Big Wapwallopen Creek. Located on Memorial Drive, the park is the site of the Fairview Township Honor Roll, which lists names of township veterans. (Courtesy of Darlene Miller-Lanning.)

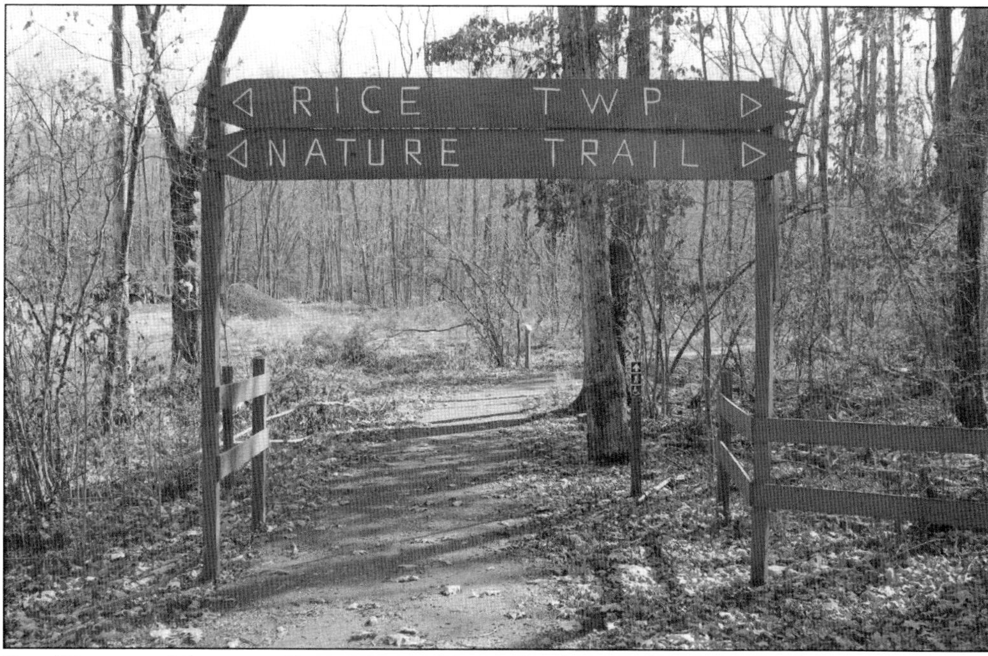

RICE TOWNSHIP MUNICIPAL PARK NATURE TRAIL. Facilities at the Rice Township Municipal Park include a nature trail, tennis courts, ball fields, and a playground. Rice Township also maintains a pavilion at the Ice Lakes recreation area, a popular spot for fishing and ice-skating. (Courtesy of Darlene Miller-Lanning.)

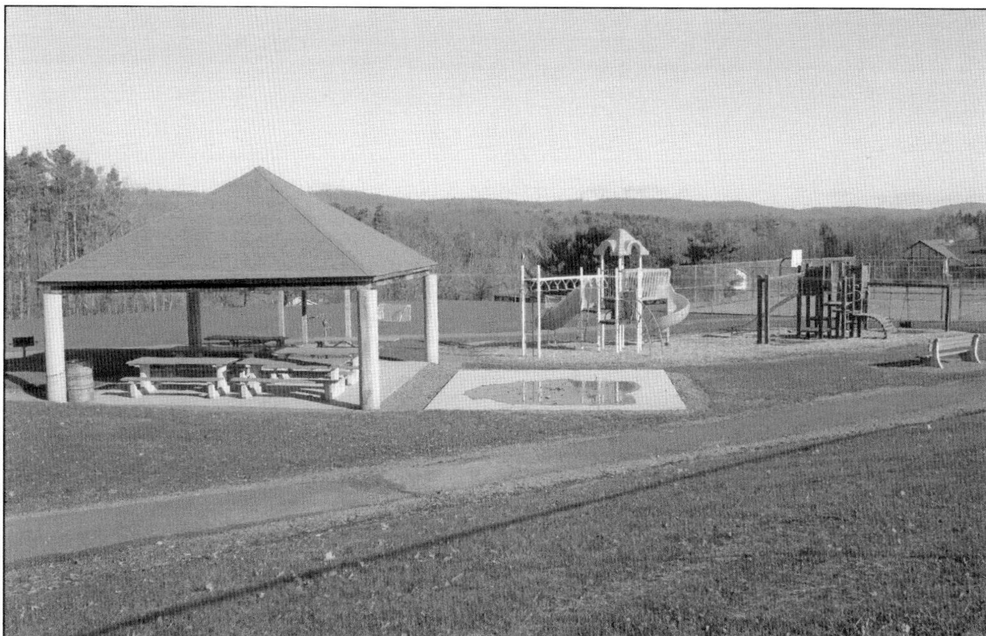

SLOCUM TOWNSHIP MUNICIPAL PARK. Slocum Township Veterans' Memorial Park was established in 1978. Located at the corner of Slocum and Schmid Roads, the park offers a view of surrounding mountains as well as playing fields, picnic areas, playground equipment, and exercise trails. (Courtesy of Darlene Miller-Lanning.)

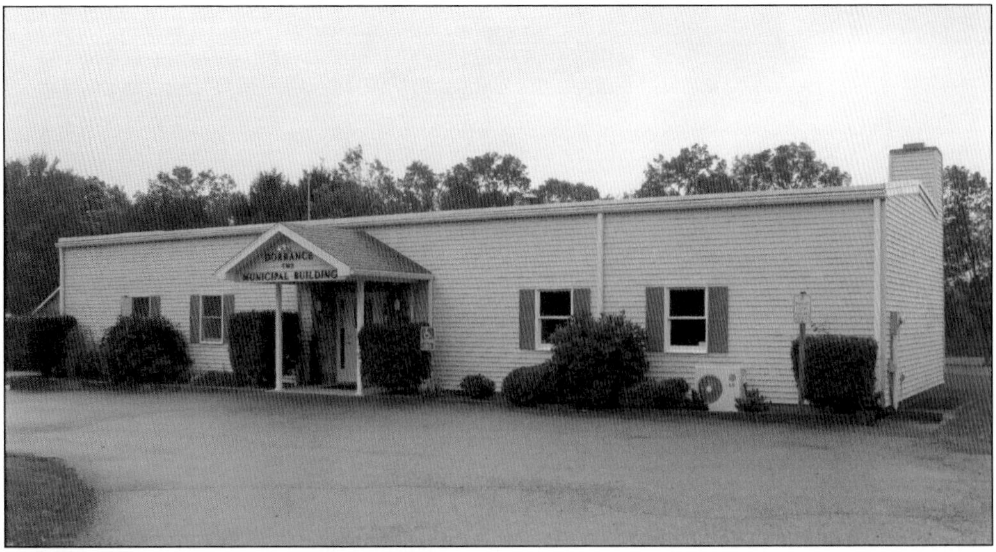

Dorrance Township Municipal Building. Municipal offices for Dorrance Township are housed in the former Dorrance Township School, which was constructed on Blue Ridge Trail in 1950. The adjacent Dorrance Township Municipal Park opened in 1978. (Courtesy of Darlene Miller-Lanning.)

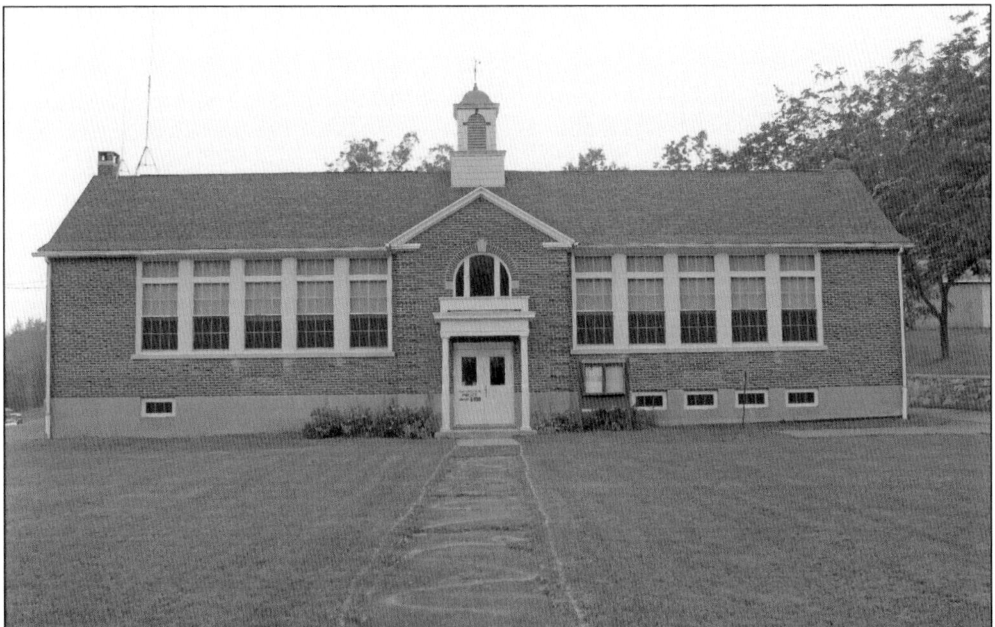

Nuangola Municipal Building and Library. The former Nuangola School on Nuangola Road, built in 1934, now serves as the Nuangola Municipal Building and Library. (Courtesy of Darlene Miller-Lanning.)

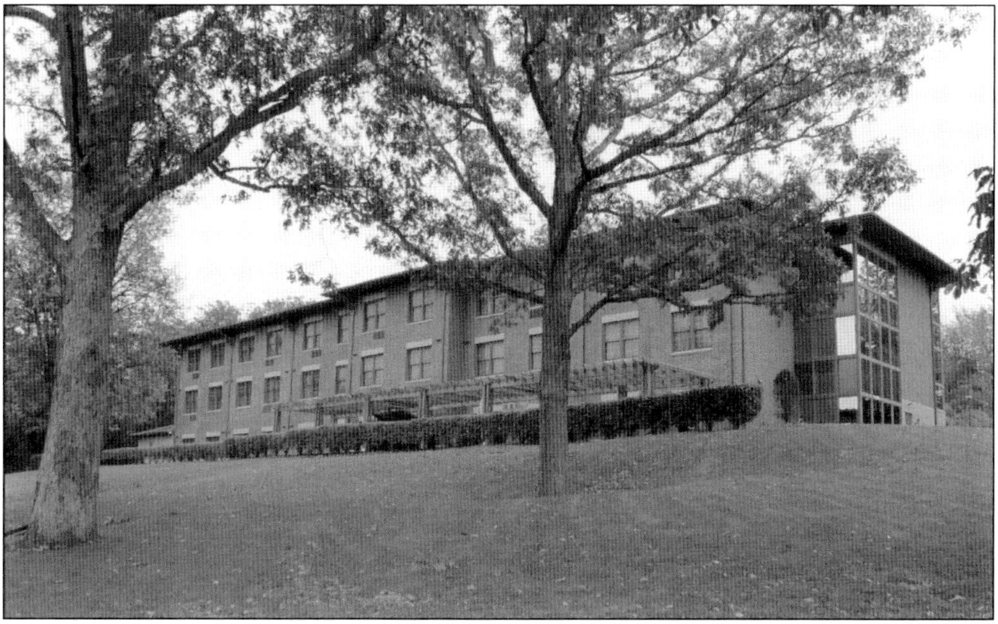

WRIGHT MANOR. The Wright Township School was built as a WPA project in 1937. While the building was demolished in 1997, the Wright Manor senior citizens' apartment complex now occupies the school's site on South Main Road. (Courtesy of Darlene Miller-Lanning.)

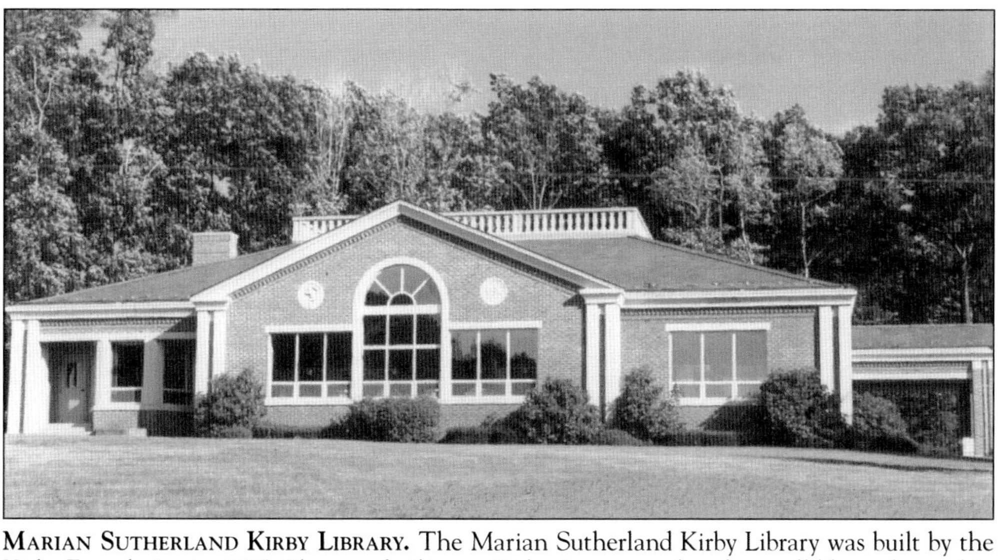

MARIAN SUTHERLAND KIRBY LIBRARY. The Marian Sutherland Kirby Library was built by the Kirby Foundation in 1985. The new facility on Kirby Avenue replaced a small library located in a house at the corner of Park Drive and Route 309. The Kirby Library is a member of the Luzerne County Library System and offers many public programs, including children's activities and book discussion groups. (Courtesy of Mountain Top Photo.)

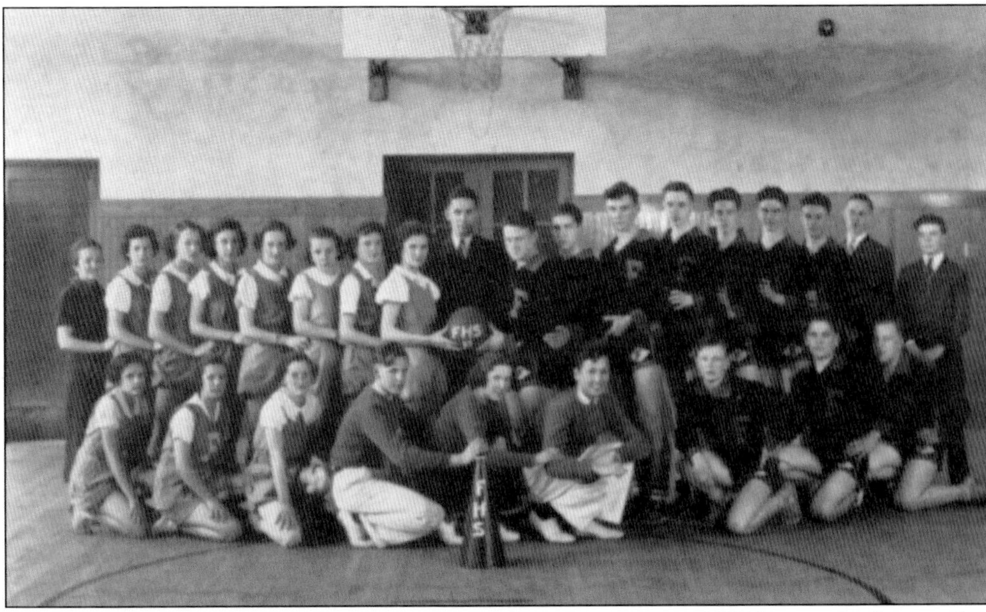

Fairview High School Basketball Teams and Cheerleaders. In 1937, boys and girls attending Fairview High School had the opportunity to join basketball teams and a cheerleading squad. The teams played in the Mountain Interscholastic League and celebrated at season's end with a banquet. (Courtesy James and Edith Miller.)

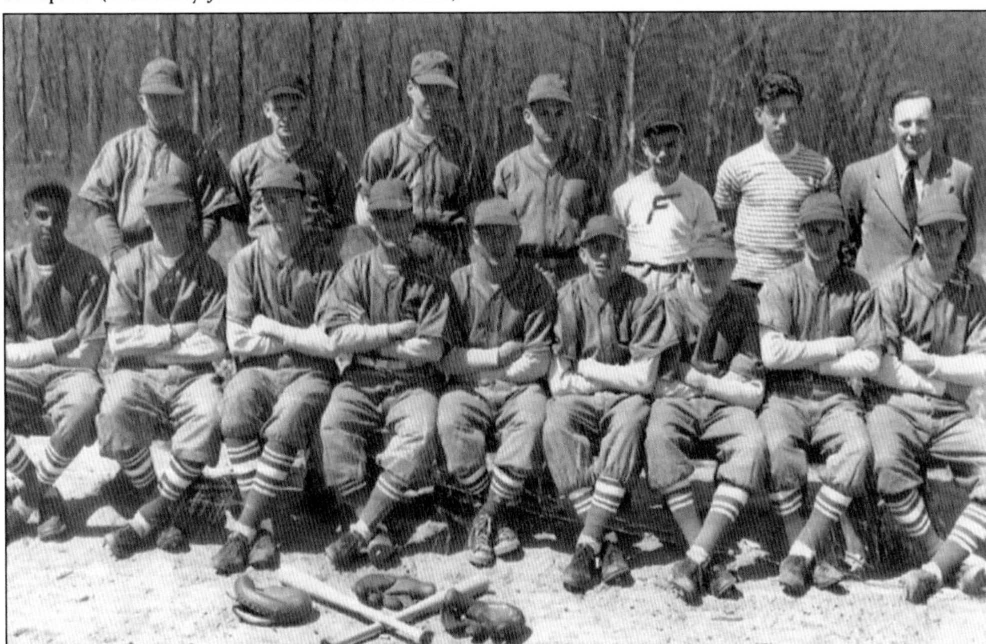

Fairview Indians Baseball Team. Community sports have always been popular in Mountain Top. Local teams like the Fairview Indians played in the early 20th century. The Mountain Top Area Recreational Association continues this tradition, as do the youth basketball league, youth soccer association, little league, and baseball and softball association. (Courtesy of the Mountain Top Historical Society: *Pieces of the Past.*)

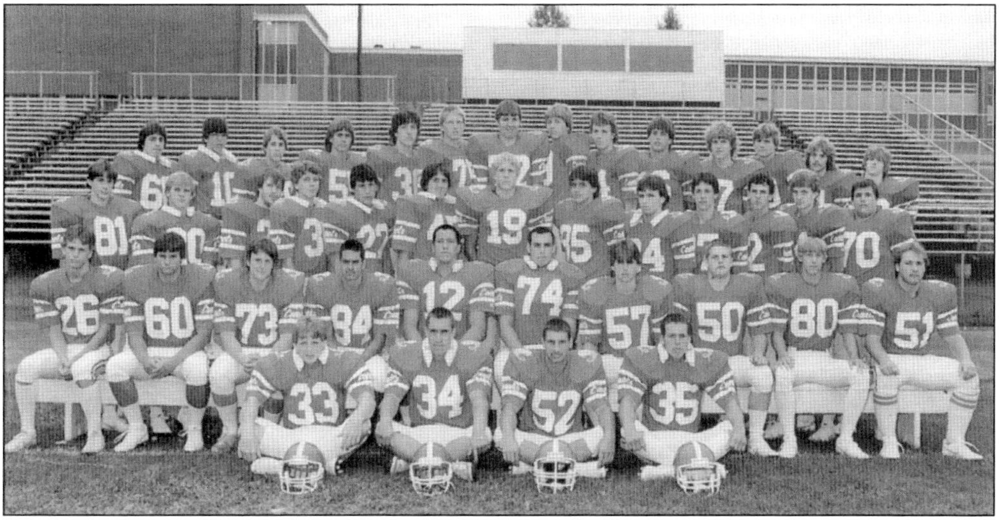

Crestwood Comets High School Football Team. The Crestwood Comets football team won the Eastern Conference title in 1985. Football is one of many sports in which Crestwood students may participate. Others include basketball, baseball, softball, volleyball, soccer, hockey, wrestling, track and field, cross-country, swimming, tennis, golf, and lacrosse. (Courtesy of the Mountain Top Historical Society: *Pieces of the Past.*)

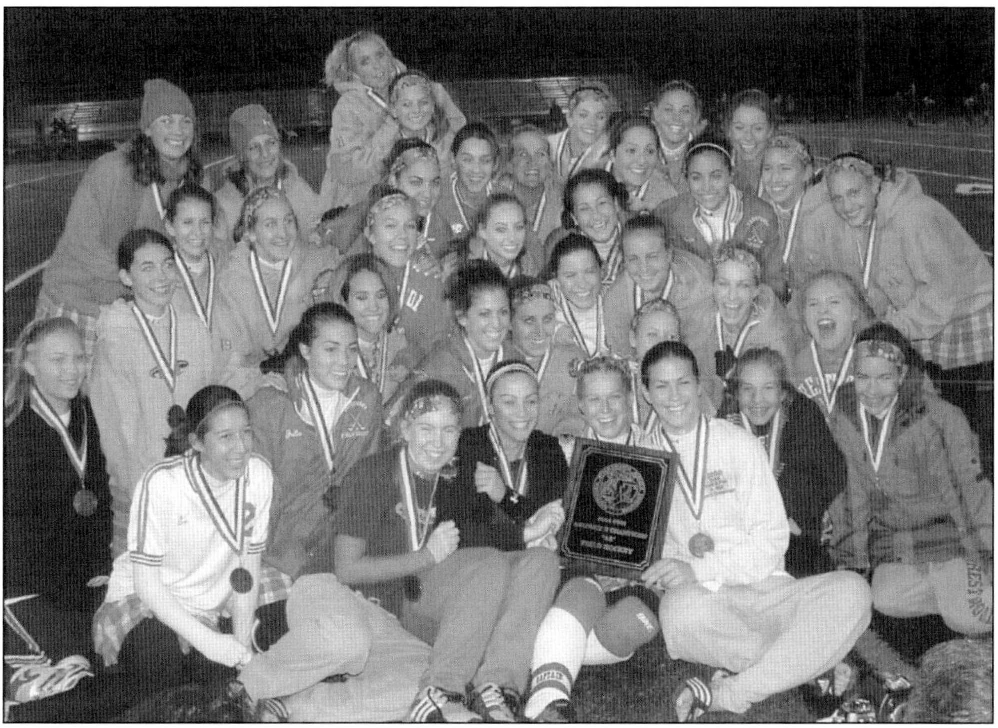

Crestwood High School Girls' Field Hockey Team 2003–2004. Since the 1980s, the Crestwood girls' field hockey team, coached by Elvetta Gemski, has regularly competed in state tournaments. In 2004, team members successfully defended their District II and PIAA Class AA state championship, finishing with a 26-0 record. Members of the "Big Red Machine" have gone on to play at the college level and compete in the Olympics. (Courtesy of David Suitch.)

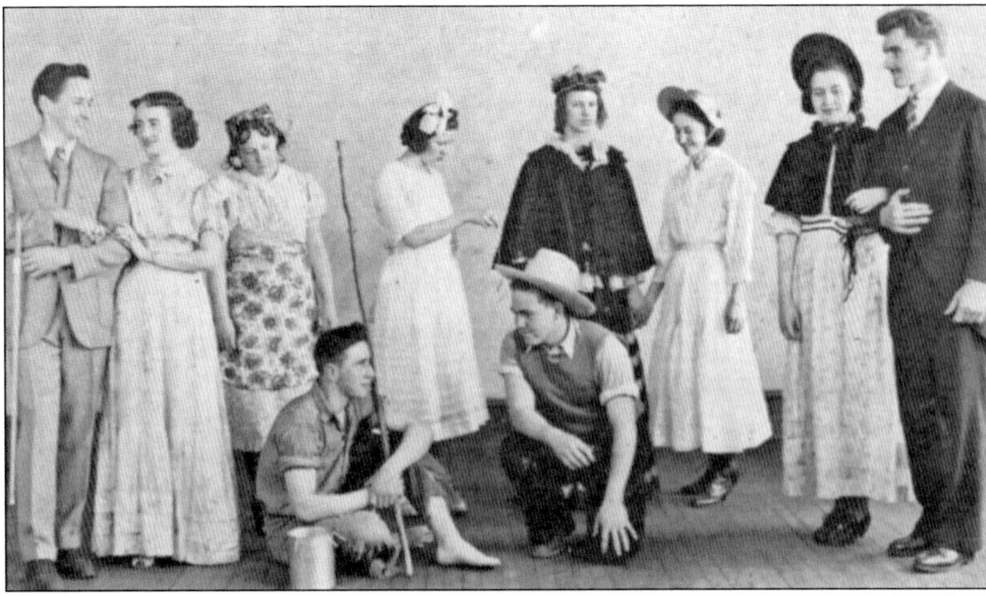

FAIRVIEW HIGH SCHOOL CAST OF *HUCKLEBERRY FINN*. In 1937, Fairview High School students performed the play *Huckleberry Finn*. (Courtesy James and Edith Miller.)

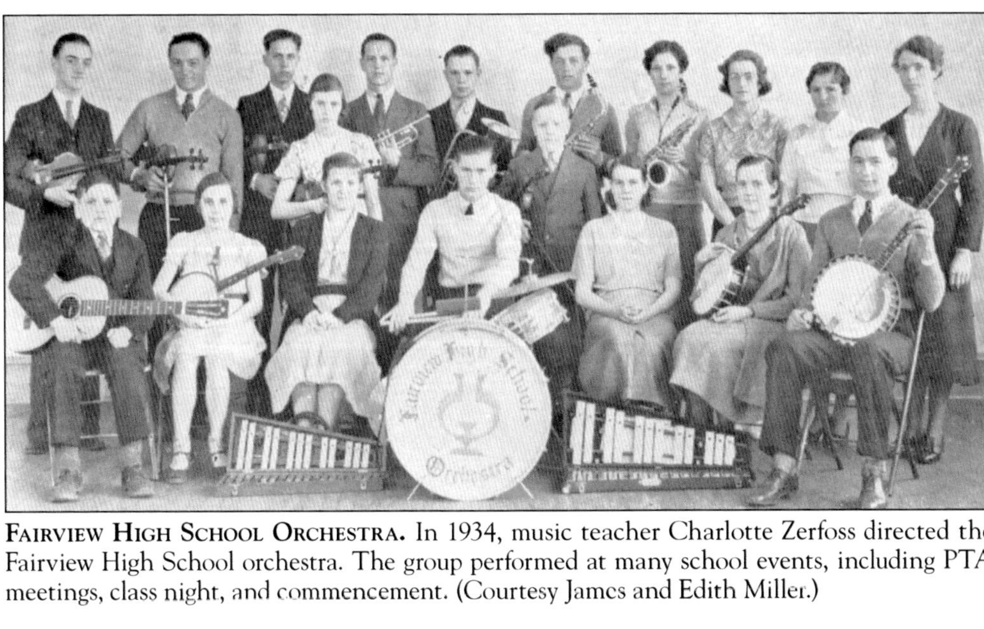

FAIRVIEW HIGH SCHOOL ORCHESTRA. In 1934, music teacher Charlotte Zerfoss directed the Fairview High School orchestra. The group performed at many school events, including PTA meetings, class night, and commencement. (Courtesy James and Edith Miller.)

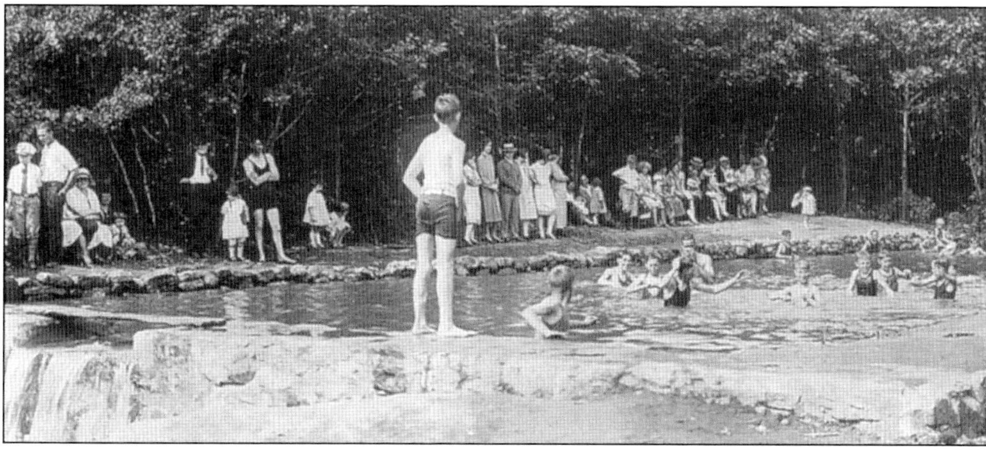

Swimming at Camp St. George. In 1925, the St. Boniface Church branch of the Knights of St. George in Wilkes-Barre purchased a site for a summer camp along Watering Run. A swimming pool constructed along the creek provided campers with a place to cool off. While overnight camping ended in 1964, the camp is still used for picnics and reunions. (Courtesy of the Mountain Top Historical Society: *Pieces of the Past.*)

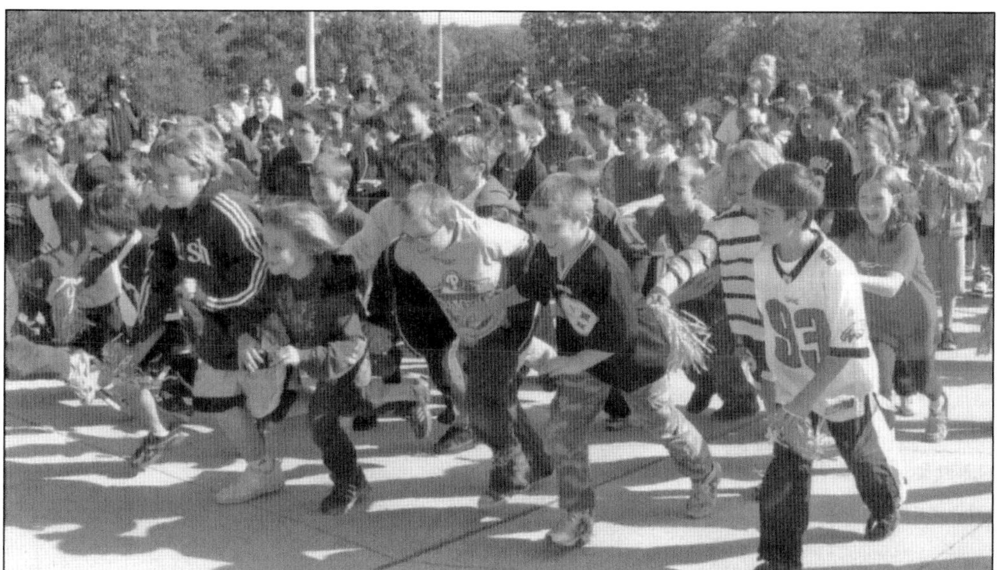

Rice Elementary Race for Education. Each year, students at Rice and Fairview Elementary Schools participate in a Race for Education to raise funds for their PTAs. St. Jude's School also conducts a Race for Education. The events celebrate physical fitness and school spirit. (Courtesy of Rice Elementary School.)

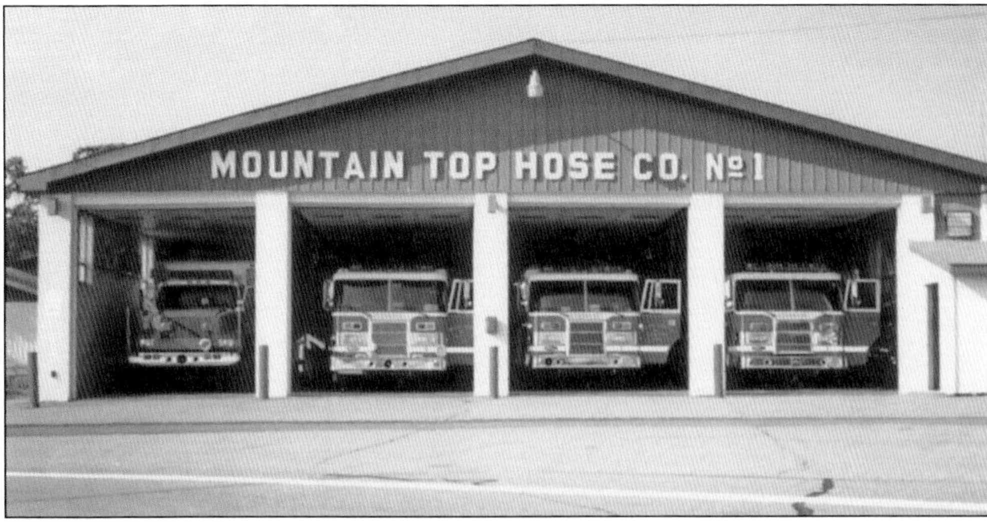

Mountain Top Hose Company No. 1. The Mountain Top Hose Company No. 1 was established in 1939. Trucks and equipment were housed in the Fairview Township Municipal Building until 1975, when a new facility was constructed on Woodlawn Avenue near Route 309. (Courtesy of Mountain Top Photo.)

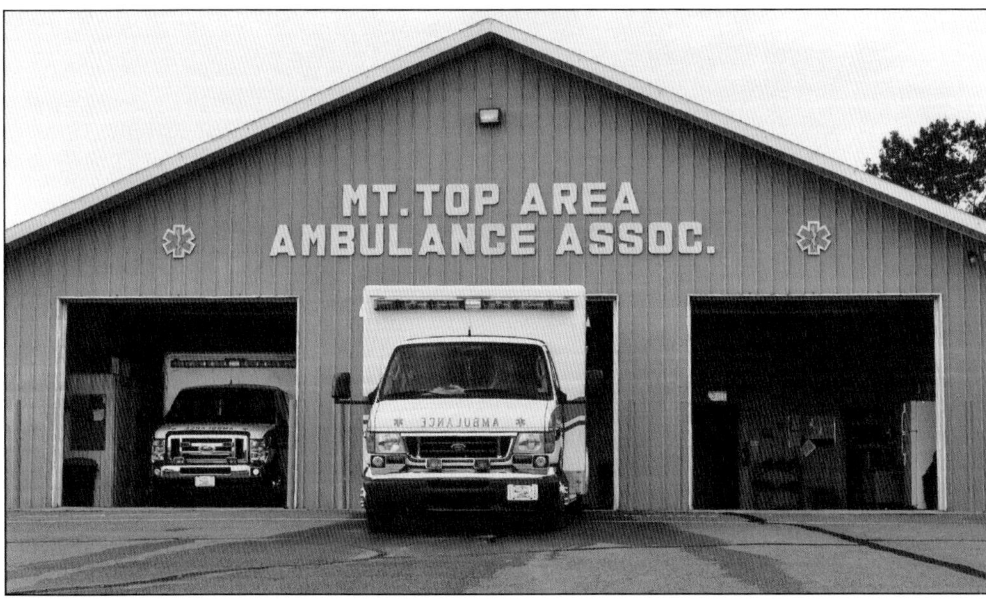

Mountain Top Community Ambulance Association. The Mountain Top Community Ambulance Association was established in 1952. Today, the association headquarters, which features a heliport for emergency transports, is located at the intersection of Woodlawn Avenue and Route 309 near the Mountain Top Hose Company No. 1. A second facility is located near the Rice Township Municipal Park. (Courtesy of Mountain Top Photo.)

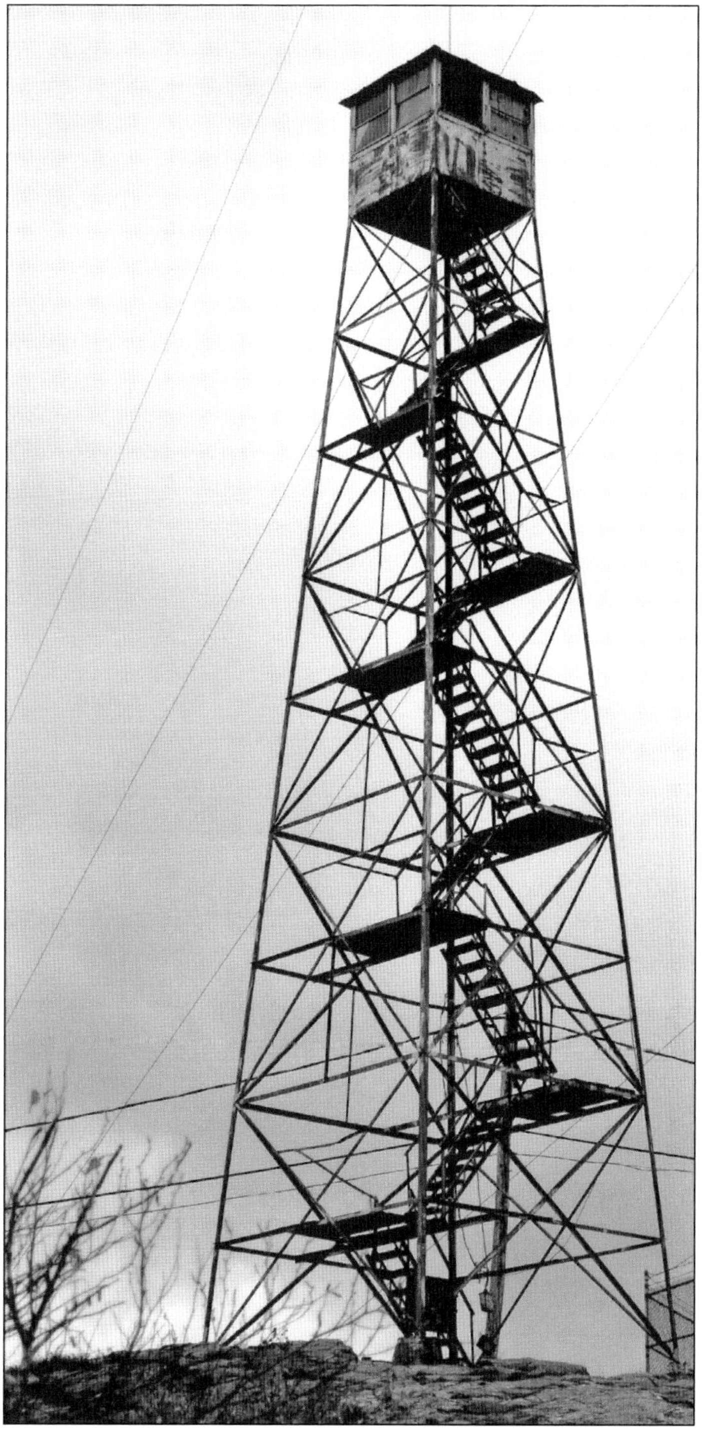

FIRE TOWER ON PENOBSCOT MOUNTAIN. In 1923, the Pennsylvania Department of Forestry constructed a 65-foot observation tower on Penobscot Knob at an elevation of 2,140 feet. Lookouts posted in the tower had a wide view of the surrounding territory, which they scouted for forest fires. (Courtesy of Mountain Top Photo.)

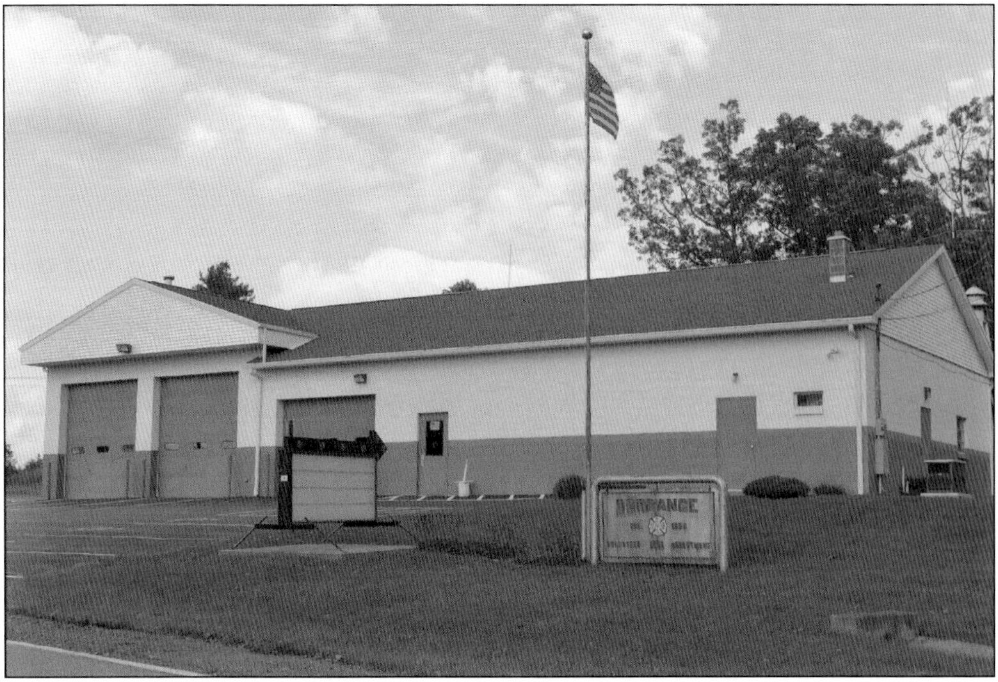

DORRANCE TOWNSHIP VOLUNTEER FIRE DEPARTMENT. The Dorrance Township Volunteer Fire Department was chartered in 1958. It is located on St. John's Road near the former Fey's Grove. (Courtesy of Mountain Top Photo.)

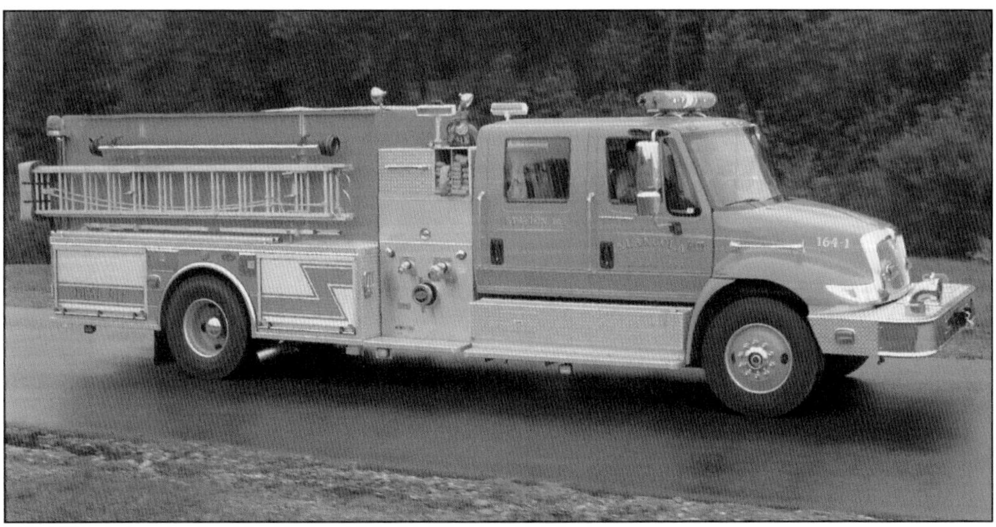

NUANGOLA VOLUNTEER FIRE DEPARTMENT ENGINE NO. 164-1. The Nuangola Volunteer Fire Department was established in 1958. It is located on Nuangola Road near the intersection of Lake and High Streets. (Courtesy of Darlene Miller-Lanning.)

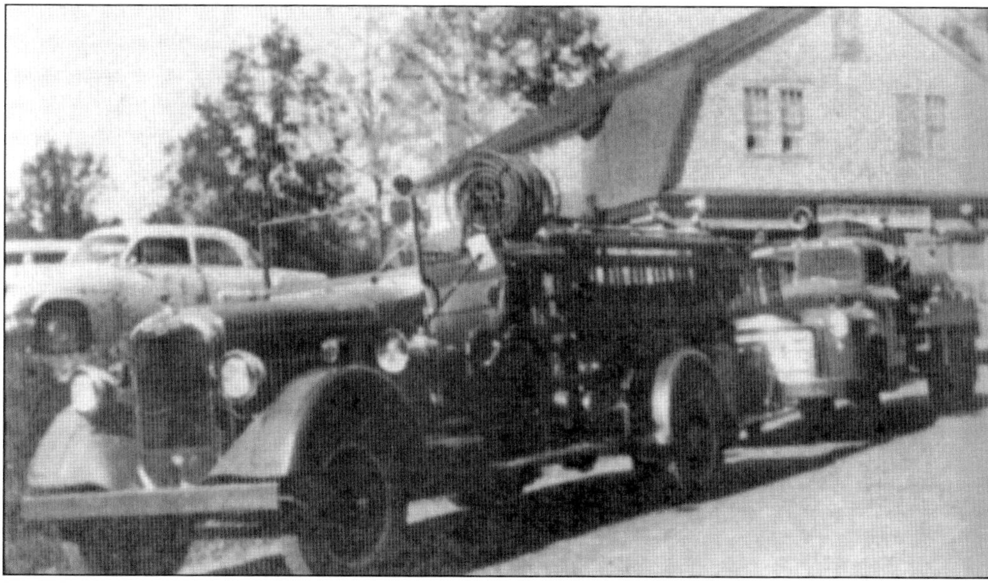

Rice Township Volunteer Fire Department. Rice Township Volunteer Fire Department was established in 1954. Located on Nuangola Road at Nuangola Station, it occupies the structure built by Fred Pettit as a brood house in the 1920s. (Courtesy of the Mountain Top Historical Society: *Pieces of the Past.*)

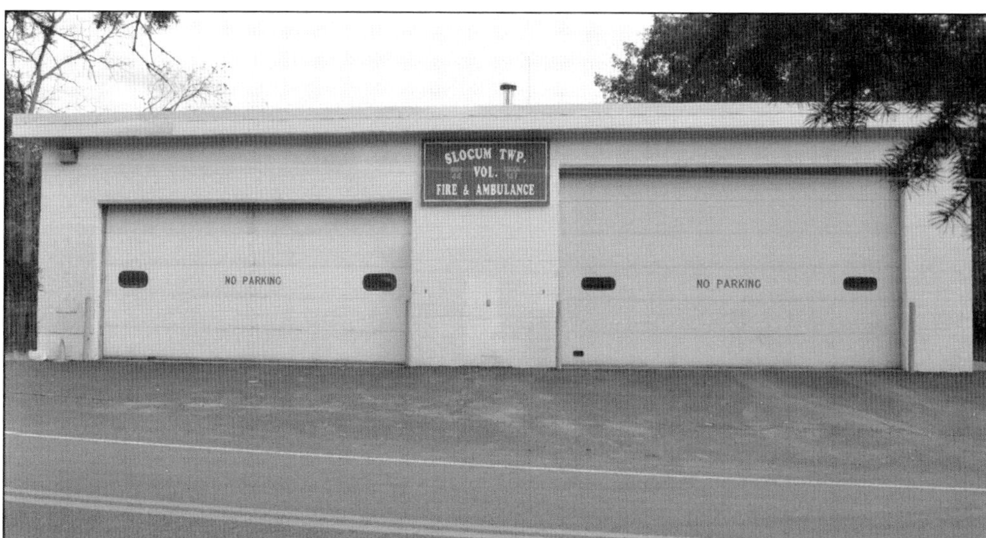

Slocum Township Volunteer Fire Company. Located on Slocum Road, the Slocum Township Volunteer Fire Company was organized in 1957. The organization works closely with the Slocum Township Volunteer Ambulance Association, formed in 1977. (Courtesy of Mountain Top Photo.)

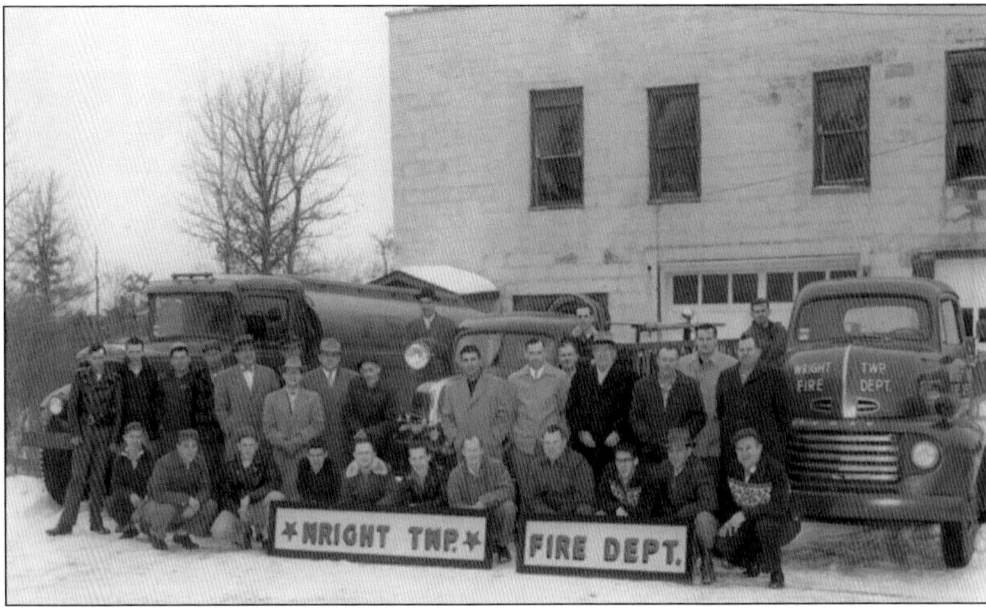

WRIGHT TOWNSHIP FIRE DEPARTMENT. Members of the Wright Township Fire Department, founded in 1955, included Joe Thomas, Ken Thomas, Bob Smith, Hillard Lamoreaux, Hubert Smith, Bob Jakubowski, John Legault, Ben Edwards, Skip Barry, Tony Modrovsky, George Grazul, Richard Fisher, John Sachs, Rowland Hildebrand, Aaron Hess, Michael Kwochka, Carl Sachs, James Walters, Noel Adams, John Thomas, Ronald Wren, George Pollock, Paul Youngblood, Ronald Williams Sr., and Jack Miller. (Courtesy of the Mountain Top Historical Society: *Business Directory*.)

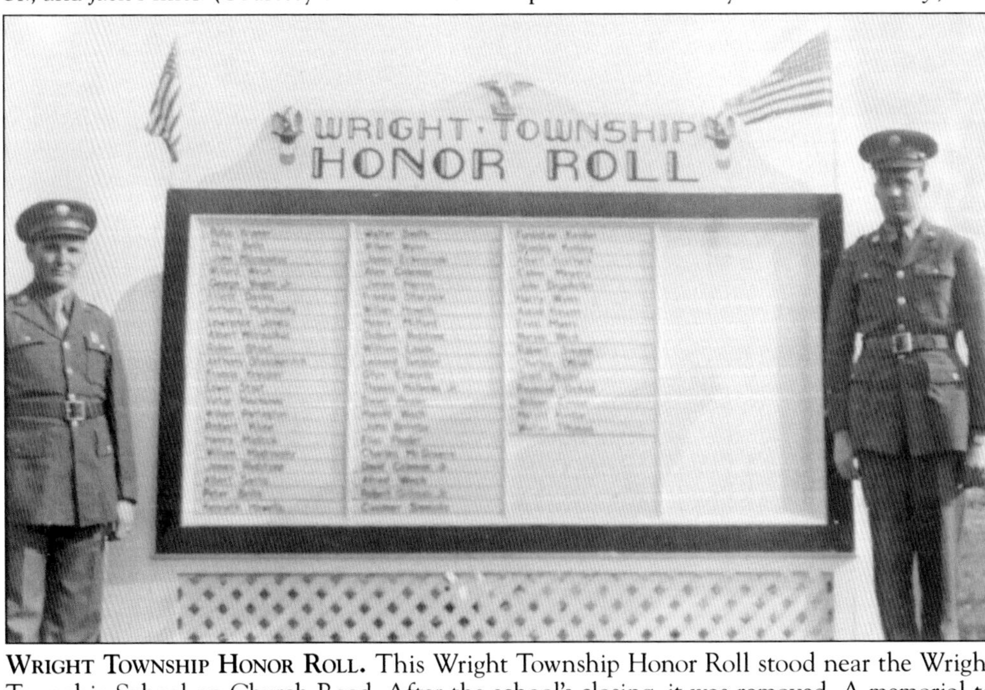

WRIGHT TOWNSHIP HONOR ROLL. This Wright Township Honor Roll stood near the Wright Township School on Church Road. After the school's closing, it was removed. A memorial to all those who gave military service was erected at the Wright Township Municipal Building. (Courtesy of the Mountain Top Historical Society: *Pieces of the Past*.)

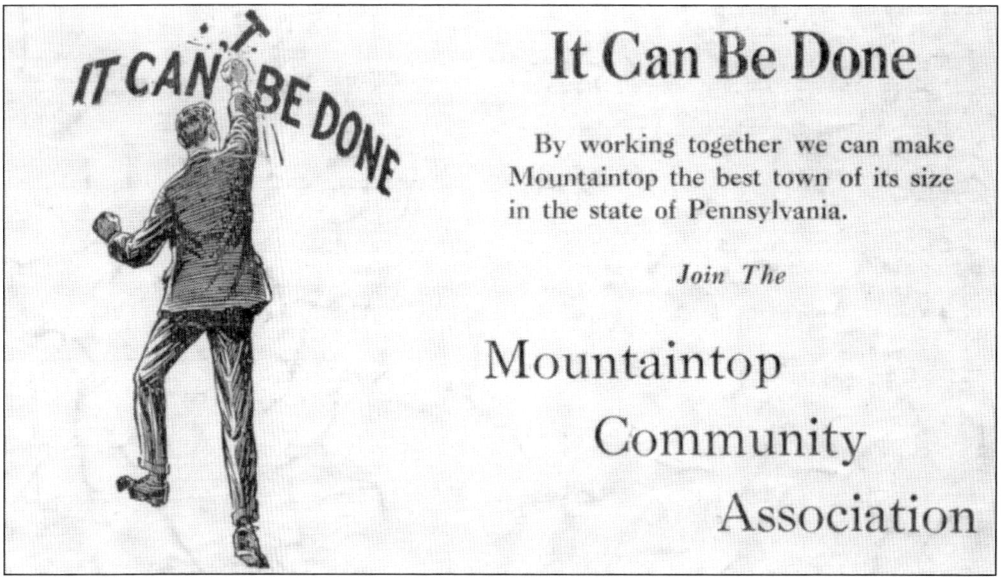

"It Can Be Done." In 1929, the Mountain Top Community Association published a half-page ad in the *Fairview High School Annual* expressing faith in community solidarity during difficult economic times. The spirit of this early civic group continues today in organizations like the Mountain Top Lions Club, Kiwanis Club, Welcome Club, and Mountaintop on the Move, founded in 1950, 1962, 1969, and 1986, respectively. (Courtesy James and Edith Miller.)

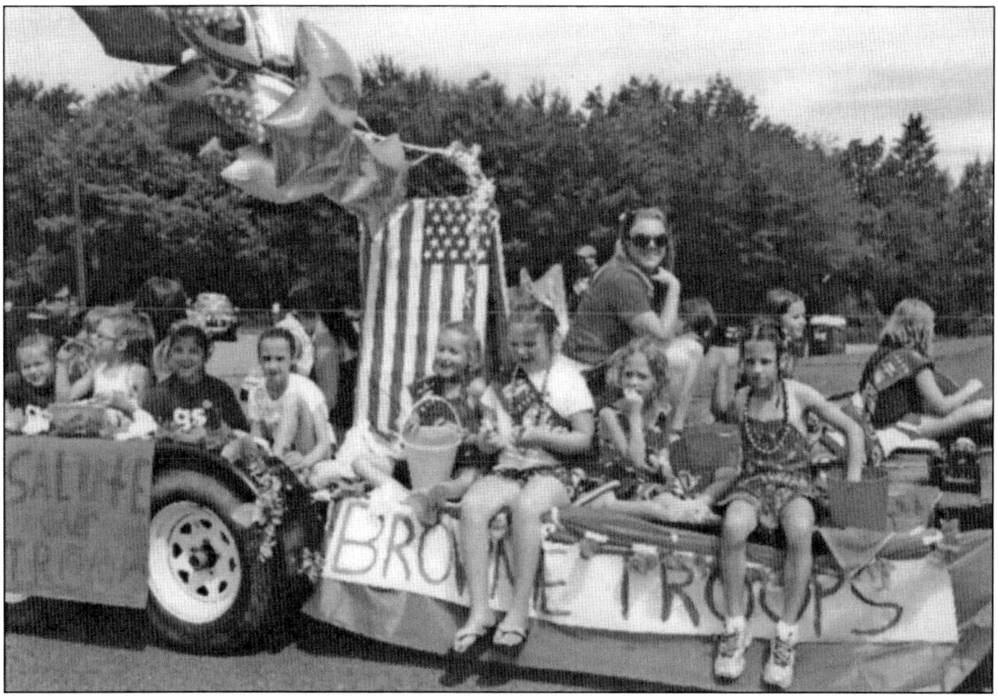

Independence Day Parade. In 2011, Mountaintop on the Move sponsored its 25th anniversary Independence Day Parade. Many local residents and organizations participated in the parade, which followed Route 309. Among them were local Brownies who created a float celebrating a "Support Our Troops" theme. (Courtesy of Katie Larsen-Lick.)